T0276954

INDIANS

ADVANCE PRAISE FOR THE BOOK

'Namit Arora is one of the most acute observers of contemporary India, and in his new book he extends his gaze to the past. Resourcefully researched and elegantly written, *Indians* deepens our sense of the wonder that was India' —Pankaj Mishra, author of *Age of Anger: A History of the Present*

'Namit Arora brings an inquiring mind, a clear head and a light touch to bear on a miscellany of Indian history's foundational texts and most significant sites. *Indians* is illuminating, absorbing and a joy to read. I defy anyone to peruse it and not feel richly rewarded by its insights'—John Keay, author of *India: A History*

'Namit Arora is the finest kind of travel companion: curious, well read, even-tempered and imaginative. Touring India's oldest cities with him is an acute pleasure. Arora dissolves the time between the past and the present, revealing how complex and diverse India has always been, and how, by misunderstanding our history, we run the danger of mismanaging our present. *Indians* is both timely and necessary'—Samanth Subramanian, author of *This Divided Island: Stories from the Sri Lankan War*

'Namit Arora has created a gem of a book that is a joy to read. It defies categorization, as it seamlessly combines travelogues, historical accounts and biographies. This approach brings alive ancient, medieval and modern India in such a manner that you can almost touch and feel the centuries and millennia as they pass by. It takes a remarkable feat of insightful writing to cover such a long period within a single volume while also avoiding a top-down perspective. An easy, entertaining and engaging book'—Tony Joseph, author of *Early Indians: The Story of Our Ancestors and Where We Came From*

'Possessed by wanderlust, Arora takes the reader on an intricate and perceptive journey through India, against the weight of the past and challenges of the present. In this beautifully crafted travelogue, Arora celebrates the momentous and the everyday in India's history, offering astute observations on its cultural fabric, illuminating its richness and frailty with insight and compassion. A brilliant and original achievement'—Assa Doron, author of *Life on the Ganga: Boatmen and the Ritual Economy of Banaras*

'Namit Arora takes us on a delightful journey through six magnificent archaeological sites and offers eloquent accounts of several major travellers of India. A gripping read with scholarly rigour, this book will interest both general readers and scholars'—Devangana Desai, author of *The Religious Imagery of Khajuraho*

INDIANS

A *brief* HISTORY *of a* CIVILIZATION

NAMIT ARORA

PENGUIN
VIKING

An imprint of Penguin Random House

VIKING

USA | Canada | UK | Ireland | Australia
New Zealand | India | South Africa | China | Singapore

Viking is part of the Penguin Random House group of companies
whose addresses can be found at global.penguinrandomhouse.com

Published by Penguin Random House India Pvt. Ltd
4th Floor, Capital Tower 1, MG Road,
Gurugram 122 002, Haryana, India

First published in Viking by Penguin Random House India 2021

Photographs courtesy of Namit Arora

10 9 8 7 6 5 4

The views and opinions expressed in this book are the author's own and the
facts are as reported by him which have been verified to the extent possible,
and the publishers are not in any way liable for the same.

Names have been changed to protect privacy.

ISBN 9780670090433

Typeset in Minion Pro by Manipal Technologies Limited, Manipal
Printed at Replika Press Pvt. Ltd, India

www.penguin.co.in

MIX
Paper from
responsible sources
FSC® C016779

This is a legitimate digitally printed version of the book and therefore might not
have certain extra finishing on the cover.

To
Usha Alexander

Contents

Introduction

The Lost Worlds of India

What does it mean for a world to vanish? As a kid, when I first came across the term 'lost cities', I was mesmerized. A whole city lost? *Lost?* How can that happen?

We live with the illusion that our physical and cultural worlds have a certain solidity and stability, that despite inevitable change, they will endure long after us, bearing our legacy and progeny. We maintain this illusion even when we're aware of the many lost worlds that archaeologists have dug out—astonishing places like Machu Picchu, Angkor Wat, Memphis, Mohenjo-Daro and Persepolis. Since such lost worlds first captivated my imagination as a boy, I've visited dozens of them but I've lost none of my fascination for them.

The idea of writing this book was born on the road around 2004. During the preceding fifteen years, since 1989, while I studied and worked in the United States and Europe, I visited India only on short trips to see family. But smitten by wanderlust and bored with my profession (which only paid well), I often took time off from work to backpack solo in countries across Latin America, North Africa and Asia. I began to feel, as historian Miriam Beard wrote, that 'travel is more than the seeing of sights; it is a change that goes on, deep and permanent, in the ideas of living'.

As I changed over those fifteen years, so did India, and I longed to discover it afresh. Happily, so did my life partner whom I'd recently met. In 2004, she and I took a two-year break from our jobs to travel in India. We visited 110 destinations in twenty states: natural and historic sites, mountains and coasts, lost cities and bustling metros. Eager for experiences, we stayed in humble hotels and travelled by foot, bus, train, boat, car, scooter, bike, rickshaw, camel and more. I also began to keep a photo journal on *Shunya.net*.

This was a life-transforming experience. I loved so many of the places we visited. Each one threw up new questions. When we returned to the US, they stayed with me, leading me to deeper reading and reflection, revealing both new continuities and dead ends between India's past and its contemporary society. I wrote short essays on some of these places. Slowly, a more coherent idea of India's civilizational trajectory began to take shape in my mind, anchored around my earthy and often romantic encounters with some of its most thrilling sites and monuments.

At the same time, I noticed how interest in the past was surging in India. Modernity, capitalism and nationalism were fuelling in us Indians a desire to understand our place in the world in new ways. More than ever before, we now visited historical sites and hungered for new narratives about them: What had happened here? Why did it end? Too often, sadly, the popular new narratives are dull, untrue, or driven by chauvinism—instead of scholarly rigour and a humanistic temper, where openness, evidence and empathy lead the way. And how we see our past is increasingly shaping our idea of India and where we want to go as a society.

In 2013, my partner and I permanently quit our professions and relocated to India for the long term. After completing a book of essays and a novel, I returned my attention to the places that had captivated me in those previous two years of travel—the lost and found worlds of ancient and medieval India. I now decided to write about their remarkable stories at length.

I looked for sites that spanned north and south, and a wide swathe of time. I settled on six. It's hard to say why I chose these specific sites and not others. It was partly my idiosyncratic desire to understand these six lost worlds better. Each represented a distinct past in a land of many pasts. I saw them as the keys to a deeper understanding of Indians. Each promised a good journey too—a realm of mysteries and rewards that are hard to spell out.

I began planning a book that combined archaeological travel writing with narrative history. I hoped to find the essence of each site's inhabitants—their defining beliefs, customs and institutions; their struggles and living conditions—and their legacy in the cultural mosaic of India. I would lean on both diverse scholarship and primary sources, such as archaeologists' reports as well as the accounts of famous past travellers, many of whom had visited this distinctive land beyond the river Sindhu (Sanskrit for Indus)—a word used by the ancient Persians to also refer to the subcontinent and all its inhabitants (pronouncing 's' as 'h'), a non-religious, ethno-geographic descriptor. What did these travellers think of the Indians they met and what challenges of cross-cultural understanding did they face? Alongside, I would present my own experience of these sites and encounters as a traveller. In short, I hoped to bring alive these sites, past and present, in rich and evocative detail, combining the big picture with telling minutiae and quirky anecdotes. In doing so, I hoped to illuminate the most consequential trends, transformations and fault lines of Indian civilization.

I was inspired to write such a book, a book of connecting the dots, of relating ideas and emotions of our ancestors with our own. With my task cut out, I began gathering the sources and making travel plans to revisit the six sites. Three years later, I had this book.

On Approaching the Past

How should one tell the story of a lost world? By being truthful, one might say, by sticking to the facts. But what does that really mean? Facts are one thing, their interpretation another. Facts don't explain how they became facts, or why we care about some facts more than the other facts—only stories do that.

Inseparable from every story is the storyteller's sensibility, shaped by her politics, identity and culture. This is nothing new; it has always been true of all stories, including my stories in this book. There is no impartial or omniscient chronicler of events, no 'scientific' history. The storyteller's subjectivity and bias are woven into the very selection of what she considers to be salient facts and the weight she assigns them in her narrative.

Strictly speaking, 'all stories are fictions', wrote historian Hayden White. In the words of a critic, White held 'that while historical facts are scientifically verifiable, stories are not. Stories are made, not found in the historical data; historical meaning is imposed on historical facts by means of the choice of plot-type, and this choice is inevitably ethical and political at bottom'.[1]

Yet, while there are no 'neutral' or 'objective' stories, among people who share certain standards of truth and morality, some stories are decidedly superior, possessing more explanatory power than others. And perhaps the best tool human civilizations have evolved to identify such stories is modern scholarship, which attempts to expand knowledge about cultures and texts, subject to ongoing revision based on new evidence, fresh analysis and debate by a diverse community of scholars. This tool does not—at least not by design—put the cart of interpretation before the horse of facts. Rather, it is an enterprise in which historical knowledge evolves led by new facts and persuasive interpretations. It's not perfect, but alternatives divorced from such an approach seem to me decidedly worse.

As historian Modris Eksteins writes in *Walking Since Daybreak*, 'It is not possible to write history without preconception. It is possible, however, to write history with layers of suggestion, so that history evokes, history conjoins, it involves. History should provoke, not dictate meaning. It should be a vehicle rather than a terminus.' The result, one hopes, is an account that both opens up and advances new understandings of the past.

I've read scores of historians in my adult life. I've liked some more than others. Who, in my view, makes a good historian? One with ample sensitivity, imagination, depth of perception, the right distance and the ability to synthesize vast bits of social knowledge. One who tries 'to see the world as its members saw it, and understand, to the extent possible, what it was like to live in it'.[2] One who labours over linguistic clarity and analytical rigour and frets about the quality of her sources and being truthful to herself. One who possesses a judicious *sense of history*, the kind that comes from sustained reflection on human societies across time and place.

Furthermore, she knows that historical sources can lie, that things are often not what they seem. Indian court chroniclers often inflated the political, cultural, military and sexual exploits of their patrons. Classical Athenian art can lead us to overestimate the social status of women in that society, as Khajuraho's erotic art can convey a misleading view of most women's sexual freedom in the time of the Chandelas. Ancient and medieval travellers, who rarely spoke local languages, often recorded errors, hearsay and matters 'lost in translation' as truth. Consider: If a far descendant of ours, studying Sweden in early twenty-first century, looked at the Swedish books of that period, she would find a high proportion of crime fiction and may conclude that crime was a major concern there compared to other countries. In fact, Sweden has a relatively low crime rate but a penchant for crime thrillers. A good historian cultivates a fine-tuned radar to assess what conclusions are supportable by what evidence.

Unfortunately, historians can also be accomplices in political games. Some, more than others, interpret past events to favour a particular group. While it's true that no one owns history, some historians are clearly more partisan—like those who wilfully flout or conjure up evidence, or are led by a hegemonic sense of identity. Such history writing—often zealously undertaken from what is defined as 'our perspective'—is less about elevating scholarship, and more about honing majoritarian pride in a social group. Histories written from such insular points of view thrive by inflating the fears, resentments and tribal affinities in the reader—and exacerbate civil and communal strife.

In my storytelling, I wish to promote neither pride nor shame in our past, but to increase understanding of the diverse and complex journeys of our ancestors. I see the past as a dynamic interplay of migration, conflict, mixing, coexistence and cooperation led by various existential motives. I write not from any 'our' perspective but from *my* perspective, which accounts for both cultural and material factors, and is not aligned with any single ideological view. I've gained from many views and aspire to be as fair-minded as I can be, while striving for intimacy, immersion and analysis. I'm not inclined to take pride in things I did not help create, but I do believe in celebration and wonder—and there is plenty in the Indian past worthy of both, as I hope the reader will find in the following pages. At the end of the day, what will always make a 'better story' of the past is the reader's discernment in the present.

The Arc of My Story

Following this introduction, six chapters on major sites alternate with five chapters on major travellers. In this way, I zoom across nearly 5000 years of India's past while reflecting on some of its most brilliant eras—and their breaks and continuities with Indian social life today.

I begin with Dholavira, a Bronze Age metropolis of the Harappan Civilization in the Rann of Kutch, discovered only in 1967. Thriving between 2600–1900 BCE, it is best known for its water harvesting and fine reservoirs. I examine the ancestry of the Harappans, what they excelled at and what distinguishes them from other civilizations of the day—such as not turning up any evidence of temples, wars or armies, and seemingly possessing a flatter social class hierarchy. I consider the languages they likely spoke, their undeciphered script, theories about their demise, and how their legacy lives on today in our lives. I talk to the ecologically vulnerable locals from the nearby village of Dholavira, after which the prehistoric site is named and whose residents too had lived with ecological vulnerability.

After the decline of Harappan cities, Aryan migrants from Central Asia arrived by 1500 BCE and mixed with the locals. A nomadic-pastoralist people, the Aryans brought a proto-Sanskrit language, an early version of the Vedas, new forms of social hierarchy and the horse. After a gap of more than a thousand years since the fall of the Harappan cities, the next cities arose mostly in the Gangetic Plain in the first millennium BCE, moving India from prehistory into the age of decipherable texts, and the time of the Buddha, Mahavira and the early Upanishads. I present some fascinating observations by Megasthenes, Greek ambassador to the Mauryan court in Pataliputra, c. 300 BCE—including a custom where Mauryan men sing and play music to soothe angry elephants. Ashoka's missionary work helped make Buddhism a pan-Asian religion.

I then visit Nagarjunakonda in Andhra Pradesh, a lost world found in 1920. Once called Vijayapuri, it was the capital of the Ikshvaku Kingdom (c. 220–320 CE) that traded with Rome and whose Buddhist institutions were mainly patronized by wealthy women. Among its remains is the only amphitheatre found in ancient India. I take an imaginary walk through the ancient city and consider the ideas of Nagarjuna, founder of the 'Middle Path' school of Mahayana Buddhism—best known for the concept of *shunyata*—and one of the greatest philosophers of all time.

By the mid-first millennium CE, Chinese pilgrims began to arrive on perilous journeys to India. They came seeking Buddhist scholarship and authoritative texts. I present highlights from the surviving records of three of them—Faxian, Xuanzang, Yijing—that provide us vital portraits of Indian social and religious life between 400–700 CE. The 'first and chief difference between India and other nations', wrote Yijing, 'is the peculiar distinction between purity and impurity'. They described ongoing tussles between Brahmins and Bodhisattvas. These Chinese monks' records, translated in the nineteenth century, helped rediscover India's Buddhist antiquity (after Buddhism declined and vanished from India, its texts, monuments and even the Buddha himself were forgotten by the Indians).

One such rediscovery was Nalanda Mahavihara, a Buddhist monastery in Bihar often considered the first university in the world. Between the fifth and thirteenth centuries, monks from across Asia came here to learn grammar, logic, philosophy, theology, astronomy and medicine. I wander its tranquil ruins and attempt to conjure up the lives of its monks in the seventh century. I introduce their famous teachers and their notable theories, examine the university's financing and more. In the late first millennium, both Indian Buddhism and Nalanda declined for reasons surprisingly different from those peddled in popular histories. I reflect on the stark contrast between Bihar's illustrious past and its dismal present.

In 1001 CE, Mahmud of Ghazni began his infamous plundering raids in the subcontinent. In this period, Alberuni—a brilliant scholar, scientist and polyglot—spent thirteen years studying Indian society and culture. I consider his account of India, which he had written to provide, in his own words, 'the essential facts for any Muslim who wanted to converse with Hindus and to discuss with them questions of religion, science, or literature'. Few pre-modern travellers can match his insights into Indian life and thought. His account shows that on the eve of the Turko-Persian invasions, Brahminical society wasn't exactly a picture of intellectual and moral well-being that many now fondly imagine it to be.

I board a train to see the temples of Khajuraho, famed for their erotic art. Built between 950 and 1100 CE, they were later swallowed up by a forest and eventually discovered as archaeological ruins by a British engineer only in 1838. I seek answers to what every modern visitor likely wonders: What does this erotic art mean? How did a culture that exalts penance and renunciation depict sex so vividly on temple walls, next to their gods? What social milieu permitted such depictions that scandalize Indians today? And why did this tradition disappear entirely from temple art across India? For a site as famous as Khajuraho, it's astonishing that most popular histories and local guides get the answers almost entirely wrong.

I next turn to the Italian merchant and explorer, Marco Polo, and his social portrait of the Coromandel Coast. Returning home to Venice from China in 1292 CE, Marco spent a few weeks or months in the kingdom of the Tamil Pandyas near modern Thanjavur, before sailing up the Malabar Coast. He noted that people eat with only their right hand and keep the left for 'unclean' tasks, avoid putting their lips on drinking flasks and consider darker skin more attractive. After Marco, additional portraits of the Malabar Coast came from Ibn Battuta of Morocco, Abdur Razzaq of Persia, Afanasy Nikitin of Russia and others, who also describe striking family norms that have gone extinct along with many social habits and prejudices that survive today.

I then visit the breathtaking ruins of Vijayanagar in Hampi, Karnataka. Once the capital city of the Vijayanagar Empire (c. 1336–1565), it was famed for its wealth, military prowess and cosmopolitanism. How did it acquire all the riches that foreign travellers gushed about? Was Vijayanagar a self-conscious bastion of Hinduism heroically resisting Islam for centuries, as Hindu nationalists claim? What is its legacy in south India? For such questions and a sense of its rulers, economy, trade, social customs and festivals, I lean on both scholars and visitors like Razzaq, Niccolo de Conti of Italy, and Duarte Barbosa, Domingo Paes and Fernao Nuniz of Portugal. Near Hampi, I also meet Krishna

Devaraya, eighteen generations apart from his famous namesake and royal ancestor.

I then turn to François Bernier, a French physician who spent twelve years in north India (1658–69), mostly working for a nobleman in Aurangzeb's court. A rationalist steeped in the mindset of the emerging Enlightenment in Europe, he wrote about the pomp and the glitter of the Mughal court, as well as the fine architecture of Delhi and Agra. Eager to explain the recently discovered principles of blood circulation, he was known to cut open living goats and sheep before his horrified hosts in Delhi. His insightful analysis of the causes of the dismal social and economic conditions of ordinary Indians in pre-colonial India also reveals how woefully unprepared Indians were for the cultural and economic onslaught of European imperialism.

Finally, I visit Varanasi, a city inhabited since antiquity. Archaeological remains of its lost worlds, including ancient Kashi and Sarnath, date to early first millennium BCE. Steeped in religious mythology, Varanasi has been home to many major and minor faiths and intense sociopolitical contestation. Although it is often seen as a centre of Hindu orthodoxy, it has a rich, pluralistic past and is equally the city of Kabir and Ravidas. In a city that relies on the business of pilgrimage and death, I look at two of its core communities that operate along the Ganga: the Mallah boatmen and the Dom workers on the cremation ghats.

I see this book as my ongoing conversation with these sites and travellers. It began fifteen years ago and a snapshot of it is frozen in these pages. Over time I may well revise some of my opinions; regret that I forgot to say some things, or didn't say them well enough; and at times be surprised at how well I articulated my view. This book will also continue to remind me that all my immersion in lost worlds is largely to better understand my own.

Gurgaon, January 2020

The Mysteries of **Dholavira**
(2600–1900 BCE)

The road to Dholavira cuts across a dazzling landscape of salty mudflats before entering Khadir Island. I'm travelling across to the island's western end, to the archaeological site of Dholavira, a nearly 5000-year-old city of the Harappan Civilization.

It is mid-afternoon in early April and the mercury is pushing 40°C. The pale hues of this desert land contrast with the colourful attires of women of various castes and semi-nomadic pastoral groups: Ahir, Meghwal, Rabari, Jat and others. I ask my taxi driver to stop for a photo, and a group of Ahir women receive me with curious stares and giggles, much as I recall from thirteen years ago in 2006, when I first visited Dholavira.

This is the Rann of Kutch, an area in north-western Gujarat comprising about a tenth of the state, bordering Pakistan. In prehistoric times, the Rann ('salt marsh') was a navigable extension of the Arabian Sea. It later got closed off from the sea by siltation and possibly also by seismic upheaval. Nowadays, during the monsoon, rain and seasonal rivers fill up the low-lying areas of the Rann, aka the 'white Rann', with water that turns brackish from the residual salt encrusted upon the ground. In some parts, the locals get out in boats and harvest shrimp. When the waters begin to dry up, flamingos migrate to its wetlands from northern climes.

Surreal scenes greet dry-season visitors: the cadavers of wooden boats, abandoned by the locals, on unevenly dried mudflats. Some people go off-road and drive on to this 'white Rann', taking care to avoid any remaining slushy spots. Heat mirages make distant landmarks hover in mid-air. In the moonlight, the salty white terrain glows; without the moon, the Milky Way often lights up the night sky.

Settlements in the Rann are limited to a few *bets*, or grassy island–plateaus above the salty mudflats. Khadir, about 500 sq. km in size, is one such island that hosts the remains of the ancient city of Dholavira. Discovered in 1967 and excavated only after 1989, Dholavira is among the five largest Harappan cities known today, along with Harappa, Mohenjo-Daro and Ganweriwala in Pakistan, and Rakhigarhi in India. They represent the first-ever urban culture in the subcontinent, with well-planned 'cities, developed social classes, craft and career specialists, writing and long-distance trade with Mesopotamia, Central Asia, and even with the countries at the mouth of the Red Sea'.[1] As we'll see, their cultural legacy still thrives in modern Indian culture.

Khadir has no perennial rivers, lakes or springs. It also gets little rain, making it a harsh environment to live in. At least since Harappan times, Khadir has had a shallow potable aquifer. Its farmers have long grown crops like millets (jowar, bajra), green gram (mung) and sesame by supplementing rainwater with groundwater using hand-drawn wells. The archaeological site gets its name from the village of Dholavira (population 2500), a short walk from the ruins.

Further east, in the Little Rann of Kutch, is a wildlife sanctuary that protects the endangered khur, or Asiatic wild ass, a shy, handsome animal that can sprint at 70 km per hour. It lives on a few bets in the Rann. Only a few thousand khurs survive, though luckily, their numbers have risen since my last

Figure 1. Structures atop the 'citadel' of Dholavira

visit. The sanctuary also has wetlands where local and migratory birds nest, including cranes, storks and flamingos. The flamingo—delicately perched on one leg, neck down, looking for shrimp—seems to me an apt symbol of vulnerability in this era of climate change. Here and there a desolate camp is planted upon the crusty dirt, where a family or two join forces to eke out a living by mining salt from the saline groundwater; this is a major local industry. Legend has it that when a salt worker dies, the soles of his feet survive the cremation—a lifetime of salt pan labour bakes them so hard that even fire cannot fully consume them. The mined salt is transported in Tata lorries and heaped into many hillocks of salt around a nearby railhead. Unlike today, salt was once a precious commodity, creating proverbial obligations to those 'whose salt one has eaten'.

I stay in a *bhunga*, the traditional round hut of the Kutch region, at the Dholavira Tourism Resort, an unpretentious hotel that's a short walk from the ruins. Built by the state, it's run by a committee of Dholavira villagers headed by the sarpanch, and its profits are invested locally. At the archaeological site in the morning, three men—a caretaker and two guides—are playing cards on a stone bench. Though tourism has risen since my last visit, I see no other tourists. The caretaker says that the site now averages three to five visitors daily in this off season, whereas thirteen years ago, in the same season, I had been the first visitor in three days. An Archaeological Survey of India (ASI) museum with an auditorium has come up as well.

The ASI, led by archaeologist R.S. Bisht, excavated Dholavira over fourteen winters, from 1989–2005. Hundreds from the Dholavira village worked at the digs. The older of the two guides in front of the museum has worked with Bisht himself. The younger guide offers to show me several attractions in addition to the site: his Meghwal neighbourhood in the Dholavira village—one of its many neighbourhoods that are segregated by caste; the glow of the white Rann on the upcoming full moon night; unexcavated Harappan sites on Khadir Island where broken beads and pottery can still be found on the ground; a stone quarry used by the ancient Dholavirans; and a hill replete with wood and seashell fossils. Good thing I'm here for at least a week.

The Rise of the Harappans

The Harappan Civilization (aka the Indus Valley Civilization), alongside the Egyptian, the Mesopotamian and the Chinese, counts among the world's greatest Bronze Age civilizations. 'Civilization' here usually refers to urban life enabled by agricultural surpluses, specialized occupations, social stratification, writing or other symbolic communication, and monumental architecture. Lasting from 3300–1300 BCE but thriving in its mature form between 2600 and 1900 BCE, the Harappan Civilization exceeded all other Bronze Age civilizations in both population (estimates range from one to five million) and geographic spread (nearly a third of modern India's size).[2] It 'was the most extensive urban culture of its time, about twice the size of its equivalent in Egypt or Mesopotamia'.[3]

The Harappan Civilization, discovered as recently as 1924, pushed back antiquity in the subcontinent by 3000 years. British archaeologist, Sir John Marshall, announced the discovery of Harappa and Mohenjo-Daro with great flourish in the *Illustrated London News*. In the preceding decades, many of its finds had been reported and studied, but the excavated artefacts had failed to fit existing theories; specialists couldn't decipher its symbols. Clearly this was something new. This groundwork had made Marshall's 'discovery' easier. Marshall himself had no clue about the age of the artefacts until, weeks after his

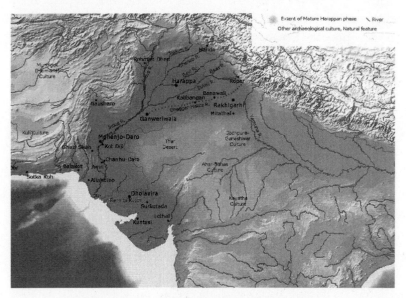

Figure 2. Spread of Mature Harappan Civilization[4]

announcement, it emerged that similar artefacts had also been found in ancient Mesopotamia. Funnily, an Indian archaeologist, Devadatta Ramakrishna Bhandarkar, had visited Mohenjo-Daro in 1911–12, but had 'thought the site was not old because the bricks looked modern to him'.[5] More Harappan sites were soon discovered, totalling thirty-seven by 1947. Today, over a thousand are known, from tiny hamlets to fortified cities with up to 50,000 people.

A great deal has been learnt about the Harappans since Marshall, but we may now be in one of the most exciting times in the study of the Harappan Civilization and its aftermath. Scientific scholarship, led by a large international study in population genetics and human migrations, has now decisively clarified a range of timelines, revealing fresh insights into the Harappans and how they are related to us. Recent findings from archaeogenetics tell us that the Harappan Civilization arose several millennia after two population groups collided and mixed as far back as 10,000 BCE. The first group was a local population of hunter-gatherers, the direct descendants of the earliest successful wave of modern humans who had left Africa at least 70,000 years ago and settled in the subcontinent at least 65,000 years ago.[6] The second group was a population of West Asian hunter-gatherers who migrated to the subcontinent before the advent of agriculture in the Fertile Crescent. It now appears that agriculture either arose independently in the subcontinent, or was imported in subsequent millennia by cultural rather than genetic diffusion from West Asia.[7]

As with other ancient civilizations, the Harappan Civilization largely arose along rivers and coasts. The rivers included the Indus and the extinct Ghaggar-Hakra (some scholars, with contested evidence and dubious motivation, call this the Saraswati River of the *Rig Veda*).[8] Scores of sites in Gujarat like Dholavira, Lothal and Surkotada arose on the Arabian Sea coast, or along nearby rivers. 'Indus Valley Civilization' is therefore inaccurate; many scholars prefer 'Harappan Civilization', honouring a convention in which the first discovered site's name is adopted for the whole.

As elsewhere, the Harappan Civilization too was marked by a set of advanced skills and practices. These include 'domestication of animals; cultivation of wheat, barley, and other grains; growing of fruits; building of houses; organization of society in cities; spinning and weaving of [cotton] textiles and dyeing them various colors; the use of the potter's wheel and the decoration of wares; river [and sea] navigation; the use of wheeled vehicles; the working of metal [copper, tin, arsenic, lead, silver, gold and electrum]; writing; fashioning of ornaments from faience, ivory, bone, shell, and semiprecious stones'.[9]

Harappan cities had specialized trades, markets, the fanciest goods and high culture, and had smaller towns and villages around them. City dwellers traded with farmers and herders in villages, and probably also with nomadic people and hunter-gatherer tribes in nearby forests. From the villages and the hinterlands, the city-dwellers received raw materials like metals, semi-precious stones, timber and, of course, food grains, conveyed by bullock carts or pack animals. There is no evidence that Dholavira was the capital of a unified region, but it seems reasonable to speculate that it was a trading hub for scores of Harappan sites and other nearby peoples. Archaeologist Gregory Possehl sees Dholavira as 'a regional center of authority, a hub of communications, an ancient caravanserai for traders and travelers'.

The Harappans seem to have lived in a heterarchy rather than a hierarchy, implying that across the entire Harappan realm, there was no overarching authority. Its far-flung regional centres were likely independent and decentralized, but localized hierarchies of power can be inferred from the plan of their cities. Further, their public works required a steady supply of labour, likely funded by taxes. What also unified them across the entire region was a common material culture (and perhaps a substantially common spiritual culture), though they were also ethnically diverse and had distinctive local features and priorities.

For instance, the Harappans were united by a common writing system. They had a uniform system of weights and measures, starting with a 50 mg weight, an astonishing feat of precision for its day. They all made similar beads, bangles, pottery and square seals. Their metallurgy was alike, with kilns fired at controlled temperatures up to 1200 °C. They forged similar tools like axes, hammers, chisels, saws, sickles, drills, nails, needles, textile looms, cattle ploughs, fishhooks and fishing nets. Their homes have turned up comparable razors, blades, copper mirrors, mortars, pestles and querns. They had similar architecture, town planning, drains and manhole covers, and brick-lined wells 'ingeniously built with tapering bricks to prevent them from collapsing'. In some riverine sites, including Mohenjo-Daro, every third house on average had a private well, in addition to the public wells. 'Many houses had waterproof bathing platforms and privies. Waste water was channeled away through pipes and chutes into covered drains that ran along level streets. The cesspits of these drains were regularly emptied.'[10] Their cities were usually oriented along cardinal directions. They seemingly also had a numbering system, at least in commercial use, that mixed binary and decimal—binary for small numbers, decimal for large.

The Harappan sites also had a fair bit of internal diversity, often shaped by geography. For instance, Dholavira lay in an arid zone and, compared to northern sites, focused a lot more on water harvesting and storage; its trade and material culture was more maritime than riverine; its funerary structures took many forms and differed from other regions' Harappan sites—they were largely cenotaphs, devoid of human bodies, suggesting different cultural beliefs (more on this below). Pottery and seals varied regionally in style and iconography.

Dholavira: The Great Metropolis of the South

The most striking feature of Dholavira today is its water management system. One gets the sense that, because of necessity, every drop of water in this arid land was saved. The city is spread over 200 acres, and about 10 per cent of it is taken up by sixteen rock-cut and/or stone-block-lined reservoirs of various sizes. They harvested water from catchment areas in the city as well as from two monsoon-season rivulets, Mandsar and Manhar, which they had dammed. Linked by intricate channels and dams, the reservoirs encircle the city's residential core. The largest of the five reservoirs excavated thus far could store nine times as much water as an Olympic-sized swimming pool and over a hundred times more water than the Great Bath of Mohenjo-Daro. Dholavira's planned residential centre, surrounded by waterbodies, must have made a visually appealing sight, and perhaps a source of pride for its residents.

Archaeologists speak of seven cultural stages in Dholavira's evolution. The settlement began around 3000 BCE with a walled fortress on a hill, and was clearly built by people who were already technologically advanced and valued urban planning. In stage two, the settlement grew northward. Stage three saw a spurt in creativity: new buildings and reservoirs came up, along with big gains in pottery art. Then came a big earthquake that damaged the fortress. Dholavira's mature phase spans stages four and five, from 2500–2000 BCE, when most of its monumental structures—gateways, fortifications, reservoirs—were built, along with a profusion of pottery, inscribed seals, weights, beads, and items of gold, silver, copper, ivory, shell, faience, soapstone, clay and stone. The fifth stage saw rising levels of impoverishment and urban decay, ending with a temporary desertion of the city, perhaps after a breakdown of its water harvesting system.[11] Then came a brief revival in stage six, at least on the citadel—a new group of Harappans arrived, who left a different cultural stamp on the artefacts from this stage. In the last stage came a group that built an entirely new style of homes, which were circular—the bhunga, like my room in the local hotel. However, the city kept shrinking, until it was finally abandoned around 1500 BCE. As with much else about

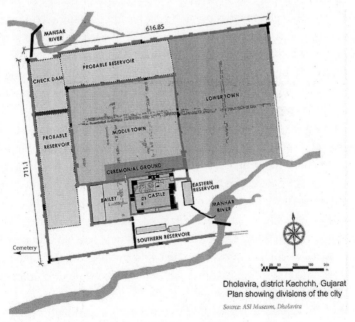

Dholavira, district Kachchh, Gujarat
Plan showing divisions of the city
Source: ASI Museum, Dholavira

Figure 3. Site plan of Dholavira with major divisions

Dholavira in particular and the Harappan Civilization in general, no one is sure why this vital urban centre ended when it did. We do know, however, that Dholavira outlasted other well-known cities like Mohenjo-Daro and Harappa by up to two centuries.

Three major sections of the city have been identified: 'citadel', 'middle town' and 'lower town', in descending order of prosperity and civic amenities. To the south, on higher ground, is the citadel, where the elites presumably lived. It is enclosed in thick fortification walls of stone, with pillared guard rooms just inside the locking gates, as in medieval forts. To the north of the citadel is the middle town, and the lower town is to its east. The middle town had larger homes and an enclosing wall of its own, suggesting that people of a higher class lived there than in the lower town, who were protected only by the outer city walls.

The massive walls of the citadel has towers and five gates, each with a different design. Inside, there are remains of a 'castle', with its concealed passageways; sewage and water harvesting drains; stairs and chambers, some with chiselled pillars of finely polished limestone. East of the castle on the citadel is the 'bailey' area, with homes of people presumed to be servants to those in the castle and perhaps also granaries (some dispute this interpretation). Many of the seven settlement stages, which span a depth of 14 metres, are visible in certain excavated parts of the citadel, though most stages lie buried. What's visible today doesn't always correspond with the city's mature phase. Overall, less than a fifth of the site has been excavated.

Among the most impressive finds on the citadel are its intricate network of storm-water drains, 'with slopes, steps, cascades, manholes (air ducts/water relief ducts), paved flooring and capstones'.[12] Its arterial drain was large enough for a person to walk through. A deep well atop the citadel was once fitted with ropes and leather buckets—a stone at the edge has rope marks—and the extracted water then cascaded down rock-lined channels to a small water reservoir, and to a bathing tank for the citadel's residents. Who occupied this privileged spot, and what social organization supported them? All we have now is informed speculation (more on this below).

Both the middle and lower towns functioned as residential quarters, with streets and homes laid out on an approximate grid-like plan. Many bead and metal workshops have also been found, suggesting that these areas were not only residential. Among other trades, the locals cut, polished, etched, and drilled beads with high artistic and technological skill. Many homes seem to combine a workshop area, a washroom and residential quarters. As with most ancient cities, the rooms, even in the middle town, are small by today's middle-class urban standards—they're more like the rooms in our urban slums. Kitchens seem scarce, suggesting the use of communal kitchens. In the first three stages of the city, people used white and pink clay 'for plastering nearly all the structures whether defensive walls, roads, streets, ceremonial ground, or the walls and floors of private houses'. But this changed abruptly in stage four, 'as if under a royal decree or by a resolute public consensus'.[13] Dholavirans kept dogs as pets, and figurines often depict them with collars. Stray dogs likely roamed the ancient city as they do today in urban India.

Water harvesting drains that fed the city's reservoirs ran throughout the city. However, perhaps due to the city's limited supply of water, sewage drains were built only on the citadel, not in the middle or lower town. Most houses in the middle and lower towns had internal drains

Figure 4. Gate and wall between middle and lower towns

that emptied outside into portable waste-water pots, like the earthen *matkas* of today. These served as sullage jars—used mainly for fluid waste, human and industrial—which were periodically emptied beyond the city walls into the sea. For defecation, ancient Dholavirans likely went outside the city walls with a lota in hand (as some people still do today in the Dholavira village).

Figure 5. 'Citadel' and north gate, overlooking the 'stadium'

Figure 6. Symbols on the signboard of Dholavira. Author of sketch: Siyajkak; CC BY-SA 3.0

Between the citadel and the middle town is an open field, 285 m x 47 m, which was once enclosed on all four sides by stepped grandstands, in either three of four tiers. The space has been dubbed a 'stadium', which Bisht reckons may be the 'earliest and the largest stadium found so far in antiquity'.[14] Besides sports, the 'stadium' may also have hosted 'royal' or religious ceremonies, festivals, public executions, performances or markets.

Overlooking this stadium is the citadel's north gate, the most monumental of all gates. Perhaps big announcements were made from its high vantage point to thousands of people gathered below. On this gate hung the famous three-metre-wide signboard of Dholavira, with its ten mysterious symbols. Each symbol, made from gypsum inlaid in wood, was about 14 inches high, the largest size found anywhere in the Harappan realm. They must have been legible from the stands across the stadium. For all we know, it could well have said, 'Save water!'

Walking around, I often spot pottery shards on the ground, some painted, some as large as my palm. They came from pots that were up to one metre tall. I pick up a smooth piece of a stone bangle worn by a Dholaviran four millennia ago. Perhaps a mother scolded her child for breaking it. Dholavira, it appears, was 'one of the greatest centres for making stone beads' and has yielded 1270 drill bits and many stone polishers, the largest from any Harappan site.[15] Notably, the castle itself had many bead-making workshops. My guide points out bits of semi-precious stones lying about—carnelian, chert, quartz, chalcedony, serpentine, jasper, agate—many from mines in Kutch. He shows me greenish copper slags from the smelting process used to purify the ore. Children's toys, whistles, dice, sling balls, hopscotches, game boards carved on stone blocks and even a smoking pipe have been found here. Perhaps then, too, small crowds gathered around players hunched over a board game under a shady tree. Around 225 seals, of steatite (soapstone) and other materials, have been found (soft steatite stones were finely carved, polished and fired in a kiln to harden them). 'They carted many truckloads of material to Delhi,' claims the guide, where it now lies in ASI facilities. He also points out some of the bones of animals that the Harappans ate: goat, sheep, cow, buffalo, deer, fish, rabbit, chicken, wild pig, wild ass and more. The Harappans hunted too; seals from many other Harappan sites show 'encounters with wild and ferocious animals'.[16]

A great mystery surrounds the walls of Dholavira—from its outer city walls to internal walled neighbourhoods. Its city walls are several metres thick; three of its four corner towers have been excavated. But it's unclear from whom such thick defensive walls were meant to protect the residents. Dholavira was then literally on an island! None of the usual threats—wild animals, enemy states (there were likely none), pirates from the sea, or hostile tribal groups (how many could have been there on the island to be a threat?)—would have required stone walls that are many metres thick and high. Nor are there moats around them. Some speculate that the walls guarded against sea storms and tsunamis, but the walls had gates and weren't watertight. Perhaps they withstood earthquakes better. Or perhaps the walls were part of a still-unknown cultural or religious project. Asko Parpola, a Harappan Civilization scholar and author of *The Roots of Hinduism* (2015), has suggested that their purpose may 'have been to impress people and thus reinforce political power'.[17] Unfortunately, not much can be said here with certainty about what drove their need for such massive fortifications.

Indeed, Dholavira's gigantic reservoirs and fortification walls are its monumental works, rivalling the Pyramids of Giza in ambition, effort, design planning and mobilization of labour. The Herculean civil engineering makes one wonder what drew Dholavirans to this hostile arid land in the first place (maybe it was much less arid in 3000 BCE, as has been proposed), and how much collective thought and energy went into the hydraulic projects. It must have required a large labour force and a centralized bureaucracy. Notably, Harappan cities offer no evidence of slave labour, nor 'depictions of people being bound or captured',[18] though it's worth remembering that an absence of evidence is not evidence of absence.

At its peak, the walled city of Dholavira had an area under 0.5 sq. km, slightly larger than Vatican City. It perhaps had a population of 10,000–15,000, and was almost as dense as Delhi today. Interestingly, much of it was for pedestrians only. 'There is no evidence of rut marks on the main streets of Dholavira,' writes Bisht, suggesting that they 'didn't allow bullock carts or any kind of vehicular traffic inside the city'. Rut marks do appear at the entrance gate to the stadium, which may have been from carts conveying goods to a market there, or perhaps participating

Figure 7. A reservoir on the south side; citadel visible on top

in sports. Many people must have lived outside the city walls too, especially farmers and herders, likely in homes made of perishable materials. Perhaps artisans as well, who may have come to the city to its workshops and to sell their wares. At least three other Harappan settlements within half-a-day's travel by bullock cart have also been found on Khadir Island.

Beyond the City Walls of Dholavira

Further west, past the western wall, lies the city's necropolis with hundreds of unmarked burials. Most are about the same size and contain funerary objects like pots and beads, with some burials a little better endowed than others. However, all but one of the three dozen excavated burials are symbolic or cenotaphs, i.e. without human remains. It's not clear what they did with the bodies. Bisht has proposed that Dholavirans had switched to another method of disposing the dead while still raising memorials. A couple of the burials are architecturally far more elaborate than the others, with more lavish objects. They contain multiple burials added over time in layers, turning it into a mound—perhaps belonging to a set of people related in some way across hundreds of years, whether from a single family or owners of a hereditary title or conferred honour. Due to the absence of human remains, the precise relationships of those buried here remain unclear. This represents an entirely novel form of burial in the Harappan realm.

Other Harappan sites display a range of funerary practices. Mohenjo-Daro hasn't revealed a cemetery at all. Harappa, Kalibangan and Rakhigarhi have cemeteries where burials with bodies outnumber cenotaphs, but even taken together, these burials represent only a small fraction of those who must have died.[19] Some scholars have speculated that burials, whether or not with human remains, were given only to members of a certain class and/or ethnicity. What funerary treatment did the rest receive? Cremation is an obvious possibility but archaeological evidence for it is extremely weak (evident only at one small site, Tarkhanwala). Perhaps cremations were held far away from the city, and they didn't collect the ashes to bury in the cenotaphs. Perhaps the dead were consigned to the river or the sea, a practice that has a long history in India (even today certain kinds of people are consigned directly into the Ganga). No one knows for sure. However, at least based on a sample of the exhumed bodies, Harappan life expectancy seems fairly good for that era—'nearly half of the individuals reached their mid-30s and almost one-sixth lived beyond the age of 55'.[20] Many of them had dental caries and likely suffered toothaches.

What did they think about their afterlife? What daily fears and hopes did they harbour? What were their myths, anxieties, humour, repressions, prejudices? Until the Harappan script is deciphered, much of how we answer these questions amounts to informed speculation at best. The script, presumably logo-syllabic, has yielded 400 plus unique symbols (versus 600 plus for Sumerian Cuneiform) on seals, pottery, metal and other artefacts. Parpola feels 'sure that just one language was used in writing the Indus script, because the sign sequences of its inscriptions are repeated throughout' the Harappan realm.[21] Written from right to left, the inscriptions contain only five symbols on average, which some claim make unusually short texts for a linguistic script. Over a hundred claims of decipherment have failed to convince most scholars. Three scholars have even argued that the Harappan symbols don't represent a linguistic script, and may be a system of communication akin to modern traffic signs.[22] This means, they say, that instead of coding a significant portion of a spoken language, the script only represents 'nonlinguistic symbols of political and religious significance'. This has been robustly challenged by Parpola and other scholars. The Harappans certainly knew about the Mesopotamian Cuneiform writing system, so they knew the value of a script. Perhaps theirs was not a full but a partial writing system. Even such basic matters remain unresolved.

It's unclear how the script will finally be deciphered, unless we chance upon a bilingual text for its inscriptions—a Rosetta Stone of sorts. If such a thing exists, it may be in Mesopotamia, where the Harappans traded actively. I personally hope their inscriptions turn out to be a script that encodes vivid information, and that it gets deciphered in my lifetime, revealing the Harappans based on their own words and unlocking more of their mysteries for us.

One afternoon, the younger guide takes me to the quarry from where ancient Dholavirans mined the beautiful multihued stones found all over their city. We ride his 100-cc motorcycle, going north on unpaved hilly, stony roads through arid scrubland. After seeing the quarry, we continue north, looking for an unexcavated Harappan mound, one of a few on Khadir. This region is under close surveillance by the Border Security Force (BSF), especially since the terrorist attack in February 2019 in Pulwama, Kashmir. We learn from a passing jeep of BSF jawans that to go further we'll need permission from a faraway office, a process that might take weeks and possibly end in denial.

But when the jawans disappear from sight, we push on, risking the consequences. On one uphill stretch of rocky terrain, the bike stalls and tips over. We fall but escape lightly, with just a knee abrasion in my case. I'm soon drawn to an enchanting quality in this part of the island, to its undulating hills and the great views it offers over the gleaming white Rann. The terrain is also rich in fossils and variously coloured and textured stones. When we stop to wander up a slope, I stash a few seashell fossils in my pocket. A couple of miles later, perhaps shaken by the fall, the guide gets cold feet, raises the spectre of detection by the BSF, and advises that we turn back.

What's clear is that Dholavirans engaged in an epic struggle against the elements. Their entire city strived to wrestle order out of a hostile environment, and did so for over a millennium. Perhaps the elements got worse over time, but why did they choose this struggle? With the area's water resources clearly not ideal for agriculture, what economic activity could have driven the city's fortunes and sustained people for centuries in this harsh environment? Some scholars believe that Dholavira was a regional hub of maritime trade and commerce (the Rann was then navigable to the Arabian Sea and beyond).

The Harappans traded internally and with others, both overland and on waterways. Porters and bullock carts moved goods overland. From the sea near Dholavira, ships went upriver to Harappa with salted and/or dried marine catfish. They sourced raw materials from far and wide: copper, shell, semi-precious stones. Skilled artisans must have travelled often, spreading similar technologies and fads. Going by discovered seals, beads and weights, the Harappans also traded with Sumer and Akkad in Mesopotamia, and with Dilmun people on the islands of Failaka and Bahrain in the Persian Gulf. In these parts, the

Harappans were known as the people of Meluhha—possibly close to a name the Harappans had for their own territory—and were perhaps seen as a source of luxury goods like carnelian beads, lapis lazuli, gold dust, ivory, pearls, fine timber and exotic animals. The Harappans may have returned with dates, wool textiles, incense and more.

All this trade appears to have been led by the Harappans, who built seagoing vessels that went along the coast to Mesopotamia. Based on surviving terracotta models from the nearby trading port of Lothal (then on the sea), these vessels include a sailboat, 'a flat-bottomed barge-like boat', 'a heavy boat, with a broad stern, and pointed prow' and a catamaran.[23] These and other innovations in seafaring may have happened at Dholavira and Lothal. A ship depicted on a seal shows a central cabin and two land-seeking birds. Many of their ships were large and sturdy enough to even transport water buffaloes to Mesopotamia, for which there is inferential evidence. Some Akkadian seals refer to an expat community of Harappans in Mesopotamia. One describes the owner of the seal as 'Silusu, interpreter of Meluhha language'. A Sumerian-style burial found in Harappa suggests that Mesopotamians lived in that city too.[24]

On stone benches under a tree outside the museum, I chat with the two guides. They are both from the Dholavira village. They take pride in their village becoming famous by association with the ancient site, but there is also a sense of resentment towards the ASI. The guides claim that the government, at the ASI's behest, forcibly acquired farmland around the site (c. 2012), for which they paid the villagers a mere Rs 2900 per acre. People still farmed this land, beneath which lay more reservoirs of the ancient city. 'The price was an insult,' says the older guide, turning gloomy. 'Better to have given them our land as a gift.' The matter is now in court in another town; the villagers are ill-organized, they have to bear the costs of travel and litigation, and the case might take years or even decades to resolve. The guides also allege that after the digs were done, none of those who worked for years on the digs with Bisht were given permanent government jobs at the site or the museum.

Most guides also resent that all credit for the discovery of Dholavira went to J.P. Joshi of the ASI, with no mention at all of two villagers, Shambhudan Gadhavi, master clerk and amateur geologist, and Velubha

Sodha, former sarpanch, who had earlier found the site, picked out some beads and pottery shards, and sent them to the Kutch Museum in 1967. Joshi was then working on Surkotada, a later Harappan site in Gujarat that thrived between 2100 and1700 BCE. Joshi recognized the artefacts from Dholavira at once, and was immortalized by history, even before turning up on site, allege the guides. Despite the enabling work done by others, John Marshall too got all the credit for the discovery of the Harappan Civilization. Such is the way of the world, laments one guide. He asks whether I, in my writing on Dholavira, would help set the record straight.

One afternoon I accompany a guide to the Dholavira village, designated a 'smart village' by the Gujarat government. Outside their dairy cooperative, we run into the sarpanch. Potable water is a huge problem here, he tells me. Some years ago, with the growing use of submersible water pumps, the shallow aquifer on Khadir Island began to go dry. Deeper borewells found only brackish water, unsuitable for all but a few salt-tolerant crops used mostly as livestock feed.

This ecological blow raised the farmers' vulnerability to droughts. Many shifted to raising cows, buffaloes and goats; some farmers and farm labourers migrated out; a few joined the nascent tourist economy and other trades. In a mere generation, producers became importers of grains and vegetables. The state now sends drinking water tankers to villages on Khadir Island, and has put a reverse osmosis filtration plant in Dholavira village for the brackish groundwater. The output is then sold at one rupee per litre. The villagers hope that the state will buy them an Israeli mobile desalination unit to make 100,000 litres of drinking water per day from the brackish groundwater. Others dream of a canal from the Narmada River, whose water already doesn't reach the sea. This seems like the future in most of Kutch, India's largest district. No one seems to be inspired by the ancient Dholaviran approach to this problem.

The Harappan Imagination

What was the unique genius, or at least what were the most distinctive qualities, of Harappan versus other early civilizations? 'The Indus polity and Indus society look totally unlike their contemporary equivalents in Mesopotamia,' writes Andrew Robinson in *The Indus: Lost Civilizations* (2015). Unlike in Mesopotamia and Egypt, archaeologists have not found any military grade weapons or war damage in Harappan cities, nor any depictions of war, armies or prisoners on Harappan seals or pottery, which otherwise depict a large range of subjects, including real and mythical fauna, flora, symbols, bullock carts, hunting scenes, people wearing jewels and elaborate headdresses, and mother goddess figures. This apparent lack of a warring culture is often attributed to their lucky geography—tucked between the north-western mountains, the eastern desert and the southern sea—which, it is said, shielded them from external enemies.

The Harappans, apparently, did not even wage internal wars. This is often explained by saying that the riverine Harappan cities were well provisioned, with no scarcity of food or other resources, reducing the impetus for conflict. However, Parpola believes that violence likely accompanied major transitions, as from the early to the mature Harappan phase, though there is no hard evidence (some early Harappan sites have turned up ash and debris, which may have resulted from either violent or accidental fires). Indeed, an *entirely* peaceful civilization is an idle fantasy, and Occam's razor points to other conclusions. After all, most cities had thick walls with watch towers. All the knives, spears and arrowheads discovered—presumed by some scholars to be used for hunting—could have been used against other groups of humans (one seal shows two men spearing each other while a woman, or a goddess, stands in the middle holding their free hands). There may well have been conflicts over fertile farmland, forests, water, taxation or certain resources that may not have been as plentiful as presumed. Still, the lack of loud and clear indicators of war or standing armies, so commonplace in other civilizations, is a striking feature of the Harappan Civilization.

Further, Harappan cities have not revealed monumental, or even humble, temple structures, a great puzzle for scholars. There aren't any equivalents of the temples and pyramids of ancient Egypt or the ziggurats of Mesopotamia. Some say the Great Bath of Mohenjo-Daro had a religious purpose but this is highly speculative. Or perhaps the Harappans built religious shrines and large sculptures from perishable materials like wood. In any case, while there are hints, we have no clear sense of Harappan gods and rituals, or whether they had any temples or priests.

Scholars have offered divergent interpretations of seals with possible religious content: a handsome seven-inch sculpture of a man named 'priest-king', who could well have been an aristocrat; a seal named 'proto-Shiva' that depicts a multi-headed, seated figure in a yoga-like pose, one of 'several other yogi images in the corpus of Mature Harappan materials';[25] another seal that shows a female (deity?) standing under a Bodhi tree with its heart-shaped leaves, a figure kneeling before her in supplication and seven standing figures watching them; other seals that depict mysterious objects and rituals before a unicorn; the swastika motif appears often; some female figurines have a paste-like substance along the middle parting of their hair; a stone object in the shape of a phallus has been identified; two terracotta male figurines have erections; a small terracotta object in Kalibangan resembles the familiar Shiva lingam.

All this is very tantalizing. There can be little doubt about cultural continuities. Harappan beliefs clearly shaped later religions of the Axial Age in the subcontinent. Quite possibly, Indian ideas of meditation and even renunciation have Harappan origins. But it's difficult to draw firm conclusions about this, or about what the Harappans themselves believed, at least until the script begins to speak. Scepticism is essential: The deciphered Mayan script revealed how wrong many scholars were about the beliefs they had attributed to the Mayans (such as being peaceful).

The Harappans did not build monumental sculptures, such as of kings or gods, as did the Mesopotamians and the Egyptians. This doesn't make them any less complex than others, writes Possehl, rather it's an alternative way in which a civilization, with a 'highly complex sociocultural system, has expressed itself'.[26] They did make fine miniature art, as in seals and beadwork. And while their figurines aren't notable for their artisanship, they still evocatively depict their people 'in great variety, with many poses: sitting in chairs, lying on beds, holding babies and animals, kneading bread, and other things that people do to round out their existence,' writes Possehl. Animal puppets, in which a bull might shake its head or pull a cart, reveal a playful sense of humour, perhaps designed to amuse children. There are some fantasy creatures too, but 'on the whole, the Indus peoples in their art, as in other aspects of their lives, come across as people with a practical bent, a tendency to deal with and represent the real world as they [and we] see it'.[27]

That said, what jumps out as the Harappans' greatest monumental work is the city itself, a marvel of urban design and engineering, city-wide sanitation systems that include the first indoor toilets in the world and sophisticated water management. 'Probably not until later Roman times did people devise so many clever construction techniques to deal with comforts and discomforts related to water.'[28] They also excelled at shipbuilding and long-distance trade—another reason to think that they had centralized authority and bureaucracy to mobilize labour, develop trading networks and organize long-distance shipping expeditions.

Figure 8. Eastern gate and entrance of the citadel

Harappan cities of the mature period (2600–1900 BCE) had some walled neighbourhoods with larger buildings and better provisions, suggesting that an elite class resided there. But not everyone agrees. There is 'no justification' or archaeological support for this presumption, says archaeologist Jonathan Mark Kenoyer.[29] In fact, in certain stages, the 'citadels' in Dholavira and Mohenjo-Daro were hubs of artisanal–industrial activity. There is no evidence of royal palaces; homes differ in size and provisions but not by much. Sanitation and water wells were available to all. Based on the bones of the dead, the rich and the poor seem to have enjoyed similar access to nutrition. Their burials too display a narrow range in their sizes and types of funerary objects. However, as noted earlier, burial practices may have varied across individuals, or social groups.[30] That the Harappans had a social class hierarchy is clear enough. What's remarkable is that this hierarchy seems so much flatter than in other ancient (or modern) civilizations.

To illustrate how unusual the Harappans seem, Robinson describes a Mesopotamian royal burial chamber where scores of other people were sacrificed and buried along with the king to assist him in his afterlife, adding that, 'No burial even remotely resembling this lavish Sumerian burial has turned up in excavations in the Indus area. Indus burials, which are relatively rare, contain the very simplest of ornaments, such as a shell bangle, no weapons and no hint of human sacrifice, whether of menservants or courtiers.'[31]

Based on all that we know today, it seems reasonable to say that the unique genius of the Harappans lies in building elaborately planned cities, and forging what seems a relatively egalitarian and non-warlike society. If only *this* could fire up our modern nationalists, I muse, rather than whether or not the Harappans created the Vedas or spoke proto-Sanskrit (more on this ahead).

The dining room in my hotel is also a round bhunga. At night it doubles up as a bedroom for the workers at the hotel. A set meal with papad, daal, a vegetable, ghee-coated chapattis, rice, salad, achaar and chhaachh comes for Rs 125, and a breakfast of upma or poha for Rs 70. The TV plays either IPL matches or Lok Sabha 2019 election news. The dining room is abuzz with flies. Little frogs hop in. 'Many more come in the monsoons,' says the only server in the restaurant. As a kid growing up in Gwalior, I saw frogs very often, but haven't seen one in years in our cities—not the least because frogs are undergoing a massive die-off globally. The server, a chatty middle-aged villager, had earlier showed me wood and seashell fossils he had collected on his outings with geologists. He knows that India was once joined with South Africa, before it broke away a 'long time ago'.

'Bisht worked very hard,' the server says in Hindi about Dholavira's lead archaeologist. 'Some people asked him, if the Aryans were not outsiders—as he held—why are there no horse bones here and at other sites? He never had a good answer. He half-heartedly cited the findings at Surkotada, though he knew that the "horse" reported there was really khur [Asiatic wild ass].' The server shrugs, 'I don't know where that debate is now.'

That silly 'debate', I tell him, thanks to genetics, is now officially over; the Aryans indeed came from outside.[32] He nods and flashes a smile. Earlier in the day, one of the guides had also said that Bisht interpreted many findings in Dholavira through a Vedic lens.[33] 'One shouldn't bring *dharam* into scholarship,' the guide had sagely said. 'It doesn't come to any good.'

After a hot day I yearn for a cold beer and silently curse the powers that have made Gujarat a dry state. For those in the know, a guide told me, prohibition is a joke; country liquor is available in every village. Mafias in Ahmedabad deliver liquor at home like pizza. The Harappans, going by a distiller excavated at a site in Sindh, were perhaps the first people in the world to distil alcoholic beverages.[34] A Harappan artefact is said to 'represent the press used to make soma, a hallucinogenic drink known from later Vedic texts' composed in the subcontinent.[35] As I sit thirsting for a beer, it seems to me that in at least one way, Gujarati politicians have regressed to the Stone Age.

The Decline of the Harappan Civilization

The mature Harappan age lasted an impressive 700 years (longer in some parts, including Gujarat). No one is sure why their industrial production and long-distance trade declined and their cities began depopulating after 1900 BCE, or why their script went out of use after 1800 BCE. There is no evidence yet of war, invasion or an epidemic. It appears to have been a slow, uneven process of urban collapse, desertion and dispersal, until its last vestiges vanished everywhere by 1300 BCE. How did archaeologists detect this civilizational decline? Robinson explains:

> In the most recent levels of Harappa and Mohenjo-daro the early excavators found distinct signs of deterioration in the conditions of houses, drainage and urban existence. At Mohenjo-daro, huts were poorly constructed out of used and often broken bricks; kilns were built in the middle of streets; and some bodies were left unburied . . . Moreover, painted pottery largely gave way to plain wares and inscribed seals were no longer in use.

Similar signs of decline occurred at Dholavira too. Across the realm, the decline, however, had regional variants, was non-linear, and even had halting, temporary revivals, often led by different cultural groups dubbed 'post-Harappans'. After its final demise, it took nearly a millennium for the next cities to arise in the subcontinent—in faraway Gangetic Plain— with no apparent awareness of their Harappan predecessors. Oddly, the subcontinent seems to have lived without a successor writing system for over a millennium, until the rise of the Brahmi script that we know from Ashoka's edicts. By then, the script must have been in use for a while, and evidence of its earliest use has turned up in Anuradhapura, Sri Lanka, in 6–5 centuries BCE.[36] It's currently safe to say that the flame of a literate urban civilization wasn't lit again for over a millennium.

One theory for the demise of Harappan cities blames regional climate change that likely caused a sustained drop in monsoon rains, making the entire region more arid and impairing the ability of the agricultural hinterland to feed its cities.[37] Support for this theory comes from the common depiction of animals like rhino, buffalo, elephant and tiger, which thrive in wetter climes. Another theory blames earthquakes, which likely altered the path of Indus River, impacting Harappa and Mohenjo-Daro, and turned the Ghaggar-Hakra River from a perennial Himalayan-sourced river into a monsoonal one, impacting Ganweriwala and Rakhigarhi. More frequent flooding, as in Mohenjo-Daro, may have caused more outbreaks of malaria or cholera, making people leave, but the evidence for this is still weak. It's also possible that new beliefs and material conditions led to a breakdown of earlier social relations between the city and the village, making it harder for the city to raise taxes from its rural hinterland. In other words, the cause of their demise is very much an unsettled debate, and likely involved multiple factors.

Whatever the cause, the Harappans and their descendants began moving east and south—a process already underway for millennia but had now gathered momentum—some to the Ganga–Yamuna plains, many more to the southern parts of the subcontinent. DNA analysis shows close genetic proximity between the Harappans and modern south Indians.[38] Even the Harappan language was very likely proto-Dravidian. Support for this comes from the proximity between modern Dravidian languages and Elamite, a deciphered but extinct language of Iran with a logo-syllabic script. Speakers of proto-Elamite, which however remains undeciphered, were neighbours to the Harappans and traded with them. Another strong

clue is an isolated pocket of a Dravidian language, Brahui, a close relative of
Elamite that still survives in Baluchistan, where the Harappans lived. Brahui
today has 300,000 speakers; their ancestors very likely did not migrate there
from south India. Parpola has highlighted 'Dravidian loanwords in the
Vedic language, including the oldest available source, the Rigveda'.[39]

In short, independent evidence from three disciplines—linguistics,
archaeology, genetics—now makes it fairly certain that the Harappans
spoke one or more proto-Dravidian languages (and possibly other
languages; they inhabited a large region). Their collapse in the northwest
was followed by the third major influx of migrants into the subcontinent,
of a people who called themselves Aryans. Never in their wildest dreams
could these Aryans have imagined that they'd be the source of so many
incendiary debates and culture wars 3500 years later!

The Aftermath of the Harappan Civilization

Harappan seals, pottery, figurines and animal bones reveal many real
and mythical animals—dog, tiger, birds, wild ass, 'unicorn, humped
bull, elephant, rhinoceros, water buffalo, short-horned humpless bull,
goat, antelope, crocodile and hare'[40]—but not horse, one-humped camel
or donkey. The horse appears in the subcontinent *after* the collapse of
the Harappan Civilization. It likely arrived in numbers along with the
Aryans from Central Asia, a horse-riding nomadic–pastoralist people
with perhaps some knowledge of crops. What also accompanied them
was their language and religion: proto-Sanskrit, proto-Vedas and Vedic
gods—mostly male gods, such as Indra, Agni, Mitra, Varuna, Rudra
and Surya, and a few female gods, such as Usha and Prithvi. They used
iron, revered fire and the cow (though they also slaughtered it and ate
beef),[41] and preferred cremating the dead. By the time these Aryan
herders entered the subcontinent—in the middle centuries of the second
millennium BCE—urban Harappans had largely dissolved into rural life.

Notably, the Vedic lore of the Aryans mentions defensive armour,
weapons, chariots and warfare against dark-skinned foes named Dasas.
But the Dasas were not Harappans, who no longer lived in fortified cities
by the time the Aryans reached the Indus Valley. Based on the styles of
Dasa forts described in the Rig Veda, Parpola and others have argued

that the Dasas were proto-Sakas, a pastoralist group of the Central Asian steppes, and 'the major fights between the Aryans and the Dasas probably took place not in the Indus Valley but in the Indo-Iranian borderlands, en route to the Indus Valley'. Nor does the description of the Saraswati River in the Rig Veda fit the Ghaggar-Hakra River that dried up c. 2000 BCE, and instead maps on to the river called 'Haraxvaiti (in Avestan) or Harahuvati (in Old Persian)', which is very likely the Arghandab River, or less likely the Helmand River, both in modern Afghanistan.[42]

After the arrival of the Aryans to the Indus Valley, the locals (rural descendants of the Harappans) probably saw them as an aggressive bunch and their encounters were likely not all peaceful. One indicator of this is the very skewed genetic footprint of the Aryan male in later populations, despite the fact that, like all migrating groups, they had come with entire families. According to a scientific study in 2017, 'Genetic influx from Central Asia in the Bronze Age was strongly male-driven, consistent with the patriarchal, patrilocal and patrilineal social structure attributed to the inferred pastoralist early Indo-European society.'[43] Further, while archaeologists haven't found any telltale signs of war or invasion, it's reasonable to expect that the locals would have initially resisted the imposition of the Aryan language, religion and culture, since that's how such encounters usually play out.

The Aryans also brought with them a form of social hierarchy with priests at the top—a proto-varna system without endogamy (i.e., marrying only within a specific social group). They had no linguistic script and the need for it was reduced due to the lack of an urban civilization. The priests may also have impeded the rise of a script that might have democratized their oral chants and deflated their esoteric powers. Notably, such instincts seem alien to the Harappan ethos, given the ubiquity of the artefacts with their script on them. For instance, their script often appears as graffiti-like scribbles on stone blocks in non-elite parts of Dholavira, and as messages stamped on pottery items used by ordinary people (possibly brand or ownership details?).

After a millennium of mixing and migration in the subcontinent, numerous sites arose in the Gangetic Plain, whose settlers had learnt 'to fire a more durable and sophisticated series of ceramics known as painted gray ware (PGW)', writes historian Sudipta Sen.[44] They evolved social formations 'in which clans, lineages, and tribes began to yield to new ruling councils and kings'. From this came new urban life, hybrid cultures, languages, pantheons and religio-spiritual ideas that we now associate with mid-first millennium BCE India. These developments had strong contributions from both the Aryan and the Harappan substrates. New political and social conflicts en route also seem to have inspired many of the stories in the great epic Mahabharata.[45]

Could the Harappan social hierarchy have included endogamy based on occupation, i.e., a proto-caste system? Did a hereditary group of manual scavengers clean the sullage jars of Dholavira homes? Current archaeology and genetics consider this unlikely (more ancient DNA analysis of Harappans may provide conclusive evidence). Scientists trace the earliest instances of endogamy to the first millennium BCE, probably more than a millennium after the Aryan migration into the subcontinent; mixing of populations was the norm until then. Thereafter, mixing coexisted with a few groups practicing endogamy, which eventually led to a more widely endogamous caste system.[46]

But can we say which cultural substrate—the Aryan or the Harappan—drove the creation of the caste system? A strong clue comes from the fact that Aryan genes register far more strongly in the higher castes, who are also lighter skinned on average. Further, DNA evidence has shown that endogamy first appeared and became the norm 'among upper castes and Indo-European speakers'.[47] Indeed, as many scholars have long argued, the roots of the Indian caste system almost certainly trace back to the Aryan substrate.

Further, patriarchal practices like Sati, too, appear to be a legacy of the Aryan substrate. Sati's earliest noted occurrence in India dates to the fourth century BCE, as recorded by two first-century-BCE writers, Diodorus Siculus and Strabo. Though now mostly associated with India, sati also occurred back then in the Near East and Europe, among descendants of earlier migrants of the root proto-Indo-European culture, the Yamnaya—also the parent culture of the Indo-Aryans. In the fifth century BCE, Greek historian Herodotus wrote about a Thracian tribe where the 'most beloved wife' of a dead husband—deemed so by family and friends, and intended to be a coveted honour—was sacrificed and buried with him. A century later, the Thracian wife of Philip II, father of Alexander the Great, was burned on her husband's funeral pyre, as per the custom of her people. In the first century CE, Roman historian Tacitus observed that in a Germanic tribe (descended from the Yamnaya), 'the wife refused to survive her husband, but killed herself in order to be burnt on the same funeral pyre as him'. He noted that many other tribes disliked widow remarriage. In the tenth century CE, Arab historian Al Masudi noted sati among Slavic and Russian tribes (also descended from the Yamnaya) in the Caucasus region and in India.[48] Such funerary customs have a distinctly patriarchal script. They're qualitatively different from those of ancient Egyptians, where servants were sometimes sacrificed and buried with an important man. Sati was likely alien to the Harappans, but in the mixed culture that arose later, it gained a foothold among the warrior elites and became part of the Indo-Aryan cultural legacy in the subcontinent.

In the last decades of the twentieth century, however, cultural chauvinism reared its ugly head in the scholarship of Indian prehistory. A host of Hindu nationalists and 'motivated scholars' (almost entirely brown or white Hindu men) began championing an alternative view of the Aryan migration, arguing that there was no Aryan migration at all![49] That the Aryans and the Harappans were one people, both 'fully indigenous'. They claimed that the proto-Indo-European language family, of which Sanskrit is a part, was created by these indigenous folks and taken to the west—the Out of India Theory (OIT). This also implied that the Harappans spoke proto-Sanskrit and codified it in their as-yet-undeciphered script, that they composed the Rig Veda, which describes their own fortified cities like Dholavira.[50] Such bogus 'scholarship', as is now amply clear, has fed hordes of middlebrow Hindutva ideologues since the 1980s. Armed with little knowledge and misplaced pride, well-heeled urban Hindus began to confidently assert that the Aryan Migration Theory was 'discredited'. Countless websites carry this fake news.

In fact, the 'controversy' about Aryan migration was never an honest disagreement among scholars. Parpola, for instance, has long considered it 'impossible' that 'the Vedic Aryans were indigenous to South Asia'.[51] The massive weight of evidence from linguistics, philology, and archaeology—though it had gaps that its rivals tried to exploit—has long favoured what's now being proven or refined by population archaeogenetics, a field whose impact on ancient history may end up being as significant as radiocarbon dating (1949).[52]

The OIT was motivated by bad politics rather than by good scholarship. Beneath its shallow veneer of science lay an insecure and parochial Hindutva project all too vested in proving that Vedic texts and Sanskrit were primordially indigenous to the subcontinent. If Hinduism could be shown to be a 'native' religion, it would foster Hindu pride and nationalism and render Islam and Christianity 'invader' religions. However, to the extent the Rig Veda, Sanskrit, and priestly fire rituals are seen as foundations of modern Hinduism, to that extent Hinduism too, it turns out, is an 'invader' religion, arriving with the Aryans from Central Asia. As these facts trickle down, it'll be interesting to watch how Hindutva ideologues devise new tricks to preserve the nativist claims and supremacist beliefs that underpin their project of Hindu nationalism.

The Harappan within Us

Many modern Hindus revere the Sanskritic Vedas as the fountainhead of their religion, but the Harappan substrate that lives on today is both older and arguably more pervasive, especially in what we might call 'folk Hinduism', with its mother goddesses, guardian deities, reverence for certain trees and animals and perhaps even spiritual-meditative practices. Harappan female figures in terracotta, possibly goddesses, 'with full breasts, rounded hips, and the hipline belt or girdle called the *mekhalā*', resemble the *yakshis*, symbols of fertility, on the Buddhist stupas of Bharhut and Sanchi, 'with the same well-endowed figure and the same hipline *mekhalā*'.[53] Conch shells appear at many Harappan sites, though we can only guess what purpose they served. In his splendid book, *Early Indians* (2018), Tony Joseph has noted many material continuities, too, and how 'the way in which we carry on the traditions of Harappan Civilization are too many to count'.

> The way houses are built around courtyards; the bullock carts; the importance of bangles and the way they are worn [as in the famous bronze figurine, 'the dancing girl', a style still common

in Kutch]; the manner in which trees are worshipped and the sacredness of the peepul tree in particular; the ubiquitous Indian cooking pot and the kulladh; the cultic significance of the buffalo; designs and motifs in jewelry, pottery and seals; games of dice and an early form of chess [dice and chess like boards have been found at multiple Harappan sites]; the humble lota which is used to wash up even today; and even the practice of applying sindoor and some measurement systems.[54]

'Personally,' Robinson concludes about the Harappan Civilization, 'I am drawn to what appears to be its success in combining artistic excellence, technological sophistication and economic vigour with social egalitarianism, political freedom and religious moderation over more than half a millennium. If further investigation were to show this attractive picture to be accurate, the Indus civilization would also be a hopeful sign for the future of humankind.'[55] Robinson's view has flourish and humanistic allure, though, if and when the script is deciphered, I suspect he will be proven partially wrong. Until then, what we have is akin to a melodious song in an alien language and whose lyrics remain mysterious to us.

Leaving Dholavira, travelling 100 km southeast, I stop to see the Harappan ruins of Surkotada located by an extinct river that flowed into the Rann. It too has a 'citadel' and a 'lower town'. In its time, Surkotada saw two waves of 'post-Harappans', newcomers who ushered in new styles in materials and objects. It too has a 3.5 m thick fortification wall, nearly as thick as that of Dholavira, and a significant feat of engineering.

On the road to Ahmedabad, I already miss Dholavira and its stark vicinity. Stories swirl in my mind—of villagers, site workers, guides, hotel staff. After this second visit, I'm even more in love with this mysterious site. For opening a vista to my ancestors who still continue to shape my present, it even feels a part of my personal history.

The Harappans invite us to ponder the deepest questions about human nature and culture. Facing ecological challenges as we do today, Dholavirans responded with immense creativity and resolve. Perhaps it is their vulnerability and struggle that make them more endearing to us. Given the looming climate crisis, will our modern age last longer than their mature period of 700 years?[56]

Megasthenes's India

(c. 300 BCE)

India is 'the most easterly part of the inhabited world', wrote the Greek historian Herodotus (c. 484–25 BCE). Only a barren desert lies beyond. The Indians, most numerous of all people, are 'almost as black' as Ethiopians. They live in myriad tribes and speak many languages. India's animals and birds, he wrote, are the largest in the world and its wild trees make 'a kind of wool' that's better than sheep's wool, and from which the Indians make clothes.[1]

To the classical Greeks of the fifth century BCE, India was above all a land of the weird and the creepy. Herodotus never visited India yet recorded legends without scepticism, such as its gold-digging ants bigger than foxes and faster than all animals on earth; a tribe called Padaei whose elderly or ill members are promptly killed, cooked and eaten by their closest friends; tribes that eat raw fish and tribes that eat only wild vegetables; further, all these tribes have sex in the open like herd animals and their men naturally produce black semen.

The reality was much less fantastical. In the preceding millennium, Indo-Aryan culture had evolved with strong Harappan influences. This culture became dominant in the north and found a home in several political units known as *janapada*s. Their literate elites spoke Sanskrit while the rest spoke one of the many Prakrits derived from Sanskrit.[2] By the sixth and fifth centuries BCE, new cities had arisen across the Gangetic Plain. New trades and lifestyles had emerged. Kingships coexisted with nascent democratic republics, which, like Athens later on, did not survive the march of monarchy and empire.[3]

In these new cities, people were debating some very bold and original questions: What is the nature of reality and how do we know it? Where does consciousness come from? Are virtue and vice absolute or mere social conventions? Wandering philosophers thrived in a marketplace of ideas. These included radical materialists, chronic fatalists, self-mortifying ascetics, diehard sceptics, devoted pragmatists, artful sophists, saintly mystics and the customary miracle mongers.[4] 'Rivalries and debates were rife,' writes historian Romila Thapar. 'Audiences gathered around the new philosophers in the kutuhala-shalas—literally, the place for creating curiosity—the parks and groves on the outskirts of the towns.'[5] This was the time of the Buddha, Mahavira and the making of the Upanishads.

In the centuries ahead, the Greeks would learn much more about the Indians. A catalyst for this was Alexander of Macedon's invasion of Punjab (327–25 BCE). Alexander, after defeating the Achaemenid Persians and sacking their capital, Persepolis, crossed the Hindu Kush Mountains via the Khyber Pass and approached the plains of the Indus. News of his 50,000 seasoned warriors set off a strong self-preservation instinct in King Ambhi of Taxila, and he promptly allied with Alexander. For this act, he was called the first royal 'traitor to his country' by a twentieth-century Indian nationalist. But Ambhi had 'nought to gain by resistance except the annihilation of his illustrious city and the applause of a very remote posterity', writes historian John Keay.[6]

Continuing east, Alexander ran into King Porus and defeated him in a hard-fought battle on the banks of the Jhelam. Impressed by Porus's bravery and dignity in defeat, Alexander restored to him his kingdom and pressed on across Punjab, amassing more territory. He wanted to go all the way to the Ganga but after eight years of war, losses from their battle with Porus, and rumours of mighty armies ahead, his exhausted troops rebelled near present-day Amritsar. Alexander sulked but was forced to abort his mission. His army began its return to Macedonia by sailing down the Jhelam and the Indus for many months and then via the sea and along the coast.

In Punjab, Alexander had met some ascetics that the Greeks recorded as 'gymnosophists' (naked philosophers). They had apparently given up all vanity and saw death with contemptuous indifference. They held 'that all men are held in bondage, like prisoners of war, to their own innate enemies—the sensual appetites, gluttony, anger, joy, grief, longing, desire, and such like—while it is only the man who has triumphed over these enemies who goes to God'.[7] Alexander was intrigued and ordered their master, 'Dandamis', to come see him or else face beheading.

Dandamis bluntly refused. 'Let Alexander terrify with these threats those who wish for gold and for wealth, and who dread death . . . Go, then, and tell Alexander this: "Dandamis has no need of aught that is yours, and therefore will not go to you, but if you want anything from Dandamis come you to him."' This raised Alexander's admiration for the ascetics. He persuaded one of them to come along—'Calanus', a candidate for being 'India's first cultural emissary'. His fellow ascetics denounced Calanus for selling out and leaving 'to serve another master than God'. Calanus later left a deep mark on generations of Graeco-Roman writers with his eerily calm public self-immolation after an illness, where he climbed 'on his own funeral pyre'.[8]

It's fair to say that Alexander's foray had a marginal political impact on the subcontinent. Just two years later (323 BCE), aged thirty-two, he died in Babylon on his way back home, perhaps from typhoid. His death set off a war of succession. When the dust settled, some of his generals ruled different parts of his fragmented empire. Much of Asia west of Punjab was usurped by Seleucus Nicator, founder of the Seleucid Empire (312–63 BCE).

Meanwhile in Taxila, goes a popular legend, a man of 'humble origins' (which most likely implies lower caste) named Chandragupta Maurya was plotting to overthrow the unpopular king of the Nanda Empire in Pataliputra. Alexander may have met young Chandragupta and inspired him. His strategist was Kautilya (Chanakya to some), 'a devious and disgruntled brahmin who had been slighted at the Nanda court'.[9] The duo forged political and military alliances and led a victorious war in which, claims a Buddhist text, 'thousands of elephants, horses, charioteers, and infantry were slaughtered, and the headless corpses danced in a frenzy on the bloody battlefields'.[10] The duo then founded the Maurya Empire, c. 321 BCE. These were early days for both the Seleucid and Maurya empires. After skirmishes in the north-west in which the Mauryans gained control over the Indus Plains, both emperors saw wisdom in concluding a peace treaty (303 BCE). Seleucus apparently married his daughter to Chandragupta and received 500 elephants, inaugurating a long era of neighbourly trade relations.

Alexander's cultural impact, however, was larger than his political impact, and it went both ways. The accounts of his literate generals, like admiral Nearchus's, helped demystify India to fellow Greeks at home (though their taste for bizarre exotica remained). At least two Greek philosophers, Pyrrho of Elis and Anaxarchus, had travelled with Alexander and met the gymnosophists. Henceforth, atop an earlier trickle, 'Indian ideas entered the Hellenistic and Mediterranean world' more steadily, influencing many schools of thought in Greece and Rome, such as Pyrrhonism, Stoicism and Neoplatonism.[11]

A few decades later, Ashoka, Chandragupta's grandson and heir to the Mauryan Empire, embraced Buddhism and sent out missionaries across Asia, including to Afghanistan and Central Asia. One of his rock edicts in Khandahar was inscribed in Greek. Buddhism spread rapidly in these parts and across India. A century later, Menander (aka Milinda), a Greek-origin king in the subcontinent's north-west, even embraced Buddhism, apparently following a discussion with the sage Nagasena (their dialogue appears in the Pali text *Milind Panha*).

The Greek substrate of the Seleucid Empire also influenced Indian culture, as neighbours often do, notably through the sublime Gandhara style of Buddhist art. Greek astronomical ideas strongly influenced Indian astronomy.[12] In early Sanskrit texts, the Greeks appear as 'Yavana', a term later used for all foreigners from the west of India. As Keay writes, Alexander had effectively 'prised open a window on the East through which emissaries would pass, ideas would shine, and prying eyes would covet'.[13] One such emissary was the Greek Megasthenes, sent by Seleucus to Chandragupta's court, c. 300 BCE.

Approaching Megasthenes

Little is known about the early life of Megasthenes. He was probably born around 350 BCE and likely spent part of his life in Arachosia, near modern Helmand in south Afghanistan, serving a governor of Alexander. He spent at least a few months, possibly a few years, in Pataliputra (modern Patna), the Mauryan capital. He may have died around 290 BCE.

Megasthenes wrote an account of his Indian sojourn, *Indica*. Sadly, the original text is lost; only parts of it survive as paraphrased text by Graeco-Roman authors, including Diodorus Siculus, Strabo, Pliny the Elder and Arrian. (E.A. Schwanbeck compiled all such fragments in 1846 to make the text that now passes as *Indica*, and J.W. McCrindle translated it into English in 1877.[14]) But these authors paraphrase unreliably, add their own masala or include ideas from other sources, and often contradict each other. This makes it hard to draw accurate inferences about the original.

One inference that seems secure is that Megasthenes was an immensely curious man. He also comes across as an animal lover, especially drawn to elephants in India. He recognizes their intelligence and accurately records their lifecycle, mating posture and several other behaviours. He describes how they're captured and domesticated for war, and how Indians cure the animals' wounds. He also records a charming custom. When an elephant is angry and won't be pacified by mere food, its handlers 'sing to it their native melodies, and soothe it with the music of an instrument in common use which has four strings and is called a *skindapsos*. The creature now pricks up its ears, yields to the soothing strain, and its anger subsides'. This ancient custom will delight those who provide music therapy to elephants in sanctuaries today.

However, Megasthenes, like Herodotus, seems to have written down both what he saw and what he heard. For the places he did not visit, he displays poor judgement in recording absurd hearsay as truth. He mentions people with the ears of a dog and only one eye in the middle of the forehead; people with no mouths and mere orifices for nostrils, who live on the odours of roots and flowers; a pygmy tribe less than 27 inches tall; people who live a thousand years; people with ears reaching down to their feet; people with feet turned backwards; and so on.

Perhaps he was playing to a gallery at home used to such tropes of 'incredible India'. Or, as Schwanbeck suggests, perhaps he placed excessive trust in his native informants, likely royal Brahmins or other literate courtiers, who solemnly related tall tales about the rakshasas, pishachas and Mlecchas in the forests and lands beyond.[15] To the extent the latter is true, his account may also be a revealing window into Brahminical social attitudes of the day.

Three centuries later, Strabo and Pliny criticized him for 'deviating into fables' too gullibly, even as they found other parts of his account useful. Fortunately, the outlandish sections are few in number, and for the places he did visit, including Pataliputra where he was an ambassador, his account is more sober and seems based on personal observation and experience. His errors there tend to be the kind that could've been occupational hazards for any traveller of his day. What, then, did Megasthenes observe in Mauryan India?

The Mauryan World in 300 BCE

Megasthenes calls Pataliputra ('Palibothra' in his account) the greatest city in India. It lies at the confluence of rivers Ganga and Son. Shaped like a parallelogram, 15 km x 3 km, the city is enclosed by a wooden wall with slits for shooting arrows. It has 570 watchtowers and sixty-four gates (averaging one gate every 500 m). Around the wall is a defensive moat, 180 m wide and 15 m deep, which also carries the city's sewage. If Megasthenes is right, Pataliputra's dimensions would make it the largest city of the ancient world—'twice as large as Rome under Emperor Marcus Aurelius'.[16]

Much of the city, including the king's palace, is made of wood. This is because, explains Megasthenes, Indian cities located on floodplains are 'built of wood instead of brick' and 'cities which stand on commanding situations and lofty eminences are built of brick and mud'. (Later Mauryan kings did build with stone, but this may partly explain the relative lack of archaeological remains of Pataliputra. Besides fragments of the wooden wall at many sites, the most notable find has been 'a Mauryan pillared hall of [eighty] polished sandstone monoliths comparable to the pillared palace at Persepolis in modern Iran".[17] More discoveries may yet happen—much of ancient Pataliputra lies unexcavated beneath modern Patna.)

The land is fertile and enables two harvests a year, writes Megasthenes. Fruit trees abound and rivers are aplenty. Thanks to the 'abundant means of subsistence', people exceed 'ordinary stature',

possess a 'proud bearing', and are 'well skilled in the arts'. They hold
truth and virtue in high esteem, and 'accord no special privileges to the
old unless they possess superior wisdom'.

The people of this kingdom are called Prasii (likely a Greek rendition
of the Sanskrit *prācya*, or 'east'[18]). They 'observe good order' and live
'happily enough, being simple in their manners and frugal'. That said,
they also 'love finery and ornament. Their robes are worked in gold,
and ornamented with precious stones, and they also wear flowered
garments made of the finest muslin'. 'Attendants walking behind hold
up umbrellas over them: for they have a high regard for beauty, and avail
themselves of every device to improve their looks.'

This wasn't just a penchant of the Prasii. Even the wealthy folk of
Punjab, wrote Nearchus, 'wear earrings of ivory' and 'use parasols as a
screen from the heat'. They wear elaborately trimmed shoes of white
leather, with multicoloured soles 'of great thickness, to make the wearer
seem so much taller'. Others dye their beards 'according to taste'. 'Some
dye their white beards to make them look as white as possible, but others
dye them blue; while some again prefer a red tint, some a purple, and
others a rank green.'[19]

Elite Prasii men 'marry many wives, whom they buy from their
parents, giving in exchange a yoke of oxen'. 'Some they marry hoping
to find in them willing helpmates; and others for pleasure and to fill
their houses with children.' Megasthenes writes, 'The wives prostitute
themselves unless they are compelled to be chaste'; but he offers no
explanation for this puzzling remark. The king is cared for by 'women,
who are also bought from their parents'. The king leaves his palace not
only in times of war but also to judge cases in court, to offer sacrifices
and to go hunting, which he does with great fanfare and is accompanied
by two or three women hunters by his side. The 'king has in his pay
a standing army of 600,000 foot soldiers, 30,000 cavalry, and 9,000
elephants: whence may be formed some conjecture as to the vastness of
his resources'.

Strabo's paraphrasing of Megasthenes suggests that the kingdom
has 'an aristocratical form of government consisting of five thousand
councillors, each of whom furnishes the state with an elephant'.
Megasthenes, via Diodorus, suggests that in earlier times, cities had 'the

democratic form of government', but in his own time, administration was centralized. It seems to have some features of the idealized bureaucracy advocated by the *Arthashastra* of Kautilya, who may have been Chandragupta's chief minister (at best, only parts of the surviving *Arthashastra* date from his time; much of the text was created by later authors as late as third century CE[20]). Megasthenes lists a range of officials that run the bureaucracy of the state—overseers of markets, trade, the city, harbours, soldiers, water sluices, roads, births and deaths, land use, taxation, weights and measures, foreigners, etc.—though it's unclear how far out of Pataliputra their reach extended.

Theft is very rare and people leave their homes and property unguarded. As for punishment, Megasthenes writes, 'A person convicted of bearing false witness suffers mutilation of his extremities. He who maims any one not only suffers in return the loss of the same limb, but his hand also is cut off. If he causes an artisan to lose his hand or his eye, he is put to death.' A sales tax of 10 per cent is levied and any 'fraud in the payment of this tax is punished with death'. It's not clear how often this happened (it's common across ages to have poorly enforced criminal laws on the books).

'They never drink wine except at sacrifices. Their beverage is a liquor composed from rice instead of barley, and their food is principally a rice pottage.' Apparently, they always eat alone and 'have no fixed hours when meals are to be taken by all in common, but each one eats when he feels inclined'. Three centuries later, Strabo wagged a finger at this tidbit, adding, 'The contrary custom would be better for the ends of social and civil life' (as was common with the Greeks). Megasthenes's observation is puzzling; perhaps Strabo erred in paraphrasing it. Megasthenes likely meant that each family ate alone, not communally. Or perhaps he may have seen that in upper-class families, the head of the household ate first and was served apart from the family, a custom common until recent times.[21]

Indians, wrote Megasthenes, are divided into seven castes. The first is *philosophers*, few in number but in 'dignity preeminent over all'. Presumed 'dear to the gods', they conduct sacrifices and funeral rites for which 'they receive valuable gifts and privileges'. He mentions two types of philosophers: 'Brachmanes' and 'Sarmanes'—Brahmins and

Sramanas (monks of Buddhist, Jain and other heterodox sects). The Brahmins guard their esoteric knowledge and do not communicate it even 'to their wives, lest they should divulge any of the forbidden mysteries to the profane'. However, 'women pursue philosophy with some of [the Sramanas]'.

The second caste is *farmers*, the most numerous of all. They're seen as 'public benefactors' and no one harms them even during war. They live in the countryside and 'pay a land-tribute to the king, because all India is the property of the crown, and no private person is permitted to own land'. They also 'pay into the royal treasury a fourth part of the produce of the soil'. The third caste is *herders*, 'who neither settle in towns nor in villages, but live in tents' and by 'hunting and trapping they clear the country of noxious birds and wild beasts'. The fourth caste is *artisans*, makers of weapons and tools for the herders and others. They're 'exempted from paying taxes' and even get maintenance from the king. The fifth caste is *soldiers*, the second most numerous. They live 'at the king's expense' and 'when not engaged in active service, pass their time in idleness and drinking'. The sixth caste is *overseers*, tasked with administration and reporting anomalies to the magistrates. The seventh and the smallest caste is *councillors and assessors*, comprising wise people from whose ranks the king's advisers, chief magistrates, state treasurers and army generals are drawn.

But this wasn't some free-wheeling division of social labour. 'No one is allowed to marry out of his own caste,' writes Megasthenes, 'or to exercise any calling or art except his own: for instance, a soldier cannot become a herder, or an artisan a philosopher.' However, 'An exception is made in favour of the philosopher, who for his virtue is allowed this privilege', i.e., allowed to pursue other vocations and marry women from other castes—this could be how many Brahmins became councillors and assessors.[22]

What Megasthenes reports is the presence of endogamy based on occupation (the genesis of caste), though his divisions do not map on to the four varna divisions based on ritual status and purity (the philosophers enjoy a higher status, but his schema doesn't convey a strong hierarchy). Scholars have puzzled over his characterization, attributing it to confusion on his part, an interpolation by Graeco-Roman authors to make it parallel to the seven social divisions in Egypt and a few other theories. After all, Megasthenes was also wrong in claiming that there was no slavery in India. Indian sources, including the *Arthashastra*, attest to its presence though it was different from the system of slavery prevalent in Greece, so Megasthenes likely didn't recognize it as such.[23]

Mauryan India was a strange society to Megasthenes and his fellow Greeks. He could only enter it so far. He must have faced linguistic hurdles too. Perhaps he befriended Seleucus's Greek daughter, a queen of Chandragupta, and gossiped in their mother tongue about Mauryan courtiers. One gets the sense from *Indica* that he also partook in the sensuous joys of travel and discovery. He marvels at all the strange land animals and birds of India: parrots that are taught to speak and become 'as talkative as children'; apes with hair on the forehead and 'luxuriant beards hanging down their breast'; the Indian hoopoe, 'the favourite plaything of the king of the Indians, who carries it on his hand, and toys with it, and never tires gazing in ecstasy on its splendour, and the beauty with which Nature has adorned it'. If only we knew what his Mauryan hosts thought of this interesting visitor from the west.

The Void of **Nagarjunakonda**
(c. 220–c. 320 CE)

On the morning of 21 February 1920, a Telugu schoolteacher, S. Venkataramayya, from an Andhra village, Macherla, set out on an excursion with a few other villagers. He had received word from 'some cowherds about the existence of stone pillars and mounds of brick overgrown by jungle'.[1]

After going about 20 km west, they climbed the rocky Nallamalai Range where seven hills enclosed a 24 sq. km valley except on the north and west, where it was flanked by the mighty Krishna River. The river was then almost 1 km wide while still over 200 km from the Bay of Bengal.

The valley had 'an evil reputation for malaria', but they descended and entered its thorny jungle, which had a few 'gazelle, peafowl and sandgrouse' as well as venomous cobras, vipers and pythons. The valley was then home to a few Telugu Hindus and the Lambadis, a 'picturesque gypsy tribe' of pastoralists and cultivators. They lived in Pullareddiguddem, a hamlet of mud huts and thatched roofs. The hamlet had a chief called Reddi, who had a large herd of cattle, the best house and 'whose word [was] law in all local matters'.

The valley also had the Chenchus, an Adivasi tribe of hunter-gatherers living off small game, collecting honey, roots and firewood. According to archaeologist A.H. Longhurst, who worked here from 1927–31, 'The Chenchus are expert archers and trackers and even kill tigers with poisoned arrows at times.' They dwell in 'small beehive-shaped huts with mud walls and roofs covered with palm leaves and reeds'. Panthers often came down the hills to prey on livestock; occasionally, even a tiger showed up from the Kurnool forests nearby. In the ten months that Longhurst spent in the valley over four years, he 'shot six panthers to the great delight of the local villagers, and the Chenchus in particular, who actually ate the flesh of these animals'.[2]

We know nothing of Venkataramayya's dealings with the locals. What became well known was his sighting of a finely inscribed stone pillar in the jungle. He couldn't read the Prakrit inscriptions in Brahmi script but he took rubbings. Word spread to the press and

Figure 1. Pillar carving showing exercising wrestlers

officials of the British government. But it wasn't until 1926 that experts came to investigate, such as Rangaswami Saraswati, an epigraphist, and Hamid Quraishi, an ASI archaeologist and a deputy of Longhurst.

It was soon clear that the schoolteacher had reported one of the greatest archaeological finds in south India—the extensive remains of an ancient city rich in magnificent sculptures and monuments, including the only amphitheatre found in ancient India. Known as Vijayapuri, it was the capital city of the Ikshvaku Kingdom (c. 220–320 CE) and a great religious and educational centre of Buddhism and Brahminism that actively traded with the Roman Empire.

Sadly, much of the site of ancient Vijayapuri now lies submerged under one of the largest manmade lakes in the world, Nagarjuna Sagar, formed in 1960 by a dam across the Krishna River. Fortunately, before the site was submerged, a large team of archaeologists was given six years to excavate, study and relocate the most important structures of Vijayapuri on higher ground, on a hill in the valley called Nagarjunakonda ('Hill of Nagarjuna', now an island on the lake), and on the lake's eastern bank at Anupu. History buffs visit these two locations today.

I first visited Nagarjunakonda in December 2005. Heading west on a bus from Vijayawada, I passed towns and villages whose names—opaque to me because they were written only in Telugu—I kept guessing at from a paper map. The region was then infamous for years of deficient rains and drought, depleted water tables and farmers either fleeing to other regions or committing suicide to escape debt.

Thirteen years later, in September 2018, I begin again in Vijayawada, which is abuzz with new energy and enterprise owing to the state government's interim relocation here, after Andhra Pradesh was carved into two states and Hyderabad became the capital of the new Telangana state in 2014. Billboards in town show portly leaders, in traditional attire and folded hands, seeking votes for the upcoming state elections. Unlike my previous journey to Nagarjunakonda, I hire a taxi and track our drive with GPS on an alternative route.

It is late monsoon and the rains have been weak yet again. We cross the north-eastern Guntur district, where the green fields of cotton, sugarcane, pepper and vegetables have been fed mostly by canals from the Krishna and a few wells. The dam has clearly made a huge difference in these parts. My driver is Suresh, a twenty-six-year-old from Vijayawada, who has a diploma in mechanical engineering. Last year, he quit a company job in Hyderabad and returned to live with his family after his father, a forty-eight-year-old labourer, suffered a head injury and 'lost his mind'. As the elder of two children, Suresh is now the de facto head of the household, a heavy burden at his age.

I stop at the town of Amravathi, the future capital of Andhra Pradesh. This is also the site of the former capital of the Satavahana Empire, which flourished in the first two centuries CE and served as an early major conduit for the northern Indo-Aryan culture into the south. I visit the excavated remains of the Great Stupa of ancient Amravathi, which once contained the Buddha's relics, and the nearby site museum donning brickwork inspired by the Great Stupa. The Krishna River here is shallow and sluggish. Is the Nagarjuna Sagar Dam upstream not releasing much water? Or perhaps much of its water is being diverted for irrigation and other human needs? I pass places with names like Mandadam, Pedamudduru, Gudipudi, Sattenapalle and Piduguralla. I relish rolling these words around my tongue. All of this land was once part of the Ikshvaku realm, which covered modern Guntur, Krishna and parts of Nellore and Nalgonda districts.

Four hours later, I'm in Vijayapuri South once again, a village of over 10,000 people. But I recognize little of it from my previous visit. As with so many places in India, it too has grown larger, noisier, denser and unevenly prosperous. From here ferries run daily to Nagarjunakonda Island (forty-five minutes each way), including a ferry named Chamtisiri, after a royal woman of ancient Vijayapuri. In the middle of an intersection near the ferry terminal is a shiny golden statue of B.R. Ambedkar in his signature pose: raised right hand pointing forward, with the left clutching a copy of the Indian Constitution. I check into a decaying AP Tourism hotel overlooking the lake. Faded pictures of the ancient site and the dam adorn its lobby and rooms.

Excavation and Submersion

The first archaeologists to visit the ruins of Vijayapuri in the 1920s found the valley 'dotted with numerous rocky hillocks and artificial mounds covered with grass and jungle'. Many limestone pillars were still standing. From 1927–31, Longhurst's team dug up many mounds to reveal 'ruined monasteries, apsidal temples, stupas, inscriptions, coins, relics, pottery, statues and over four hundred magnificent bas-reliefs in the Amravathi style' of the Satavahana Empire.[3]

Additional ASI digs until the valley's submersion in 1960 uncovered more finds, especially by T.N. Ramachandran in 1938 and the frantic ones between 1954 and 1960 under R. Subrahmanyam. They found Stone Age tools and over hundred inscriptions and megaliths from 136 sites across 24 sq. km, suggesting 5000 years of habitation in the valley. A Neolithic cemetery and megalithic tombs from the first millennium BCE, found here and across south India, show that burial for the dead was once common among Dravidian peoples.[4] While cremation too was known, it likely grew in importance as the Indo-Aryan culture, including Brahminism and Buddhism, spread to the south from the first millennium BCE.[5] Both cremation and burial were found in Vijayapuri. Cremation was likely part of a larger cultural package from the north in which caste and its particular forms of patriarchy were key ingredients,[6] forever transforming the more egalitarian matrilineal societies of the south (possibly a Harappan legacy). Interestingly, the anti-Brahminical Dravidian Movement in Tamil Nadu has demoted cremation in recent decades, and revived 'their' ancient custom of burying the dead. Many of its leaders, such as M.G. Ramachandran, J. Jayalalithaa and M. Karunanidhi, received a funerary burial.

The finest and the most monumental finds in the valley, however, date from the historical era when Vijayapuri, the capital of the Ikshvaku Dynasty flourished here in the third and fourth centuries CE. Falling into ruin thereafter, the city was consumed by the jungle. A small settlement arose in the vicinity during the Chalukyas (from seventh to twelfth centuries) and again in the fifteenth and sixteenth centuries, but they mostly fell outside the previously inhabited area of Vijayapuri in

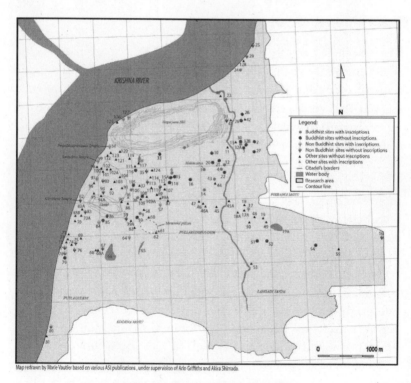

Map redrawn by Marie Vautier based on various ASI publications, under supervision of Arlo Griffiths and Akira Shimada.

Figure 2. Nagarjunakonda site map.
Source: Early inscriptions of Āndhradeśa

the valley, most of which lay undisturbed for nearly 1600 years; though levelled by the elements and the jungle, and parts of it raided by later settlers for building materials. The damage could easily have been far worse.

In the early 1950s, with many lives lost to a severe drought in Andhra Pradesh, it became clear that the region badly needed an irrigation scheme fed by a great dam. Soon, the best location for the dam was identified, which would, however, submerge Vijayapuri—arguably the most magnificent archaeological site then known in south India. A robust 'development vs heritage' debate took place in the Parliament. Was preserving our most iconic cultural heritage less important than a dam that would feed hungry millions? Both sides made strong arguments. A proposal to isolate Vijayapuri by building a high wall around it on the valley floor was floated too, but was deemed impractical. No other site was found feasible for the dam. Not surprisingly, the pro-development team won, led by Prime Minister Jawaharlal Nehru himself, who wrote, 'The idea that this place, where so much of our ancient history and culture lie hidden under the earth, should be lost forever under the new lake has distressed me greatly. Yet the choice had to be made for the sake of the needs of today and tomorrow.'[7] Simultaneously, Nehru also initiated a gigantic effort to excavate, study and document Vijayapuri, and to salvage some of its remains.

Ironically, as the pace of excavations and discoveries picked up during 1954–60, scholars realized that the site was even more significant than they had earlier thought, making its impending submergence all the more painful. But too much had already been put into motion and the decision was irreversible, leading the ASI to characterize it as an 'archaeological tragedy'.

Before Vijayapuri was submerged forever, only nine of its monuments were 'saved' and rebuilt on higher ground, detached from their original urban context.* Miniature models of fourteen other sites were made. Fortunately, the city was extensively excavated, mapped out and photographed before submersion, so we can at least imagine what a walk down its streets might have felt like. Let's go on one such city

---

* Abu Simbel was similarly 'saved' in 1964 when the Aswan Dam was built in Egypt.

walk, as if we were time travelling to it in late third century CE, observing things based on the knowledge we've gleaned from archaeology and other historical sources.

A Stroll through Vijayapuri

Let's begin our walk inside the citadel from where the Ikshvakus ruled Vijayapuri. Part of this citadel area rests on higher ground overlooking the river. It has a moat and mud-brick rampart walls. Inside is a structure, likely the palace of the Ikshvakus, along with many 'residential buildings, barracks, stables, cisterns, baths, and square wells or soak pits'. We notice two ornamental stepped bathing tanks with underground drainage.[8] The first tank is tortoise-shaped; the second is square, with a wooden superstructure, affixed with fire torches, under which the people of the citadel perhaps bathed, lounged and entertained. A great fire will eventually burn down this superstructure, leaving heaps of ash to be discovered by archaeologists 1600 years later. Similar but humbler bathing tanks exist across the city.[9]

Stepping out of the eastern gate of the citadel, we see a memorial pillar to an army chief, Mahasenapati Chamtapula, inscribed with scenes glorifying his life. This is one of the at least twenty-two such limestone pillars we'll see in the city, indicating that raising memorial pillars for prominent people is common—usually, but not always, for kings, queens, nobles or warriors. Many pillars have battle scenes honouring warriors and their victories in war. On one such pillar, a horseman with a spear battles two foot soldiers, with many men lying dead around them. Scenes like this suggest that war is an ever-present threat and even a royal pursuit. However, not far from the citadel, we're relieved to see a pillar dedicated to the foreman of the artisans; another honours a king's mother.

To the south and east of the citadel are several religious buildings. Walking east, towards the Great Stupa of Vijayapuri, we pass a few of the more than thirty Buddhist establishments found in the city, representing at least four sects, split into two broad denominations: Hinayana and Mahayana. The sounds of debate and laughter fill the streets as monks and nuns go about their day. Their monasteries often feature a pillared

Figure 3. A Buddhist monastic complex

hall in the centre, surrounded by a covered veranda and, on average, ten to fifteen rooms with terracotta-tiled roofs (about a quarter of the capacity of later monasteries at Nalanda). They have a central kitchen, dining hall and storerooms, and shared toilets with drains. The enrobed inhabitants lounge and chat, or amuse themselves with games played on boards etched into the stone floor, or toss ivory dice similar to those uncovered here. Newer monasteries, likely influenced by architectural fashions coming down from Gandhara (north-west Pakistan and north-east Afghanistan), have standing Buddha statues in apsidal shrines and adjoining stupas in brick and plaster, including one with a swastika design in brick inlay (now transplanted on Nagarjunakonda Island).

We learn that the Ceylonese, who trade actively with Vijayapuri, have been provided an entire monastery just to host their visiting monks. As a group, they patronize the more orthodox Hinayana sects that oppose image worship of the Buddha—a trend being popularized by the rival Mahayana sects and which would eventually prevail in India.[*]

---

[*] Three of these Ceylonese monasteries were called Mahisasaka, Bahusrutiya and Kumaranandi.

A fifteen-minute stroll east of the citadel brings us to the Great Stupa, which predates the Ikshvakus but which, during the early Ikshvaku rule, was renovated and grew to about 70–80 feet high and over 100 feet wide. It has finely carved relief sculpture and hosts a bone relic of the Buddha, hidden so creatively that it'll survive the plunder of treasure seekers until discovered by Longhurst around 1928 (it's now at Mulagandhakuti Vihara at Sarnath, UP).* Inscriptions at this stupa and at other Buddhist sites record the names of their major patrons, and we find it curious that the most prominent among them are wealthy women, both royal and not. Pilgrims arrive from distant places to see the Great Stupa. As with the older stupas at Sanchi and Bharhut, its relief sculpture depicts scenes from the Jataka tales and amorous couples dancing or embracing, symbolizing fertility and auspiciousness. But unlike the older stupas, it also portrays the Buddha in human form and depicts the

Figure 4. The Great Stupa of Vijayapuri

---

* The pea-sized bone relic was inside a gold box inside a silver receptacle with gold leaves, pearls and garnets. This was placed with crystal beads inside an earthenware pot in an outer part of the Great Stupa, not in the centre as was the norm. This helped it survive treasure seekers.

iconic events of his life—birth, renunciation, enlightenment, first sermon, death—and other inspirational or enchanting legends.

Further east we find the largest monastery in the city (excavated by T.N. Ramachandran in 1938 and later transplanted at Anupu; archaeologists named it after Nagarjuna), attracting student monks from far and wide (for this reason, it is now, rather exaggeratedly, called a 'university'). In its residential wing, one cell has a big limestone urn containing two teeth (archaeologists believe they belonged to Acharya Nagarjuna, who may have lived and taught at this monastery; but it's hard to be certain based on available evidence).

In a monastery nearby, we're struck by the beauty of a sculpture 'depicting the horse of the prince Siddhartha returning in grief after renunciation'. Inside another monastery is a 'beautiful carved moonstone' at the entrance of a *chaitya*, or Buddhist temple, and a 'nunnery, store rooms, sculpture workshop, foreman's seat, [and] a urinal'. Inscriptions at a monastic complex indicate that it was founded by Mahadevi Bhatideva, mother of the third king of the Ikshvaku Dynasty; another complex was founded by Kodabalisiri, sister of the same king. Other monasteries show 'an attached kitchen and refectory with courtyard' and 'an interesting drainage system'.[10]

It's now clear to us that the locals love to sculpt in stone. Their Buddhist sculpture, carved in greenish limestone, abounds with people, gods, fauna, flora and symbolic forms. On the walls of their religious and public buildings, the sculptors depict what they see unfolding around them: dancers and musicians performing; children at play; courtly events; people assembled to drink; wrestlers contesting. On one panel we see a woman in a bathtub, on another men bathe leisurely in masonry tanks, as attendants pour water from cisterns over their bodies. The panels also depict war scenes, *yaksha*s and *yakshi*s, sundry devotees, ornaments, rituals, etc. Though Ikshvaku art continues the Amravathi style of the Satavahanas, we also notice occasional Roman artistic influences in the drapery, coiffures and body shapes. We can see that the art and architecture of Gandhara, Mathura and the Sakas (Indo-Scythians) have left their mark too. A finely carved pillar, for instance, carries a charming depiction of two Sakas in their distinct style of dress.[11]

Back near the citadel and along the riverbank, the eighteen or more Brahminical temples may be the first such cluster built in south India— mostly Shaiva, a few Vaishnava, or both. The smaller temples only have a shrine chamber; the larger ones also have a pillared hall in front, with finely cut, sculpted and polished pillars. A notable pair of ornamental temple pillars, *chitra stambha*s, shows two finely carved elephants on the move, cockfights, bulls and rams, and a mysterious Amazonian woman holding a big sword with an attendant behind her. She is perhaps 'one of the *Mahatalvaris* [sword-wielding women] mentioned in the inscriptions'.[12]

We see Brahminical temples dedicated to gods like Shiva, Karttikeya, Devasena, Kubera and Vishnu. Many of these temples are inside large complexes with additional shrines, pavilions and residential quarters, where the attendant priests or servants live. Temples mostly have flat stone slabs for roofs, laid over stone or wooden beams resting on pillars and occasionally a barrel-vaulted top. They are inscribed in Sanskrit, while the surrounding Buddhist monuments are inscribed in Prakrit. Among the largest and most majestic temples is Sarvadeva, 'abode of all gods', with its pillared hall (later destroyed by fire). The temple is next to a large stepped masonry tank used for ceremonies, with its own pillared pavilion overlooking the river.

In general, the Brahminical sites are all near the riverfront, while Buddhist sites are more spread out across the entire valley of Vijayapuri, often near the city's major arteries. Buddhist sites also outnumber Brahminical ones, though the gap reduced after the third king. Besides these two belief systems, a cult of the mother goddess, suggesting fertility, sexuality and creation, is all the rage. Popular terracotta figurines depict her in a squatting pose or lying on her back, indicating either a birthing posture or readiness for sex. She is likely the non-Brahminical deity later known as Lajja Gauri, popular in central India and the

Figure 5. Mother goddess, likely Lajja Gauri

Deccan. Just north of the citadel, by the river, stands a temple dedicated to her.

Wandering a few steps further south along the riverbank brings us to a pillared hall that is a burning ghat or a cremation site. Sculptural clues and relief carvings of goddess Sati indicate that the practice of sati takes place here, at least occasionally, and is likely associated only with the warrior class.[13] From further down the riverbank, we hear the din of dock workers ferrying goods to and from the boats docked along designed piers. Travellers and touts throng the steps of the adjacent harbour, a key transit point for commerce and people passing in and out of the city.

We find a range of secular structures towards the south and east of the citadel, including residences—some with multiple rooms along a common veranda. Dignitaries and expats, such as Saka or Kushan noblemen, inhabit the finest of these homes. Each of these have a central pillared pavilion with stone floors, tiled roofs and walls built of rubble stone or standardized bricks, and finished with lime plaster. Most homes are separated from other homes by a compound wall and feature indoor plumbing—typically a brick drain leading from the house and connecting to a street drain. These drains, some open, others covered, and up to 10–12 inches wide, empty into nearby soak pits or septic tanks. Humbler homes rely more on bamboo and thatch. But even most of these have front and rear verandas and an inner courtyard beyond which lies the kitchen, pantry and an area for animals. Vessels that store grain or oil are sunk into the pantry floor.

Stepping inside many homes, we're struck by the profusion of pottery items: dishes with or

Figure 6. Pillar with scenes of social life

without lids, bowls, cups, wine jars, pots in lota and other styles, water vessels, storage jars, finials and lamps. Most of these are utilitarian in design but a few are more 'deluxe', with fancy spouts, handles and shaped like bulls or cats. Usually painted, many have fine decorations with floral and geometric designs, as well as animals and human figures, including dancers and musicians. Here and there we even find the occasional luxury of a glazed amphora.

Back along the city streets, we walk past shops and ateliers, where goldsmiths, ivory and shell artists, and glass-bangle makers ply their crafts. Shoppers haggle over piles of beads fashioned from coral, crystal, pearl, jasper and glass, as well as a range of mass-produced yet high-quality terracotta figurines, featuring yakshas and yakshis, cult goddesses symbolizing fertility, animals and so on, often worn as pendants. Carpenters, shoemakers, weavers, farmers, homemakers and experts in weapons and transport technology move from shop to shop, choosing their wares from a range of finely built iron tools and artefacts. We can smell the smoke of the nearby brick kilns.

When a deal is struck, payment is made in the coins of the realm. The Ikshvakus minted their own currency in lead coins.[14] Considerable seaborne trade between Rome and the east coast of India supplies exotic goods for sale, like amphorae and Roman coins. We might see coins issued by emperors Tiberius (16–37 CE), Hadrian (117–38 CE) and Antoninus Pius (138–161 CE). In fact, we notice a local fad of people wearing Roman coins as pendants! We witness a tussle in which a shopkeeper denounces a buyer as a purveyor of counterfeit Roman coins, which are flooding the local markets.[15] The roots of such creativity run deep in India.

Merchants and trade guilds have a powerful presence in the city, as do guilds of artisans, masons, bricklayers, tile-makers, potters, blacksmiths, confectioners and more. As a big centre of Buddhist learning, with famous teachers like Nagarjuna, Aryadeva, Dharmanandi and others,[16] the lively streets of Vijayapuri also host a colourful mix of visitors and students from many parts of India and Sri Lanka, and even an occasional one from China, alongside Brahminical priests, Buddhist monks and nuns, poets, scribes, healers, tax collectors, produce sellers, sweepers, tailors, dancers, musicians, wrestlers, and other entertainers.

Along Vijayapuri's major arteries are public baths and several pillared halls with flat roofs that serve as rest houses for traders, students, pilgrims and other visitors to this capital city that readily embraces and propagates new ideas. We see water wells and tanks, and irrigation canals fed from the river. We pass a couple of edifices with the inscription *vigata-jvar-ālaya*, 'a place for those recovering from fever', which modern scholars believe were hospitals.[17] We pass a public assembly hall and people gathered at platforms near temples to play dice, a favourite pastime. One hall, seemingly a 'club', has drinking and dancing scenes carved on its pillars, including exotic outsiders like Scythians and Kushans in their distinctive robes, and even a relief of Dionysus with a

drinking horn and a wine barrel. We hear about an upcoming dance performance at the pillared hall on the riverfront near the southern end of the city.

A delegation of foreigners passes by us, commenting on the wealth and worldliness of this fine city as they make their way to the superb bathing ghat, 75 m long and 15 m wide, next to a large temple at the edge of the city, near the citadel.[18] Built of brick overlaid by limestone slabs, its stepped design is adorned with aesthetically pleasing sculptural details, such as elephant balustrades. Some slabs are inscribed with board games.

Figure 7. Amorous couple

Nearby, stone pillars support a wooden roof, probably 'a Goods Shed and Customs House' for the considerable river-borne trade, since the only other route for heavy goods entering the valley is a narrow gorge in the surrounding hills, which can be used to ferry goods on bullock carts or donkeys' backs.[19]

Further east in the valley of Vijayapuri, set against a hill slope, is a monument truly unique in ancient India—a rectangular amphitheatre

Figure 8. Amphitheatre of Vijayapuri

that can seat a thousand spectators on at least sixteen tiers. Likely inspired by Ikshvaku contacts with Rome, it is made of brick and stone slabs, and has a covered pavilion at the top with named seats reserved for the royalty and the nobles. (Experts claim that the amphitheatre's pit, 16 m x 14 m, was designed to produce good acoustics.) It is likely used for public debates, religious discourses, music and theatre acts, and rip-roaring wrestling contests, the taste for which is evident even in the sculpture of Vijayapuri. Right above the amphitheatre on the hill is a temple with a human-sized seated figure of the Buddhist goddess Hariti, protector of children. This temple's precincts afford a panoramic view of the amphitheatre and the city.

The Rise of Vijayapuri

In late second century CE, Nagarjunakonda Valley had a small settlement called Sriparvata. An outpost of the Satavahana Empire, whose capital was at Amravathi, 140 km away, Sriparvata was home to a community of Buddhists centred around a monument that would be the precursor to the Great Stupa. It has been suggested, on slim evidence, that the settlement was at some point named Vijayapuri ('city of victory') to honour Vijaya Satkarni, a Satavahana king.[20]

In the early third century, this semi-urban settlement was ruled by Chamtamula, a feudatory of the Satavahanas. When the Satavahana Empire fell apart, around 220 CE, Chamtamula broke away and set up his own independent kingdom, founding the Ikshvaku Dynasty. Choosing the name 'Ikshvaku', he deftly linked himself to the prestigious *suryavanshi* (or solar dynasty) of Ayodhya's Rama, establishing their divine justification to rule—most likely aided by collaborating priests.

Headstrong and ambitious, Chamtamula was a devotee of Karttikeya, the god of war. It's possible that he himself renamed his new capital Vijayapuri. Though still only a chieftain, he performed the *Ashvamedha yagna*, a ritual horse sacrifice undertaken by major northern kings of the Vedic–Brahminical fold. His was perhaps the earliest instance of this ceremony enacted this far south, indicating that a lot of cultural diffusion had already happened, at least among the urban elites. This wasn't the case in c. 500 BCE when the text of *Aitareya Brahmana* described the Andhras as a non-Aryan tribe that lived south-east of the Vindhyas, beyond the northern lands ruled by Brahminical elites. Chamtamula began building the citadel, issued his own currency (showing an elephant with raised trunk) and set about expanding his realm.

Their dates aren't entirely certain, but a commonly accepted chronology of the Ikshvaku Dynasty runs a hundred years, from c. 220–320 CE, split more or less evenly between four kings: Chamtamula (c. 220–45 CE), Virapurushadutta (c. 245–70 CE), Ehuvala Chamtamula (c. 270–300 CE) and Rudrapurushadutta (c. 300–10/20 CE). Most inscriptions and the biggest Buddhist monuments date from the time of the second ruler, and most Brahminical monuments date from the time of the third. An inscription calls the third ruler *Dharma Vijayin*, and notes his aspiration to endear himself to all in the manner of Rama of Ayodhya. He bolstered Brahminism though it still likely remained a minority religion in the Ikshvaku realm. The Ikshvakus also struck alliances with other kingdoms by transferring their women to each other through marriage, as was the custom of the emerging patriarchy: women traded like, and in the service of securing, property among men.

Archaeology has shed little light on the practice of caste in Vijayapuri's social life, though modern genetic science has revealed that endogamy in the current population of Andhra Pradesh arose in the first millennium BCE, centuries before Vijayapuri.[21] This was found to be the case for many groups in the region, including today's Vysya caste group, which is about five million people strong. But it's unclear to what extent the early endogamous ancestors of the Vysya were part of a caste *system* this far south. Perhaps, to a large extent, they were. Or perhaps they practised endogamy without caste, as with Ashkenazi Jews, the Amish, and others, and later became a *jati* in the emerging caste system's hierarchy in the region; or perhaps they emerged from an endogamous caste group that had migrated from the north to Andhra lands.[22] Class, however, is apparent enough in the size and density of the housing seen across different parts of Vijayapuri.

As with the Satavahanas, a key legacy of the Ikshvakus is to have advanced into the south both Buddhism and Brahminism, and their associated arts and architectural styles. Both faiths were patronized by the Ikshvaku state but, curiously, the kings leaned strongly towards Brahminism and the queens towards Buddhism. Ikshvaku kings, following their clan tradition, subscribed to Vedic rituals and Puranic worship of Brahminical deities—as evident from inscriptions and the *Ashvamedha* complex inside the citadel, where a sacrificial horse's skeleton was also found. In this, they built upon the royal practices of the Satavahana Empire. What's also amply clear is that Ikshvaku queens played an extremely pivotal role in turning Vijayapuri into a great and famous centre of Buddhism, and presided over

Figure 9. Amorous couple on a larger panel with scenes from the Buddha's life

the rise of Mahayana. This 'suggests a significant degree of power and authority vested in the women of the royal family, in spite of the fact that succession to the throne remained firmly patrilineal'.[23]

The most prominent of the royal patrons of Buddhism was Chamtisiri, the sister of the first king, Chamtamula, and mother-in-law to Chamtamula's son and second king, who married his first cousin and took four other wives. A big donor to many Buddhist sites, including the Great Stupa, Chamtisiri 'is praised, or rather praises herself, in the inscription for her munificence and compassion, especially for those who are destitute and poor. She carefully lists her material donations and asks in return for the attainment of nirvana for herself and for the welfare and happiness of all the world'.[24] A goodwill gesture common with donors of the day was to name many members of their kinship group as benefactors—Chamtisiri listed thirty relatives in one inscription—thereby hoping to accrue the merits of religious charity more broadly.

Patrons of Buddhism also included wealthy commanders and the urban merchant class. A lay woman named Bodhisiri appears in donor records at multiple Buddhist sites, including temples, monasteries, pillars and tanks. Many other Buddhist women are recorded too, such as Mahadevi Bhatideva, Chandrasiri, Mahadevi Kodabalisiri, etc. 'Ninety percent of the donors were women,' estimates one scholar.[25] 'Taken together,' writes historian Upinder Singh, 'the epigraphic evidence points to a dominant role played by royal and non-royal women in the emergence of Vijayapuri as a premier Buddhist centre.'[26] Perhaps the south's old matrilineal sensibilities, though eroding with the spread of northern culture, were still alive in Vijayapuri's social substrate. Could this also help explain the relatively better status of women in south India versus in the north even today?

Powerful women weren't just passive donors but were active participants in the spiritual–philosophical life of the community. An early Mahayana Buddhist text, *The Lion's Roar,* attributed to a woman named Srimala, a Buddhist queen of unknown historicity, is believed to have been written at Nagarjunakonda. Lost in Sanskrit and available only via Chinese and Tibetan Buddhist canons, it is 'one of the chief scriptural sources for the theory that all sentient beings have the potentiality of Buddhahood within them'. Its translator from the Chinese, Diana Y.

Paul, admires 'its egalitarian and generous view concerning women, portraying, on the one hand, the dignity and wisdom of a laywoman and her concern for all beings, and, on the other, the role of woman as philosopher and teacher'. In the text, 'Srimala is praised for her intelligence and compassion, not for her beauty or wealth, which are implicit'.[27] Advancing the then radical idea of female Buddhas, Queen Srimala embarked on the bodhisattva path, and gained the 'lion's roar' or eloquence of an enlightened being. Scholars have noted striking similarities between the textual style of Srimala, aspiring to nirvana, and Chamtisiri doing the same in her inscriptions. The Srimala text may well have been influenced by Chamtisiri herself, or written to honour her.

At its peak, the population of Vijayapuri was likely in the tens of thousands. The ASI found only thirty-odd monasteries, each with ten to fifteen cells on average, yet estimated that the Buddhist monastic community numbered 4000, which seems high. Even with two monks to a cell and some guest monks, 1000 monks seem like a better estimate. Scholars Sukumar Dutt and H. Sarkar, and art historian Elizabeth R. Stone, see Vijayapuri marking 'a transition from Hinayana to Mahayana', concluding that its Buddhist art and architecture, 'while clearly Hinayana Buddhist in origin, was built by Hinayanists who were taking the path to the Mahayana, with monks gradually acceding to both stupa and image worship' and adding Buddha shrines in their monasteries.[28] A key figure in the rise of Mahayana Buddhism was Acharya Nagarjuna himself.

What Nagarjuna Said

The name 'Nagarjunakonda' first appears in medieval inscriptions, such as of Vijayanagar, suggesting a long memory of its association with Nagarjuna, a monk-philosopher and founder of the 'Middle Path' school of Mahayana Buddhism. He likely served the cause of Buddhism under the Satavahanas but is also said to have been a citizen of Vijayapuri in the third century CE. These claims are based not on hard evidence but inferred from early Tibetan texts, written centuries later. Most likely, Nagarjuna was in Amravathi but in middle age, towards the end of the Satavahana rule, he migrated to Sriparvata, an early name for Vijayapuri. He lived and taught there in a monastery until his death; the monastery was then perhaps named after him. This also fits circumstantial evidence related to Nagarjuna's foundational role in the development of Mahayana Buddhism, which substantially happened at Vijayapuri.

Mahayana, which injected a whole new layer of philosophical abstraction into Buddhism, according to some scholars, arose far from the mainstream monasteries of the Indo-Gangetic plain and was the work of fringe monastics like Nagarjuna.[29] Often called 'the second Buddha', his work is indispensable to several Buddhist schools. 'Nagarjuna's philosophy represents something of a watershed not only in the history of Indian philosophy but in the history of philosophy as a whole,' writes Douglas Berger, a scholar of Indian thought, 'as it calls into question certain philosophical assumptions so easily resorted to in our attempt to understand the world.'[30]

Not much is conclusively known about Nagarjuna's life. Born into a Brahmin family, he became a Buddhist. Legend has it that he spent many years at a centre of learning that later evolved into the famous Nalanda University in modern-day Bihar, but there is no evidence for this at all. Many scholars consider his exposition of the concept of shunyata ('emptiness' or 'voidness') to be a critical achievement, central to a remarkable understanding of how we make sense of the world. He is best known for two surviving Sanskrit works: *Madhyamika Karika* ('Fundamental Verses on the Middle Way') and *Vigrahavyavartani* ('The End of Disputes'), which analyse the nature of reality, how we perceive it and the basis of knowledge. His works should be thought of not only as a revival of the Buddha's views on such topics—which, at the time, were losing ground to rival views within both Buddhism and Brahminism—but also as their further development. In the rest of this section, I'll delve a bit deeper into Nagarjuna's philosophy.

The Middle Way that Nagarjuna spoke of refers to the concept of dependent origination, i.e., the idea that there is no objective, mind-independent reality that's accessible to us. This contrasts with the essentialist Brahminical view of the self (atman) and reality (Brahman), which posits that there is a true and universal reality that the human mind, with effort, can know.

Nagarjuna argued instead that what we make of reality inevitably depends on the cognitive structure of our mind, rather than on anything we can identify as an innate attribute of reality itself (*svabhava*). We understand the world through concepts, and there is no escape from our conceptual categories, no firm foundation we can reach beyond them. Thus, he suggested, we are limited by our lived experience and interpretive abilities. When we realize this, it has profound implications for us. As our illusions fall away, we begin to regard ourselves as contingent beings, inextricably steeped in a reality that we shape and which in turn shapes us, rather than as beings able to detach ourselves to contemplate reality as it 'truly' is (the so-called 'view from nowhere' implicit in the concept of Brahman, or 'Ultimate Reality', of Advaita Vedanta). Such a cognitive shift, according to the Buddha, is a prerequisite for inner peace and wisdom. It grounds us in pragmatic concerns and is conducive to cultivating compassion for our fellow beings who share this world with us.

In shunyata, Nagarjuna's real achievement was a rigorous analysis of phenomena in order to reveal the incoherence of the idea that things possess an 'intrinsic nature'—an eternal existence that does not depend on anything external to it. Nor is there a Self, with an unchanging, innate essence. Instead, the Self is our own conceptual construct, with which we refer to a set of shifting psychophysical states. That we rarely see things this way is a highly pragmatic self-deception that helps us survive. We can, however, recognize this and attain the right self-awareness through continuous practice. Though the Buddha first articulated these views, in Nagarjuna's time they were considered with suspicion. Nagarjuna's careful exposition (and extension) of these views made them respectable again, and they soon became the bedrock of Mahayana Buddhism.

What theory of knowledge can work with the idea of dependent origination or 'emptiness'? A contextualist one, says Nagarjuna, in which investigative procedures are a means of knowledge only in given contexts. To Nagarjuna, our knowledge and concepts, categories and means of investigation, feed on each other. They mutually shape and justify each other in specific contexts, and rely, above all, on us reaching a reflective equilibrium about them. Or as philosopher Richard Rorty put it, 'Truth is what your contemporaries let you get away with saying.'

Nagarjuna thus leads us to the idea that we can't know the 'ultimate truth' about how things really are; rather, there is only conventional, or generally accepted, truth, one that exists within the context of our commonly accepted practices and beliefs. That said, not every conventional truth is equally valid, Nagarjuna clarifies, and some can be judged better than others, based on humanity's shared experience of that particular 'truth'. For instance, when we claim that a fruit tastes more 'acidic' than another, we rely on conventional standards based on our shared sense of taste—there is no 'ultimate truth' of the fruit tasting acidic outside the human mind.[31]

Nagarjuna's views have found strong resonance in recent Western philosophy, particularly that of the Austrian philosopher Ludwig Wittgenstein. Nagarjuna explained how we arrive at our most cherished beliefs, and how understanding this is conducive to a deep humility. In our own world of secular and religious strife—so often over 'truths' claimed to be objective or universal—his ideas emphasize the need to be always alert to context in our interaction with and judgement of others.

The Fall of Vijayapuri

The Ikshvaku Dynasty came to a sudden end around 310–20 CE, and Vijayapuri rapidly declined thereafter. Why? Most online material and mainstream history books call this a mystery. However, based on Longhurst's slim archaeological report in 1938 and ASI's very comprehensive report in 2006, two compelling theories, not mutually exclusive, seem plausible.

The first theory claims that the rising Pallavas invaded Vijayapuri from the south, defeated the Ikshvakus, and pillaged and wrecked the city so badly that it never recovered. Longhurst wrote, 'The ruthless manner in which all the buildings at Nagarjunakonda have been destroyed is simply appalling and cannot represent the work of treasure-seekers alone as so many of the pillars, statues and sculptures have been wantonly smashed to pieces.'[32] Many stupas, he continued, 'had been wantonly destroyed and many beautiful sculptures smashed to pieces'. Sculptural slabs had been 'thrown down in all directions and most of them purposely broken'. Perhaps the Pallava army also

burned down the wooden superstructure above the stepped tank inside
the citadel and the pavilion of the Sarvadeva temple, which we know
were consumed by fire. Though the early Pallavas evidently had no
affinity for Buddhism, it's quite likely that they had mostly political
rather than religious motives. There is, however, no smoking gun for
such an invasion in historical sources, only the evidence that control
of Ikshvaku lands passed after them to the Pallavas, who had been
aggressively expanding.

The second and a more plausible theory advanced by ASI
archaeologists claims that 'the mortal blow to the Ikshvaku civic life in
Vijayapuri was dealt by the river', whose levels had risen steadily over
sixty to seventy years, causing more frequent flooding and silt deposits
evident in the excavated strata. The Ikshvakus had recognized the
problem and had started building flood-control measures, including
embankments and raising the floor height of riverside temples. In the
city's last twenty years of habitation, however, the river levels rose a
whopping nine feet, submerging much of the ghat. A major jolt perhaps
came around the start of the last king's reign, when the raging river
flooded the citadel and the western half of the city, forcing people there
to migrate to the eastern part, where life apparently continued for
many years. This massive disruption likely led to a slow evacuation and
perhaps made it easier for the Pallavas to defeat Vijayapuri.

What's amply clear is that Vijayapuri declined rapidly and no
Ikshvaku records were found after 310 CE. By 320 CE or so, notes
ASI, 'political stability in the valley and secular amenities had all
declined severely' and most of its population likely moved to greener
pastures. We can only speculate what life felt like during this period
of intense upheaval. The valley soon 'became a moribund museum
of the Ikshvaku heritage of standing monuments',[33] a sad end to a
wonderful and mostly peaceful century of intellectual ferment and
artistic creativity.

The Remains of the Day

Nowadays, most visitors to Nagarjunakonda Island come for the scenic
ferry ride and picnic with family or friends under a shady tree on the

lawns. The Ikshvakus never seemed to have lived, or at least built structures, on this hill, now covered with cactus, low brush and a few trees, including Bodhi trees ('ficus religiosa'). The 3–4-km walk to the transplanted and partially restored ruins of the Great Stupa, temples, monasteries, pillars, stupas, bathing/ritual tanks and a megalithic tomb makes a pleasant and evocative excursion. Medieval structures—the ramparts of a fort and a few Brahminical temples—still stand, likely built by the Reddi kings of Kondavidu in the fifteenth century, falling successively to the Gajapati rulers of Orissa and Krishnadevaraya of Vijayanagar. All visitors and employees leave in the evening and, at night, only two guards remain on the island.

Two Buddhist monasteries, a temple, and the city's famous amphitheatre were transplanted to the lake's eastern bank at Anupu, a few kilometres south from Vijayapuri South. I take an autorickshaw there one morning. The transplanted ruins include the monastery said to be associated with Nagarjuna. There are no other visitors; the quiet serenity of the place is only punctuated by birdsong. I sit in the empty stands of the amphitheatre and try to conjure up the bustle of the time.

It strikes me that history, as an account of our ancestors' lives and times, is necessarily based on material remains—monuments, sculptures, texts, other artefacts—mostly products of organized urban life. But while such a history reveals much about the kind of species we are, it only does so partially. The lives of our ancestors were far more varied than what their material remains indicate. For instance, at the edges of Vijayapuri and beyond were other groups that left no material remains at all—the Lambadis and Chenchus of the day who couldn't have cared less about Buddhism or Brahminism, preferring animistic folk deities and mother goddesses like Lajja Gauri instead—and who made up much of the subcontinent's population at the time. In the hinterland, these groups also often provided the labour and the food surpluses that funded Vijayapuri and its forms of creative life. We could as well say that history belongs to those whose creative works survive and vibrate in the minds of later historians.

On my final afternoon, I return to the site museum on Nagarjunakonda Island. I again pore over its exquisite sculptures, artefacts and archaeological data on the ancient city, though many of

Figure 10. Nagarjuna Sagar Lake

the best pieces are in museums elsewhere and in private collections. This museum too, like many other ASI museums, prohibits photography of works that have no copyright claims and were excavated with public money. Why? 'Orders from above,' they say, 'Apply for a permit in Delhi.' Unlike my previous visit, however, this time I manage to persuade the curator-in-charge to make an exception for my writing project.

I have time to kill before the last ferry. I wander to the transplanted third-century Ikshvaku ghat, a fitting place to rest and imagine the city at its prime: its street life, homes, people. What was Nagarjuna like as a man, in the eyes of his family and friends? How sophisticated must the city's intellectual culture have been to bubble up a thinker like him. What was it like to engage in doctrinal debates, where rival schools of thought battled each other? I sit and wonder, absently staring at a lake so large that it sends small waves crashing at my feet.

Faxian, Xuanzang and Yijing in India
(400–700 CE)

I don't know many books in which 'Go west, young man!' would be a call to go to India. One such book is *Journey to the West*, 'China's most beloved novel of religious quest and picaresque adventure', published in the 1590s during the waning years of the Ming Dynasty. The novel's hero, 'a mischievous monkey with human traits . . . accompanies the monk hero on his action-filled travels to India in search of Buddhist scripture'. It allegorically presents pilgrims journeying towards India as individuals journeying towards enlightenment.[1]

The inspiration for this novel was a journey made by a seventh-century-CE Chinese man, Xuanzang (aka Hiuen Tsang), a Buddhist monk who embarked on an adventurous seventeen-year trip to India, part of which he spent at Nalanda Mahavihara, a great Buddhist centre of learning. Other Chinese Buddhists had visited India before Xuanzang, and many more would follow, but three pilgrims left records of their journeys that would survive, giving us vital portraits of the Indian social and religious life between 400 and 700 CE. These are Faxian (aka Fa-Hien, c. 337– 422 CE), Xuanzang (c. 602–664 CE) and Yijing (635–713 CE).[2] All three of them began their journeys in Chang'an (modern Xian), a multicultural hotspot and terminus of the Silk Road. They went as pilgrims seeking Buddhist scholarship and authoritative texts to take back home, but were also among the world's earliest legendary adventurers and travel writers.

Buddhism arrived in China in the first century CE with traders and missionaries from India and Central Asia along the Silk Road and later on sea routes. The Kushan Dynasty, patrons of Buddhism based in Gandhara, played a key role in its transmission. Buddhism at first gained a following among the elite in China. But far as it was from its Indian roots, Chinese Buddhism grew based less on original scriptures, and more on derivative texts and local innovations. Buddhists were often misunderstood and defamed in China. Poor translations confused followers, as did contrary ideas from different schools of Buddhism across Central, South and South East Asia.

Nascent Buddhist communities in China therefore yearned for authentic sources on which their institutions, teachings and practices could be based. Many Chinese Buddhists also longed to see the places the Buddha had once inhabited. This, and not trade, tourism or secular inquiry, became the primary motive behind the steady stream of Chinese visitors to India in the mid-first millennium CE. It helped that the Sui and Tang Dynasties in China, from around 500 CE, had begun to patronize Buddhism, which by then had gained a critical mass of followers. Yijing himself wrote biographies of fifty-six pilgrims—mostly Chinese, a few Koreans and one Central Asian, which included five he had personally met. All of them had gone to India, learnt Sanskrit, visited pilgrimage sites, studied the Buddhist religion and philosophy at monasteries like Nalanda, and returned with ideas and books to enrich Buddhism at home.[3] There were likely hundreds more in the third quarter of the first millennium.[4] Many Indian monks also went as missionaries and scholars to China but none of their observations of China have come down to us.[5]

When Buddhism in India went into terminal decline around 800 CE and died out soon after 1200 CE, nearly all of its texts were lost forever (India's humid weather didn't help). Buddhism, its monuments and even the Buddha himself, were as good as forgotten by Indians. This changed only after the travel writings of Faxian, Xuanzang and Yijing were discovered and translated by European Indologists in the nineteenth and early twentieth centuries. Their eyewitness accounts of geography, society, customs, material life and religion greatly expanded our understanding of the Indian past. Many Chinese translations of

Indian Buddhist texts, the earliest of which date to fifth century CE, were recognized as the closest approximations of the Indian originals. This was similar to the 'rediscovery' of the ancient Graeco-Roman antiquity in Europe and of ancient Greek texts we know only through Arabic translations from the 'golden age' of Islam in the ninth and tenth centuries.

Many Journeys, One Goal

Faxian was 'the pioneer of all', wrote Yijing.[6] A native of Wuyang in today's Shanxi Province, Faxian's three older brothers all died before 'shedding their first teeth'.[7] His father exposed young Faxian to a Buddhist sangha and then sent him to a monastery, where the boy apparently felt quite at home. Both his parents died when he was around ten. By the time he completed his apprenticeship and was ordained a full monk, Faxian was noted for his courage, intelligence and self-control. 'Deploring the mutilated and imperfect state of the collection of the Books of Discipline', Faxian decided to visit India to gather texts on the *Vinaya Pitaka*, or monastic rules for monks and nuns.[8] It's not clear why he had to wait until he was in his early sixties to set out on the land route to India with four fellow pilgrims.

The five pilgrims crossed the Gobi Desert, with its 'many evil demons and hot winds'. There were no tracks to follow, wrote Faxian. 'Though you look all round most earnestly to find where you can cross, you know not where to make your choice, the only mark and indication being the dry bones of the dead [upon the sand].'[9] Later, when his party had great difficulties crossing rivers, he described their sufferings as 'unparalleled in human experience'. Despite the hardships, Faxian and his companions often found Buddhist communities and monasteries across Central Asia, which aided and hosted them en route. They reached the Indian Subcontinent via Khotan, c. 402 CE, and passed Gandhara, Takshashila and the kingdom of Purushapura (modern Peshawar). By the time they reached central India, they had been on the road for six years!

Faxian spent the next six years in India and visited many sites associated with the Buddha, such as Lumbini and Rajagriha. It took him three more years to return to China by sea. He took back with him many texts 'unknown in the land of Han' aboard a large ship carrying 'more than 200 men', braving the terrors of tempests and his ship springing a leak. He travelled via Ceylon and Java, where, he writes, 'various forms of error and Brahminism are flourishing, while Buddhism in it is not worth speaking of'. After spending years translating texts, he died at age eighty-six.

§

Two centuries later came Xuanzang. Born in a conservative Confucian family near Chang'an, he followed his brother into the Buddhist monastic life at the age of thirteen. A precocious boy seemingly blessed with a photographic memory, Xuanzang mastered his material so well that he was ordained a priest when he was only twenty. Disenchanted with the quality of Buddhist texts and teachers available to him, and 'stirred up by the recollection of Faxian', he decided to go west to India, to the cradle and thriving centre of Buddhism itself. He intended to 'question the sages on points that troubled his mind' and to return with authentic knowledge and Buddhist scriptures.

Xuanzang was twenty-six when he set out on a year-long journey full of peril and adventure. He had prepared for it by learning basic travel phrases in many languages from foreigners in Xian.[10] He rode alone much of the way on his horse, crossing great deserts, mountains and rivers, braving hail and snowstorms, and, like Faxian before him, was often guided by nothing more than the bones lying on the way. Passing a desert, 'all sorts of demon shapes and strange goblins' closed in on him, vanishing only after he recited a Chinese mantra. Then, riding his horse, he accidentally dropped his water pouch and lost all of his drinking water. After going five days without a drop of water, he tells us, 'his stomach was racked with a burning heat'. He was close to death when he finally stumbled across a small oasis and found water.

Having avoided death by dehydration, he went on to escape robbers, pesky kings and other colourful characters that seem right out of B-grade Bollywood films of the 1980s. One such was the Khan of a wandering horde of fire-worshipping Turks (Khan is a title predating Islam). Watched over by a bodyguard, the formidable Khan—clad in a green satin robe, his hair hanging loose—feasted on wine, veal and music in his lavish tent with his officers 'clothed in brocade stuff'. Around them stood troops 'mounted on camels and horses', 'clothed in furs and fine-spun hair garments' and 'carrying lances and bows and standards'. The Khan and his officers were filling each other's cups with exhortations to drink more. As they became more boisterous, the music grew louder. The Khan then urged Xuanzang to abandon his pointless quest for that hot land of the Buddha, where men 'are naked-blacks, without any sense of decorum, and not fit to look at!'

But Xuanzang was unstoppable and continued past Khotan, Tashkent and Samarkand, debating Buddhists on the Silk Road and in Afghanistan, where he saw the majestic Bamiyan Buddhas. At Takshashila, he saw Buddhism in decline, ruined monasteries and one of the 84,000 stupas built by Ashoka across India (it's unclear how Xuanzang came up with that number), one that 'constantly emits a sacred light from its surface'. At last, he had reached the subcontinent.

Xuanzang was away from China for seventeen years, spending thirteen of them in the subcontinent (630–43 CE), travelling extensively and visiting the major sites associated with the Buddha's life. He seemed to have had a deeply cathartic experience at the Bodhi tree under which the Buddha is said to have attained enlightenment, whose 'leaves are heart-shaped, slender and pointed, and constantly quivering'.[11] Xuanzang learnt Sanskrit and studied for years with Buddhist masters, most notably at Nalanda, where he was under Silabhadra, a great master of the Yogacara school of Mahayana Buddhism, which Xuanzang had been drawn to from an early age. His erudition brought him great fame and royal patronage in India. In a convocation of religious scholars 'in Harsha's capital of Kannauj . . . Xuanzang allegedly defeated five hundred Brahmins, Jains, and heterodox Buddhists in spirited debate'.[12] In a flourish of religious humility, emperor Harsha even referred to himself as a servant of Xuanzang.[13]

Xuanzang gathered hundreds of Sanskrit texts, 150 relics of the Buddha, statues and other artefacts, loaded them on pack animals and returned the same way he had come. For the remaining nineteen years of his life at home, until his death at the age of sixty-two, he worked in Xian with a team of linguist monks to translate many of the 657 books that survived his journey (a few were lost while crossing the Indus) into Chinese and wrote commentaries on them. He also published an extensive account of his travels,[14] which is now an invaluable historical and archaeological record.

§

Yijing likely witnessed Xuanzang's grand funeral in Chang'an. He was then a young Buddhist monk. Inspired by 'the noble enthusiasm of Xuanzang', Yijing longed to follow in his footsteps to India. At thirty, Yijing became serious about his dream, found a sponsor for his journey and set sail on a Persian boat for the kingdom of Srivijaya in Sumatra, where he stayed for many months with other foreign scholars and learnt Sanskrit. In the preceding centuries, Indian merchants had not only brought Buddhism to South East Asia but also a linguistic script, religious texts and rituals, literature, art, architecture and countless other aspects of Indian culture, immersion in which helped Yijing prepare for India.

He arrived by sea in 673 CE at a place called Tamralipti, near modern Kolkata. There, at a monastery, he met a Mahayana teacher and stayed with him for a year, learning Sanskrit. He then travelled by foot to Nalanda with his teacher, 'twenty fellow priests of Nalanda' and 'hundred merchants', finding strength in numbers through a 'dangerous and perilous road', across 'a big mountain and bogs'.[15] En route, he was struck 'by an illness of the season' and grew 'very weak and tired'. He couldn't keep up with the group and fell behind. Finding him alone, some mountain brigands descended on him, stripped him naked and took all his belongings. He had heard the rumour that in these parts they liked sacrificing light-skinned people. Though despairing and fearful, he managed to escape. He writes, 'I entered into a muddy hole, and besmeared all my body with mud. I covered myself with leaves, and supporting myself on a stick, I advanced slowly', until he was united with his worried teacher 'calling out for him from outside the village'.

A few days later Yijing reached Nalanda, where he stayed for ten years. He also travelled in the Gangetic Plain to the places associated with the Buddha's life, such as Bodh Gaya, Sarnath, Vaisali and Kushinagar, met many teachers 'renowned for their brilliant character', and was glad for 'the opportunity of acquiring knowledge from them personally'. Yijing's extensive account of monastic life in India reveals him as a devout yet pragmatic man, full of the sort of courage that's fuelled by religious zeal, and obsessed with codes of monastic conduct. When leaving India in 685 CE, he carted home 400 books and translated many of them on a second, multi-year stint in Sumatra. Aided by a few Indian monks, he continued this work in China, translating fifty-six works in 230 volumes. He died at the age of seventy-nine, and, like Xuanzang, was lavishly honoured by the Tang emperor.

On Interpreting Their Words

How should we read the records of Faxian, Xuanzang and Yijing? Their impressions of India are fragmentary, subjective and prone to biases and vagaries of their psychological dispositions. As with all travellers, parts of their testimonies derived from hearsay, cultural misunderstandings, personal blinders, or ideas simply 'lost in translation'.

All three monks had deep religious commitments even as they were all very curious. They often relate magical events, supernatural beings and moralistic legends without scepticism, posing challenges of interpretation for the modern scholar. For instance, Xuanzang's Buddha has subdued dragons, flown in the air, turned into a serpent to deliver magical cures and fed his blood to yakshas in a previous life; we read about a tooth relic of the Buddha that emits a bright light on religious days, and a monkey who has accrued enough 'religious merit' to be reborn as a man. Certain stupas with (purported?) relics of the Buddha, such as hair or nails, are described as having magical healing properties. Bodhisattvas appear above the ocean skies to rescue people from shipwrecks. It is reported matter-of-factly that in a forest lived a 700-year-old Brahmin who looked like he was thirty.

All three pilgrims wrote from memory, sometimes years later, raising the odds of error and embellishment. At times, the traveller narrated his story to a local scholar monk who then wrote it down. Moreover, their target audience was 'one that they had hoped would see them as highly erudite, knowledgeable because they had been there, so to speak, in the place where the Buddha himself had walked, where the sacred texts were composed and preserved, and where learned masters provided daily exegeses on these texts'.[16] Eager to reform Chinese Buddhism, they often idealized Indian Buddhism in their accounts, especially Yijing. In other words, they wrote for an audience in a different cultural milieu and often pursued didactic goals, such as shaping behaviour and inspiring fellow monks at home. Much care is therefore required in interpreting their words.

And yet, their observations of social life are often quite sharp, realistic and astute. Many are wonderfully descriptive eyewitness accounts. Of course, modern historians must also rely on other sources and use their own judgement to decide what to believe and what not, as I myself have done. In another complication, however, most translations of these Chinese texts, on which nearly all Western scholarship is based, are more than a hundred years old. They date from an era when archaeological knowledge was scant, and much guesswork went into identifying sites with altered Chinese names in the originals. Further, every translation has some errors, idiosyncrasies and cultural blind spots. Is 'heretics' the right translation of Xuanzang's term for non-Buddhists, or does it betray the translator's baggage from an Abrahamic tradition? Is 'nation' the right term for the subcontinent in the seventh century? Translations by a new generation of scholars are therefore long overdue, which, one hopes, will also provide fresh new insights into these travellers' worlds.

Naming Their Destination

Both Xuanzang and Yijing call the subcontinent 'the West', made up of five parts or 'five Indies', comprising many countries (or kingdoms). Yijing reports visiting over thirty countries in 'the West' and Xuanzang thinks it is 'divided into seventy countries or so'. 'Each country has diverse customs,' writes Xuanzang. Nevertheless, it's clear that all three Chinese visitors, as outsiders, saw an ethnocultural distinctiveness about the subcontinent (likely excluding the North East, where none of them seem to have travelled); it's not clear what, if any, common identity its residents themselves consciously shared with each other. There was the notion of *Aryavarta* but it was an elite identity that didn't extend much beyond urban areas, nor across much of the southern part of the subcontinent. Nor did the subcontinental epithet Mleccha or barbarian, apply only to people outside, since it also applied to the 'primitive tribes' and other 'impure' beings who didn't belong to any of the dominant religio-cultural streams within the subcontinent.

Yijing writes that the people of 'the West' do not call themselves 'Hindu', nor give 'the West' a single name, such as 'India'. Only the tribes outside, in the far north and west, use the term 'Hindu' to refer to *all* the people—irrespective of their faith—on the other side of the river Sindhu (Sanskrit for Indus), a region that includes much of the subcontinent. Xuanzang expresses much the same view and refers to this vast expanse as *In-tu*,[17] which his nineteenth-century translator, Samuel Beal, renders as *India*. That Xuanzang uses a single word for 'the land beyond the Sindhu' suggests that he too sees something culturally distinctive about it; he even describes its salient features *as a whole*: its physical dimensions, measures of time and distance, social customs, languages, religions and more.

'Hindu', related to 'Sindhu', was then strictly an ethno-geographic descriptor, a term for those who resided in this region, and not the religious one that it would gradually become from the late medieval to the colonial era. (Western Indologists would also coin the term 'Hinduism', which included far more than just Brahminism.) In Yijing's time (as also in Megasthenes's and Alberuni's time), outsiders saw even animists, polytheists, ancestor worshippers, Jains and Buddhists as 'Hindu'. (For a rough analogy, consider how modern urban upper-class Indians might see rural India—as full of 'peasants' or 'villagers' in certain attires, though the latter may not use any unifying identities for themselves and see their different communities and lifeworlds as completely distinct.)

Traversing the Land

In terms of general prosperity, the Chinese pilgrims see India and China as mostly on par, as in the quality of buildings, clothing and food. As for people, Xuanzang calls Indians 'upright and honourable', 'not deceitful or treacherous in their conduct', and 'faithful to their oaths and promises'. 'They dread the retribution of another state of existence, and make light of the things of the present world', which suggests a strong sense of an afterlife and karmic punishment and reward. He documents 'nine methods of showing outward respect' that Indians use with each other, such as using soothing words to make requests, 'joining the hands and bowing low', 'bending the knee', 'a prostration', etc. State governance, he writes, is 'founded on benign principles', does not subject people to forced labour, and 'taxes on the people are light'. 'In their rules of government, there is remarkable rectitude, whilst in their behavior there is much gentleness and sweetness.' There are a few 'criminals and rebels' but they are 'only occasionally troublesome'.

However, such favourable generalizing about India as a whole has frequent exceptions in his regional assessments of people. While Xuanzang says nice things about many groups—people are 'simple and honest' in Multan, 'virtuous and docile' in Malwa, 'courageous and truthful' in Kanchipuram—the 'exceptions' occur twice or thrice as often. They seem like dyspeptic verdicts, offered without explanation. For instance, in Baltistan, people are 'rough and rude in character; there is little humanity or justice with them; and as for politeness, such a thing has not been heard of'. In the country of Kuluta (Kullu district in present-day Himachal Pradesh), he finds people 'coarse and common', 'much afflicted with goitre and tumours', and their nature 'hard and fierce'. Men have a savage disposition in Garhwal. They're 'vehement and impetuous' in Kalinga (Orissa), 'crooked and perverse' in Bharuch (Gujarat), 'fierce and impulsive' in Andhra country, 'dissolute and cruel' in Chola country, and 'given to indulgence and debauchery' in Sindh. In a kingdom near Varanasi, men are 'naturally fierce and excitable', and so on.

These pronouncements do not depend on whether a country has more Buddhists or 'heretics' (i.e., of Brahminical, pagan or other beliefs). He even spent many months studying at Buddhist monasteries in several of these regions and must have interacted with many locals. Did some bad experiences colour his views? In Punjab he was robbed of everything, including his clothes, and, near Ayodhya, nearly sacrificed to goddess Durga by river pirates on the Ganges. Perhaps he was simply a grumpy, irritable monk with a tendency to hastily generalize about lay people. Was he playing to a gallery at home? Or did a kernel of truth, at least sometimes, lie beneath his sweeping pronouncements?

For most places he visits, Xuanzang records their size, salient features of their geography, their rulers, occasional individual or cultural quirks, agricultural and other products, local legends and more. Most kings, he observes, were male Kshatriyas, Vaishyas, Brahmins or Buddhists. But he records some exceptions too. In the country of Brahmapura in the lower Himalayas, where people are 'hasty and impetuous', a woman has for ages 'been the ruler, and so it is called the kingdom of the women. The husband of the reigning woman is called king, but he knows nothing about the affairs of the state. The men manage the wars and sow the land, and that is all'. In a country near Bijnor, a Shudra king 'worships the spirits of heaven'. Its 'sincere and truthful' people revere 'learning, and are deeply versed in the use of charms and magic'. In Sindh too, which abounds with Buddhists, the king is a Shudra, 'by nature honest and sincere' and reverential towards the Buddha. Matipura, near Haridwar, has a Shudra king as well.

In Kannauj, the prosperous realm of Harsha, people are honest, noble and 'gracious in appearance'. Harsha had earlier greatly expanded his domain via six years of war 'by subduing all who were not obedient'. At some point, he embraced Buddhism, banned all animal slaughter for food and made violations thereof punishable by death. He joined religious debates, 'rewarded the good and punished the evil' and promoted 'men of talent'. Xuanzang admires Harsha's religious piety, temperance and generosity. 'Every fifth year, he convoked a grand assembly of deliverance (*Maha-moksha-parishad)*, and distributed the stores of his treasuries in charity' to 'the poor, the orphans, the destitute' and religious institutions. 'In all the highways of the towns and villages throughout India he erected hospices, provided food and drink, and stationed there physicians, with medicines for travelers and poor persons round about, to be given without any stint.'[18]

Xuanzang also visits Ayodhya, where people are 'virtuous and amiable'. A hundred Buddhist monasteries host 3000 monks, he writes. Non-Buddhists are 'few in number' and have ten temples. Ayodhya, this suggests, is largely a Buddhist town in the seventh century. In early fifth century (c. 406 CE), Faxian too writes about visiting its many sacred Buddhist sites. Ayodhya's flourishing Buddhist scene in the fifth century lures Vasubandhu, a monk from Gandhara, who moves here, becomes a great Buddhist master and teacher and breathes new life into the Yogacara school of Mahayana with his half-brother, Asanga, who too lives nearby. Yogacara, as developed in Ayodhya, would become one of the two leading Mahayana schools in India (the other being Madhyamaka, founded by Nagarjuna). Vasubandhu explores 'the nature of language and the proper and improper ways for a Buddhist to employ scripture and reason'.[19] Xuanzang reveres Vasubandhu and visits the old monastery in Ayodhya where he lived, and the hall where he preached to 'kings of different countries, eminent men of the world, Sramanas and Brahmins'.

The scene in Prayag (later to be known as Allahabad), however, is very different. Xuanzang finds that 'the number of heretics [non-Buddhists] is very great', who are 'gentle and compliant in their disposition'. Though he doesn't use the term Kumbh Mela, Xuanzang may have heard about it or witnessed a version of it. He documents the popular belief that by bathing at the confluence of the Ganga and Yamuna, 'all the pollution of sin is washed away and destroyed; therefore, from various quarters and distant regions people come here together and rest'. Many ascetics who gather here, he writes, practise extreme physical rites and continue 'this ordeal through several decades of years'. Xuanzang doesn't think much of these practices. Elsewhere, debating the 'opinions of the different heretical schools', he cites the Kapalika ascetics who go naked, hang human bones around their heads and necks and 'cover themselves with cinders, and think this to be meritorious'. He asks, how can anyone 'regard these things as proofs of wisdom? Are they not evidences of madness and folly?'[20] Varanasi, he estimates, has about 100 temples with 3000 priests, who mostly honour Shiva, one of whose statues he sees as 'full of grandeur and majesty'. At Haridwar, multitudes gather 'from distant quarters to bathe and wash in its waters'. He is very impressed by the Ganga, calling it wide and blue, like the ocean, and its water 'sweet and pleasant'.

The people in the kingdom of Champa (eastern Bihar) are 'simple and honest'. Their capital is enclosed by brick walls 'tens of feet high'. It has many Buddhist monasteries but they are 'mostly in ruins'. As with so many other observations, Xuanzang doesn't explain why. South of Champa lie 'great mountain forests, thick and wild', with 'many hundred wild elephants who roam in herds'. Consequently, the elephants in the army of Champa are 'very numerous. Every now and again they send elephant masters to go around and catch them. In these countries, they keep elephants for drawing carriages (or, riding). Wolves, rhinoceros, and black leopards are abundant, so men dare not go' into the forests.

In Maharashtra, 'the disposition of the people is honest and simple', though they also have 'a stern and vindictive character. To their benefactors they are grateful; to their enemies relentless'. On one hand, 'if they are insulted, they will risk their lives to avenge themselves', on the other 'if they are asked to help one in distress, they will forget themselves in their haste to render assistance'. In war, if one of their generals loses, 'they do not inflict punishment, but present him with woman's clothes, and so he is driven to seek death for himself'. This country also has several hundred fierce warriors, 'a band of champions', who enter battle after they and their elephants have drunk enough alcohol. 'No enemy can [then] stand before them', including Harsha's mighty troops. Every time these revered champions 'go forth they beat drums before them', and if one of them kills a fellow citizen in a brawl, 'the laws of the country do not punish him'.

In Mathura, Xuanzang finds lots of stupas, monasteries and Buddhists; its people are 'soft and complacent' and 'esteem virtue and learning'. Faxian too visited Mathura, c. 406 CE, noting that there were twenty monasteries on both the banks of the Yamuna, with perhaps 'three thousand monks; and [here] the Law of Buddha was still more flourishing'. Indeed, even in the second century CE, Mathura was the production hub of the earliest Buddha statues in the north, especially for the major Buddhist sites of Shravasti, Kausambi and Sarnath.[21]

South of Mathura is the 'Middle Kingdom', writes Faxian. 'The people are numerous and happy; they have not to register their households, or attend to any magistrates and their rules; only those who cultivate the royal land have to pay [a portion of] the grain from it.' If they want to go, they go; if they want to stay on, they stay. The king governs without decapitation or [other] corporal punishments.† Criminals are

---

* According to Xuanzang, the tax amounted to a sixth of the grain production.
† Xuanzang later observed this too.

simply fined, lightly or heavily, according to the circumstances [of each case]. Even in cases of repeated attempts at wicked rebellion, they only have their right hands cut off.' This was the realm of the Gupta Empire (319–543 CE).

In Magadh (in present-day Bihar), Faxian writes, 'The cities and towns . . . are the greatest of all in the Middle Kingdom. The inhabitants are rich and prosperous, and vie with one another in the practice of benevolence and righteousness.' The 'elegant carving and inlaid sculpture work' on the 'royal palace and halls in the midst of the city' of Patliputra were so sublime that, Faxian surmises, only heavenly spirits could have made them. However, by the time Xuanzang visited two centuries later, the Gupta Empire had collapsed and Patliputra had 'long been deserted', stripped down to 'only its foundation walls', and hundreds of Buddhist monasteries and Deva (i.e. Brahminical) temples lay in ruins. Modern archaeology has found only a tiny part of what remained even in Xuanzang's time.

Impressions of Social Life

According to Yijing, 'the first and chief difference between India and other nations is the peculiar distinction between purity and impurity'. He notes that the idea of clean and unclean foods and consecrating spaces for drinking, eating and sleeping is strong among both monks and laymen. People fuss a lot over the protocols of handling food and utensils. After meals, they wash hands and rinse their mouths before touching others to avoid defiling them. Xuanzang too observed that people are 'very particular in their personal cleanliness'. They wash themselves before eating and do not share dishes or eat leftovers.

Such logic, Yijing suggests, led monastic kitchens to also keep out female servants (in case they were menstruating?), though he doesn't say how this was handled in nunneries. He offers clues on this question elsewhere, when he writes that 'nuns in India are very different from those in China. They support themselves by begging food, and live a poor and simple life'. Perhaps, unlike the monks, the nuns didn't have a kitchen in their residential quarters at all. Yijing's remarks apply to Indian Buddhist monasteries in general, and there is no reason to think that his alma mater, Nalanda Mahavihara, was any different. Scholars, however, still have few reliable specifics about the life of nuns in ancient Buddhist monasteries in India.

None of the three Chinese monks mention caste distinctions inside the monasteries. But what about the world outside? According to modern genomic research, endogamy was already common seventy generations ago, at least 'among upper castes and Indo-European speakers', so it existed in the time of both Xuanzang and Yijing.[22] Of course, it is hard for outsiders to grasp the intricacies of caste even today—especially if their native informants and interlocutors are the educated elite, which must surely have been the case with the Chinese pilgrims. That said, some aspects of caste are plainly evident in their accounts. Among the four varnas, writes Xuanzang, 'the purity or impurity of caste assigns to everyone his place'. Without elaboration, he also writes, 'When they marry they rise or fall in position according to their new relationship.'

Yijing writes, 'The Brahmans are regarded throughout the five parts of India as the most honorable [caste]. They do not, when they meet in a place, associate with the other three castes, and the mixed classes of the people have still less intercourse with them. The scriptures they revere are the four Vedas, containing about 100,000 verses . . . handed down from mouth to mouth, not transcribed on paper or leaves. In every generation, there exist some intelligent Brahmans who can recite the 100,000 verses.'[23] Faxian recalls one such renowned Brahmin turned Buddhist in Patliputra, Radha-sami, who lived 'by himself in spotless purity'. He habitually washed his hands right after anyone touched them. One day, out of 'love and reverence', the king 'took hold of his hand'. A bemused Faxian adds that 'as soon as [the king] let it go, the Brahmin made haste to pour water on it and wash it'.

Towns across the country have 'wide and high' walls, writes Xuanzang, but does not say what fears led people to build them. These walls enclose tortuous streets and lanes. 'The thoroughfares are dirty' with 'stalls arranged on both sides of the road with appropriate signs'. Could the still filthy streets of modern Indian towns have such an ancient lineage? 'Butchers, fishers, dancers, executioners, and scavengers . . . have their abodes outside' the walls. 'In coming and going these persons are bound to keep on the left side of the road till they arrive at their homes.'

Yijing, too, notes that manual scavengers, 'who carry off feces and clear away filth have to distinguish [i.e., announce] themselves by striking sticks while going about; when one has by mistake touched any of them, one thoroughly washed oneself and one's garments'. Untouchability was clearly an established practice in the seventh century.

According to Yijing, 'ghee, oil, milk, and cream' are ubiquitous, as are cereal cakes, rice and fruit like mangoes and bananas. Also common, he writes, are sweet melons, sugar cane, tubers, mustard leaves and mustard oil. Xuanzang adds to this list ginger, jackfruit, pomegranates, sweet oranges and 'sugar-candy', and notes that fish, mutton, gazelle and deer are eaten. He notices alcohol use by Kshatriyas and Vaishayas, not Brahmins and Buddhists. Curiously, Yijing observes that Indians 'do not eat any kind of onions' and associate them with causing tummy aches, diseases and bodily weakness. If 'anyone uses [onions and garlic] for food,' writes Xuanzang, 'they are expelled beyond the walls of the town', along with the other dietary misfits, 'despised and scorned' for consuming the wrong kinds of meat: ox, pig, ass, dog, monkey and 'all the hairy kind'. Faxian, nearly 300 years before Yijing, described a similar social reality when he wrote,

> Throughout the whole country the people do not . . . eat onions or garlic. The only exception is that of the Chandalas. That is the name for those who are (held to be) wicked men, and live apart from others. When they enter the gate of a city or a market-place, they strike a piece of wood to make themselves known, so that men know and avoid them, and do not come into contact with them . . . Only the Chandalas are fishermen and hunters, and sell flesh meat.[24]

Yijing takes pride in the state of healing and medical science in China and considers India way behind. Some Indian home remedies puzzle him, such as foregoing food and water for days during illnesses; other practices disgust him. In some places, he writes, 'a low custom has long been prevalent, i.e., whenever a sickness arises, people use urine and feces as medicaments, sometimes the dung of pigs or cats, which is put on a plate or kept in a jar'. Yijing denounces it as 'the worst of impure filth'. He knows that *Vinaya Pitaka* itself sanctions 'the dung of a calf and urine of a cow' as medicines, at least for the skin, but even his piety can't accept this scriptural folly; he creatively tries to discredit it by saying that only a few schools of Buddhism believe in it.

When a person dies, writes Xuanzang, his friends and relatives 'strike their heads and beat their breasts'. Those who attend a funeral are deemed unclean, and must 'bathe outside the town and then enter their homes'. He also describes a haunting practice that seems a lot like euthanasia (though one wonders how much of it was entirely voluntary).

> The old and infirm who come near to death, and those entangled in a severe sickness, who fear to linger to the end of their days, and through disgust wish to escape the troubles of life, or those who desire release from the trifling affairs of the world and its concerns, these, after receiving a farewell meal at the hands of their relatives or friends, they place, amid the sounds of music, on a boat which they propel into the midst of the Ganges, where such persons drown themselves.

Brahmins versus Bodhisattvas

Brahminism and Buddhism, the two dominant games in town, had common roots and many overlapping beliefs and customs. Religious life, especially among the laity, was fairly syncretic across most orthodox (Brahminical) and heterodox (Sramanic) belief systems. But the two also had real differences, which at times bubbled up in strong mutual distrust and hostility, especially at elite and institutional levels. Faxian relates a few examples. His account, though partial to the Buddhist point of view, reveals a combative dynamic between the two groups. When Shravasti was rising as a Buddhist town and accruing monuments that honoured the Buddha, he writes, 'The Brahmins with their contrary doctrine, became full of hatred and envy in their hearts, and wished to destroy them, but there came from the heavens such a storm of crashing thunder and flashing lightning that they were not able in the end to affect their purpose.'

Xuanzang also describes a failed plot in which 500 Brahmins, jealous and resentful of Harsha's 'excessive' patronizing of Buddhism, hired a killer to assassinate Harsha. Other kings, such as of Karnagarh in Bihar and Brahmanapura in Malwa, reportedly hosted well-attended and often bitter debates—philosophical boxing contests, if you will—between Brahmins and Bodhisattvas, with the latter invariably reported as victors in Chinese accounts, and being rewarded with fame, fortune and increased royal patronage for their monasteries. Notably, many of the star Buddhist philosopher monks were Brahmin by birth, and had joined what they likely considered a more satisfying scholastic fold of inquiry, debate and mode of being.[25] This perhaps added another layer of complexity to their rivalry with former co-religionists.

Xuanzang himself joined animated debates with Brahmins in Harsha's court, and even at Nalanda. A Brahmin challenger once showed up at Nalanda and asked for a debate. He 'wrote out forty theses and hung them up at the Temple gate. "If any one within can refute these principles," he said, "I will then give my head as a proof of his victory."' When several days passed by and no one at Nalanda responded, Xuanzang sent an attendant to tear down his theses, 'trample it under foot', and invite the Brahmin to a debate. A great number of Nalanda priests gathered 'whilst he disputed with the Brahmin'. The debate soon left the Brahmin 'silent and unable to reply'. Rising up, 'he respectfully said: "I am overcome; I am ready to abide by the former compact."' Xuanzang, claiming to espouse non-violence, magnanimously pardoned his life.[26]

There were more extreme 'heretics' too, such as Shashanka of Bengal, a Brahminical king, who 'slandered the religion of the Buddha' and raided and 'cut down the Bodhi tree', 'burnt it with fire' and destroyed the monasteries around it, though he couldn't fully destroy the roots of the tree. Thankfully, writes Xuanzang, the king of Magadh lovingly nurtured the roots 'with the milk of a thousand cows', causing the tree to miraculously revive within months.

Xuanzang, in particular, but also Faxian and Yijing, travelled extensively in India, not just to the famous pilgrimage sites. 'All over India,' writes Yijing, 'there are innumerable big monasteries.' Their accounts suggest that Buddhism was well established (though Xuanzang also saw ruined monasteries in some places, perhaps indicating the start of Buddhism's long-term decline in India). From Kashmir to Sri Lanka, they saw old and new Buddhist sites and thousands of monasteries hosting perhaps hundreds of thousands of monks split between Mahayana and the eighteen sects of Hinayana (or Theravada, the preferred term now). These monks were of course drawn from a *much larger* pool of lay Buddhists.

Such a large number of Buddhists, their institutions and monasteries were sustained in part by a culture of royal patronage and evangelism inaugurated by Ashoka for his newfound faith, and later continued even by Brahminical kings such as the Ikshvakus, the Satavahanas, the Guptas, and, of course, by Buddhist kings such as Kanishka and others of the Kushan Dynasty, Harsha, the Palas and others. But it seems clear that the Chinese pilgrims spent far more time in urban areas, which tended to have a higher density of Buddhists. According to archaeologist-scholar Lars Fogelin, Jainism and Buddhism 'allowed merchants and traders to more easily interact with foreigners and each other in ways that Brahmanical caste prohibitions had formerly prevented. For this reason, Buddhism and Jainism flourished in the cities where new trade relationships were being forged'.[27] In time, partly to accrue religious and social merit, wealthy Buddhist merchants and craft guilds also began donating to Buddhist temples and monasteries.

Royal patronage is best seen not as proof of the monarchs' inherent interest in Buddhism (which they may well have had), but of their interest in legitimizing their own authority by associating with, and investing in, popular religions, and their symbols and institutions. Big religious projects dazzled the commoners. It won the royals religious merit and goodwill. It conferred on them a sort of divine sanction to rule. (Sometimes their self-interested patronizing of many faiths furthered an inclusive and 'secular state' in the Indian sense, much before the term 'secularism' came into being: that is, paying similar attention to all major religions. Take one of Ashoka's own edicts: 'The Beloved of the Gods, [Ashoka], honors all sects and both ascetics and laymen, with gifts and various forms of recognition.') Patronizing Buddhism therefore became a good strategy for the royals after it gained a critical mass of followers, which it likely had by Ashoka's time. Not surprisingly, in late first millennium CE, when support for Buddhism among the laity began drying up, so did the royal patronage (more on this in the next chapter, 'The Vision of Nalanda').

At this point, based on the historical data we have, can we say that ancient India, for well over a millennium, was more of a Buddhist land than a Brahminical one? On one hand, this seems quite plausible. 'Early Buddhism had a substantial following,' writes Romila Thapar. 'For almost a thousand years its presence was almost hegemonic.'[28] On the other hand, we don't have enough data to precisely establish the relative prevalence of Buddhist, Brahminical, Jain, Tantric, animist, polytheist, materialist and other beliefs, or their fusion forms, which was more likely what was practised by the common people.

The fact is that the Chinese monks were far more exposed to an educated urban populace of social, political and religious elites. These were the monks' local informants, and the monks' accounts reflect this bias. This urban demographic—unlike rural or tribal folk who formed the majority of Indians—patronized the elite religions and commissioned big religious works and monuments that have survived far better than the localized deities and shrines of folk religions, which were often made from perishable materials. Indeed, it's quite likely that back then most people in the subcontinent fell outside dominant scripture-based religions, and whose animism and polytheism only occasionally included a mishmash of ideas and practices from the politically dominant religions of the day. Well into the colonial era, a great many Indians—worshipping rivers, animals, trees, spirits, saints, matas and other hyperlocal deities—subscribed to beliefs and practices that only had small overlaps with the doctrinal niceties, elite gods and customs of Vedic-Dharmic religions.

Nonetheless, the accounts of the Chinese are invaluable for opening new windows into our past that continue to inform and enchant us, and for providing us the evidence we need to resist the rewriting of history to suit narrow political ends.

The Vision of Nalanda
(c. 425–c. 1350 CE)

'We Bihari *log* know the reputation we have, from America to Dubai,' the taxi driver, Kaaru, says in Magadhi-inflected Hindi, his tone a mixture of hurt pride and irritation. I had asked him about the safety of Bihar's roads after dark. We are heading south-east from Patna to Bihar Sharif, my base camp for the ruins of Nalanda Mahavihara, the Buddhist monastery often called the first university in the world, where subjects like grammar, logic, philosophy, theology, astronomy and medicine were taught to resident monks from across Asia. When I last visited in 2006, highway robberies were common. 'But no danger now,' Kaaru reassures me. 'Nitish Kumar', Bihar's chief minister for much of the time since my last visit, 'has finished off the highway gangs'.

   We soon hit a traffic jam. A truck has overturned ahead. Expecting a long delay, Kaaru turns us around, gets off the highway and takes a rural road that will reconnect us to the highway ahead of the overturned truck. It's the monsoon season and the landscape glows a radiant green in the afternoon sun. Women plant rice in fields with standing water. Other fields have corn or vegetables. Unpainted walls of village homes carry ads for hakims of the traditional Yunani system of medicine, claiming to fix *gupt rog* (hidden diseases) and restore *mardana taakat* (masculine strength)—euphemisms for sundry sexual ailments and anxieties where talking about them is still a taboo. Kaaru plays obscure Bollywood songs from my youth that I haven't heard in decades, and which now evoke a mood of nostalgic delight.

Kaaru drives through a village where Nitish Kumar spent some of his childhood years, which explains its new large public high school and hospital. While this is atypical, things in Bihar have in fact improved more broadly in the last dozen years. Its rural road network is better; most rural homes have electricity most of the time and primary school attendance is notably higher. While the overall literacy rate in Nalanda district was still only about 70 per cent in 2018, it had risen from about 50 per cent in 2006, a gain partly attributable to the government's policies and partly to rising aspirations unleashed across India by economic liberalization.

But while the fortunes of most Biharis seem better, the state still lags behind much of the country, owing to its high rates of landlessness, poverty and population growth; rampant political corruption; stronger hold of caste and its dysfunction; and poor industrial development. Its crushing material squalor goes hand in hand with some of the worst human development indicators in India. Schools impart few useful skills and suffer from chronic absenteeism and a high dropout rate. I see lots of kids with reddish-orange hair in towns and villages—indicating malnutrition and perhaps long-term learning disabilities, though fewer kids now have the distended bellies I saw on my previous visit in 2006. Journalist Mark Tully had claimed around then that 'Biharis themselves say it's the only place in the world where the state has withered away, fulfilling Karl Marx's prophecy'.

But the state has clearly sprung back and introduced moves like a total ban on alcohol, enforced with fines of Rs 50,000 and/or three months in jail. Making Bihar a dry state was Kumar's campaign promise to the people—mostly poor women fed up with their husbands wasting money on booze. Consumption has fallen sharply, though, as I later learn from a friend in Patna, there's now illicit home delivery of liquor for those who can pay. Some villagers, Kaaru says, have resorted to home brews like mahua. The cops fear these villagers and don't bother them. Something of the old jungle raj—or the spirit of lawlessness usually associated with frontiers—is alive and well in Bihar. People still resort to vigilante justice. A few days after my visit, a woman suspected of a crime in a neighbouring district is beaten by a mob and paraded naked through the streets.[1]

Jobs, too, remain scarce in Bihar. Many Biharis, up to 10 per cent in some districts, still seek their fortunes in big cities. The migrants, conduits for remittances and modern ideas, help transform their families' fortunes back home. Outmigration isn't new in Bihar. In the late nineteenth century, exploitative agrarian policies of the British and the resulting famines pushed hundreds of thousands of Biharis to go as indentured labourers to British colonies overseas, such as the Caribbean, where they worked in sugar plantations (they replaced enslaved Africans, after slavery was abolished). In the late twentieth century, one such labourer's grandson and journalist, Shiva Naipaul, brother of V.S. Naipaul, would visit and accuse Bihar of being 'the Subcontinent's heart of darkness'.

Bihar's dismal present only makes it harder to imagine its illustrious past, when it was the beating heart of the subcontinent's high culture—imagined as Sita's home in the Ramayana; birthplace of the earliest republics;[2] land of the Buddha and Mahavira, Emperor Ashoka and the Mauryas; home to the cultural radiance of the Gupta Age, with its brilliant art, drama, literature and big advances in astronomy, mathematics, metallurgy, philosophy and other secular knowledge. Thousands of students—not only from India but also from China, Korea, Sumatra, Sri Lanka, Tibet, Japan and Central Asia—once flocked to Bihar for higher studies. Indeed, for nearly two millennia, Bihar was a creative, innovative and eventful place. Now it's a model backwater. What on earth happened to Bihar, I wonder, and to its great educational institutions like Nalanda?

The Rise of Nalanda

I'm rudely awakened the next morning by a rather unmelodic muezzin's call to prayer, and later again by an even louder tuneless man chanting Hanuman Chalisa into a loudspeaker right outside my hotel room's window. What are the odds of this double whammy? I think. Silently cursing them both, I get ready and leave for the ruins of Nalanda.

I hire an 'official guide', but I'm quickly disappointed. He gets too many details wrong, makes things up on the fly and whines about 'outsider guides' who accompany foreign tour groups and earn a lot more money than the local guides. I see only a few tourists; among them is a group of Buddhist pilgrims from Sri Lanka, who indeed have their own guide. Most foreign tourists in Bihar come from the Buddhist populations of Asia.

Figure 1. A monastic complex

Our knowledge of Nalanda comes from three kinds of primary sources: archaeology, epigraphy (the study of inscriptions) and texts that survived in foreign lands after Buddhism and its texts disappeared from India by the mid-second millennium. Our chief sources for Nalanda are the writings of Xuanzang and Yijing, who spent two to three and ten years there, respectively. They've left us a portrait of its life in the seventh century, including its physical spaces, practices and rhythms of daily life, finances, curriculum and other features of its monastic community.

Legends have long traced Nalanda's origins to the Buddha himself. One that Xuanzang recorded in the seventh century CE speaks of a naga (serpent) named 'Nalanda' who once lived in a pond in a mango grove, later the site of the Mahavihara. 'Five hundred merchants,' he adds, 'bought [the mango grove] for ten *kotis* of gold pieces and gave it to the Buddha,' who preached the law here for three months. From then on, it became a site of teaching and learning, and even Nagarjuna, the leading figure of Mahayana Buddhism and a 'second Buddha' to some, was said to have taught here in the second century CE (though evidence for this is scant).

When Faxian passed through the adjoining 'village of Nala' in c. 407 CE, he noted a stupa with relics of Sariputra, one of the two closest disciples of the Buddha. Sariputra, the locals told Faxian, was a native of Nala and so was cremated at the site of the stupa. Oddly, no community of monks had grown around the relics of a figure as eminent as Sariputra. Faxian did not mention any such community. It's therefore reasonable to conclude that there was no monastery at Nalanda when Faxian visited in the early fifth century CE.

Nalanda Mahavihara likely arose a few years after Faxian's visit—during the reign of Kumaragupta (reigned c. 414–55 CE)—and lasted around eight centuries. The site's legendary links with great names may well have shaped the decision to locate the monastery there.

After its demise in the thirteenth century, Nalanda lay forgotten and buried under mounds of earth for centuries. It was Stanislas Julien's French translation of Xuanzang's travels in 1853 that kindled interest among colonial archaeologists in identifying the site, which they soon did. In 1862, Alexander Cunningham and the freshly minted Archaeological Survey of India, which he founded, surveyed the site. The ASI led formal excavations and restorations at Nalanda from 1915–37 and then again from 1974–82.

Their work uncovered eleven monasteries, six temples and a giant stupa, aka the Great Monument. The monasteries, laid out in a row, face a parallel row of temples directly across. A 30-metre-wide path runs between the two rows. Each monastery, averaging about 40m x 60m, is made of oblong red bricks, once plastered with a paste of lime and sand. In Yijing's time, there were seven monasteries, all 'very similar in general appearance and layout; if you see one, you have seen all the seven'.[3]

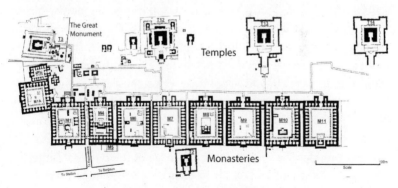

Figure 2. Excavated remains, Nalanda Mahavihara.
Author: Cpt.a.haddock; CC BY-SA 4.0

Entering one of the monasteries, I imagine being a monk in the seventh century and seeing what he would've seen: A Buddha shrine greets me by the main entrance. Walking through a thick-walled corridor, I reach an inner courtyard. It is enclosed on all four sides by two storeys of rooms, perhaps thirty-two on each floor. A veranda lines the courtyard on all four sides; stone pillars hold up a wooden roof over it. The open courtyard has a podium for lectures, a brick oven/stove, a well (with an octagonal cross-section, supposedly inspired by the eightfold path) and bathrooms with covered drains leading out.

Parts of the courtyard floors that aren't brick or stone are daubed with a mixture of dried cow dung and straw, which provides termite repulsion, thermal insulation and a cleaner, firmer surface than mud. All rooms in the monastery have walls that are multiple feet thick. Teachers and students live together in the monastery; each year before the monsoon, the eldest monks are given the best rooms. Monks training to become temple priests get a room with a purpose-built niche for a holy image, to which they offer flowers and incense after bathing each morning.

Rooms host either one or two monks and have wooden doors. The monks sit on simple chairs, wood blocks or small mats. Each morning, the monks roll up their mattresses—two sewn sheets of cloth with a layer of wool in between. Pillows are stuffed with 'home products, such as wool, hemp-scraps, the pollen of Typha latifolia, the catkins of the willow, cotton, reed, Tecoma grandiflora, soft leaves, dry moths, the ear-shells, hemp or beans'.[4] The monks store books and utensils in niches cut into the thick walls. All this reminds me of my own spartan hostel room at IIT Kharagpur, which too had just enough room for a narrow cot, a desk and a chair, and a cupboard with stone slabs for shelves.

I walk up to the Great Monument, which is still decorated with a few fine sculptural panels of stucco or stone. It has multiple stairs going to the top. In Yijing's time, it had a 'hall with mosaic floor', a seat 'made of gold and studded with jewels' and 'an image of the Buddha Tathagata' turning the Wheel of Law.[5] I try to imagine 'the ornamentation of the [Great Monument that] was delicate and superb', according to Yijing. At its base may have been the famous library of Nalanda, though a Tibetan source speaks of a library with nine storeys, which seems implausible for the building technology of the day. In any case, the library's location remains uncertain. It held the sorts of manuscripts that the Chinese pilgrims came in search of (at least eight finely illustrated palm-leaf manuscripts created at Nalanda during the Pala period still survive).

Nalanda was a place for advanced learning, not basic education. Some of its teachers both taught *and* composed path-breaking treatises and commentaries. A Nalanda education held serious cachet in the scholastic community, and it took in the best and the brightest. Or as Xuanzang puts it, they were 'men of the highest ability and talent . . . there are many hundreds whose fame has rapidly spread through distant regions'. Aspiring students had to be at least twenty years old and pass an oral exam at the monastery's entrance. They had to 'show their ability by hard discussion' and demonstrate a deep knowledge of 'both old and new books before getting admission'. No more than two or three out of ten were admitted, and even they were promptly humbled by the calibre of their teachers and co-students. Nuns were admitted too but little record of their lives survives.

Xuanzang wrote that during his time, Nalanda's population was 10,000, including 8500 students and 1500 teachers in 108 residential monasteries, each with four floors. Many scholars consider these

Figure 3. The Great Monument

numbers too high. Did Xuanzang exaggerate them for his Chinese audience to increase Nalanda's prestige and, indirectly, his own? A generation later, Yijing estimated Nalanda's population to be 3000, resident in just seven monasteries.[6] This muddies the water a great deal. Historians have tended to pick and choose between these two very different numbers based largely on their subjective analyses and purposes. Going by the archaeological evidence, historian A.L. Basham, in *The Wonder That Was India*, favoured an estimate even smaller than Yijing's. Nalanda Mahavihara, Basham wrote, 'consisted of a very large complex of buildings but it could hardly have accommodated a thousand monks in anything like the comfort described by the Chinese traveler [Xuanzang]'. Meanwhile, archaeologist H.D. Sankalia favoured an estimate of 4000.[7] In short, there is no consensus on how many monks and teachers were at Nalanda even in the century when it may have been at its prime and for which we have the maximum historical records.

Each monastery was led by a learned master, with additional teachers aiding him. Students were taught by multiple teachers and were likely split in groups based on their knowledge and interests. The teachers held their discourses in various parts of the monastery and in the temples across. According to Xuanzang's biographer, Hwui Li, 'Within the temple they arrange every day about 100 pulpits for preaching, and the students attend these discourses without any fail.'

Nalanda relied on royal patrons for its sustenance, including famous names like the Guptas of Magadh, Harsha of Kannauj and the Palas of Bengal. Seals and inscriptions on bricks, stone and copper plates at Nalanda have revealed other names too, such as the seventh-century Maukhari Dynasty of Magadh and Bhaskaravarma, a king from Assam. They variously commissioned new monasteries, temples, or gave grants of money, livestock or land. Taxes raised from all villages on this land flowed to Nalanda (Xuanzang reports 100 villages, Yijing 201), including essentials like food, clothing, lodging and medicine for all students and teachers. Each day, villagers sent 'several hundred piculs of ordinary rice' (1 picul = 60 kg), and 'several hundred catties in weight of butter and milk' (1 catty = 100 kg) to Nalanda. Though these numbers appear too large as well, this generous aid, according to Xuanzang, 'is the source of the perfection of their studies'.

One king built a high wall around the Mahavihara, likely something the monks had desired for a while. 'A long succession of kings,' writes Xuanzang, 'continued the work of building, using all the skill of the sculptor, till the whole is truly marvelous to behold.' In the ninth century, even a king of Sumatra, Balaputra, 'built a monastery at Nalanda and provided funds for the acquisition of five villages, the income from which would support the monastery'.[8]

In physical terms, Nalanda Mahavihara evolved a good deal over the centuries. Most of its structures were even rebuilt multiple times, sometimes after a fire. New layers appeared on top of old remains, often with new architectural features and sculptural decor. The monastic complex extended beyond today's ASI boundaries to neighbouring mounds that still await excavation, although some have been pillaged over the centuries for their bricks.

Sculptures excavated at Nalanda are in stucco, stone and bronze. A great many are of the Buddha himself, showing a range of poses or mudras and iconic events from his life. Bodhisattvas appear too, as well as Jambhala, the Buddhist god of wealth, and his consort, Hariti, the goddess of fertility. With the rise of Tantric Buddhism, or Vajrayana, Tantric deities appeared in the ninth and tenth centuries, such as Tara, Avalokiteshvara, Marichi, Heruka, Khasarpana, Trailokyavijaya and Yamantaka. Curiously, nearly 10 per cent of Nalanda's iconography consists of Brahminical deities, including Surya, Vishnu, Lakshmi, Balrama, Shiva, Parvati, Durga, Kubera, Skanda, Yashoda-Krishna and Saraswati, and scenes from the epics, such as Ravana with Sita (there are many exquisite samples in the Nalanda site museum). This shows that by the late first millennium, gods had crossover appeal and people had overlapping pantheons while still regarding their own sects as distinct from other sects. Clearly, other symbols and beliefs differentiated them, rather than a strict separation of their gods. This is still common, say, in Sri Lanka—where Hindus revere the Buddha and Buddhists revere gods like Kataragama (aka Murugan, son of Shiva and Parvati), Vishnu and Ganesh—even though the Sinhalese Buddhists and Tamil Hindus have long seen themselves as very distinct, and even fought a long and bloody civil war from 1983–2009.

Figure 4. Aparajita trampling Ganesha

Having said that, the Nalanda site museum, which displays less than 3 per cent of its stash from Nalanda and its vicinity, has several curious sculptures from the waning centuries of Indian Buddhism. According to the museum's panels, the Buddhist deity Aparajita is shown trampling Ganesh while Indra holds an umbrella over his head. The Tantric deity Heruka, whose crown depicts the Buddha, is shown trampling Shiva. There are other such images, including the Vajrayana deity, Trailokyavijaya, and the Buddhist deity, Vidyujjvalakarali. What might explain this dramatic and violent iconography that even flouted their ideals of non-violence? The reasons for this are likely rooted in the rise of new conflicts in the late first millennium between Buddhism and the popular new sects of Hinduism. According to Romila Thapar, 'Hostility between the Buddhists and some sects of Shaivas grew from philosophical and religious contestation, as well as competition for patronage.'[9] The Buddhists, likely on the defensive, resorted to this dramatic imagery to assert their religion's superiority to ambivalent folk.

While Nalanda was the preeminent centre of Buddhist learning in India during most of its existence, it was also part of a network of monasteries in the region, including Uddandapura, 12 km north of Nalanda; Yashovarmapura, 22 km east; and Tiladhaka, 33 km north-west. Further afield were Vikramashila in Bihar, and Somapura and Jaggadala in Bangladesh. Most of these sites have been at least partially excavated. What collaborations and rivalries did these monasteries have with each other? We don't know a whole lot but we can guess a few reasons. Historian Sukumar Dutt has argued that the Palas, the last major patrons of Buddhism in India, had started shifting funds away from Mahayana-centric Nalanda to Vajrayana-centric monasteries like Vikramashila and Somapura, which they had founded. In large measure, this shift was a response to the rising popular appeal of Vajrayana, or Tantric Buddhism—a mystical, ascetic, syncretic, magic-infused and community-involved sect of Buddhism.[10]

I spend half a day at the Nalanda site museum before returning to Bihar Sharif. I wander its streets, picking on a roasted corn on the cob daubed with salt and lemon. Buffaloes in narrow lanes vie for space with people and noisy, smoke-belching vehicles, including ornately decorated autos. With over three lakh people, minimal town planning and hardly any municipal services, Bihar Sharif is about as unlovely as it gets: open drains, fetid smells, rotting piles of refuse and hot steaming discs of bovine poo. I see no parks, pavements or public squares. The exteriors of most buildings have been left unplastered and unpainted, accentuating the town's shabby look. I wonder how all this deflating ugliness might impact the psyches of local men and women.

Amid all the chaos are vendors with cartfuls of juicy malda mangoes and fresh vegetables. Congested market lanes throng with people, suggesting enterprise and nascent consumerism. I see two old-fashioned single-screen cinema halls still going strong and Hindi film posters stuck on walls all over town. A Big Bazaar store has opened too. Next to it is perhaps the first pizzeria in town, with a bubbly young woman at the counter trying out her English with customers. Countless ads for coaching classes promise 'advanced reasoning skills' and success in competitive exams in English, maths, medicine, railways and accounting—no doubt the surest ticket out of town for youngsters who acquire them.

Rhythms of Daily Life

I return the next day and wander the evocative ruins. What better place to feel the impermanence of all things? I try to fill in the monasteries' missing walls, roofs, pillars—in vibrant colour. I imagine myself back within the quotidian life of the monks: the sounds of gongs, chants, greetings and discussions; cooking smells; unstitched yellow robes drying in the sun. In my mind's eye, I see monks praying, chatting in the veranda, queuing for the toilet, and other mundane sounds and visuals of monastic life. I see them seated around a podium for a lecture.

Does the teacher throw a piece of chalk at that dozing student in the back row?

Every morning, each student monk approaches his teacher, kneels before him and touches the ground with his forehead. The student inquires about his well-being and 'offers him toothwood and puts a washing-basin and a towel at the side of his seat'. He 'rubs the teacher's body, folds his clothes, or sometimes sweeps the apartment and the yard'. He also brings clean drinking water for the teacher and offers other services as necessary. For his part, the teacher, besides teaching the expected topics, 'inspects the pupil's moral conduct, and warns him of defects and transgressions', and in case of an illness 'nurses him, supplies all the medicine needed, and pays attention to him as if he were his child'.[11]

'It is considered meritorious to dig ponds,' writes Yijing. Sal trees are planted along these ponds that 'are fed by rainwater and are as clear as a pure river'. There are 'more than ten great pools near the Nalanda monastery and there every morning a *ghanti* is sounded to remind the monks of the bathing-hour'.[12] Monks emerge in groups to bathe in these ponds with a cloth tied around their waists. According to Yijing, 'Bathing without any cloth is contrary to the teachings of the Buddha'. These ponds were in fact carefully made tanks and the ruins still exist, filling up with rainwater during the monsoon.

Daily life is guided by water clocks—i.e., water-filled copper vessels with calibrated holes—and distinct drum beats at different hours or the blowing of conch shells. Gongs signal the start and end of events, services and ceremonies. To get some exercise, all monks take walks in mid-mornings or late afternoons.

In late afternoons or early evenings, monks join a three-part prayer service. Buddhist priests perform this service at the temple, walking

Figure 5. The entrance to a monastery

'three times round a stupa, offering incense and flowers. They kneel down, and one of them who sings well begins to chant hymns', extolling the Buddha 'with a melodious, pure, and sonorous voice, and continues to sing ten or twenty slokas'. Additional hymns and slokas from scripture are recited. Many of these 'charming compositions' contain 'high principles' and are the work of Matriketa, a 'great literary talent'. He lived long ago, writes Yijing, but is so revered that 'all who compose hymns imitate his style, considering him the father of literature'. As the ceremony ends, the assembled monks cry out, 'Subhashita! Sadhu! [Well spoken! Well done!].' Because Nalanda's population is too large to gather at a single temple, a prayer group goes from monastery to monastery, performing a shorter version of the full ceremony at every stop.

The Chinese accounts are silent on how many monks stayed away from, or disagreed with, all this ritual and idol worship, which the Buddha had expressly warned against. He had clearly overestimated the ability of his flock to live without the symbolic and emotional immediacy of having his image close at hand. Like most of us, the monks were good at compartmentalizing ideas. In a competitive marketplace of faiths, embracing such rituals and idol worship likely also made it easier to attract new converts.

Monasteries run their own kitchens, writes Yijing. Outside each kitchen is a wooden statue of Mahakala, a Tantric deity seated on a small chair and darkened with oil rubbings. He allays misfortunes from people's lives. At meal times, incense is burned and food is first offered to Mahakala. Oil lamps are lit after dark. During dinner, monks sit on low rattan chairs with wickerwork, about 18 inches apart to avoid touching each other while eating, which is said to be defiling; junior monks might sit on low blocks of wood. Trays of food are then brought out and placed before them on the ground, a surface typically made of dried cow dung and leaves.

Dinner begins with a welcome serving of one or two pieces of ginger with salt on a leaf. Next might be 'gruel made of dried rice and bean soup with hot butter sauce as flavoring, which is to be mixed with the other food [using] fingers'. Vegetables might follow, perhaps also ghee, honey, sugar, cereal cake or a seasonal fruit like mango. Vegetables are not eaten raw and are 'well cooked and eaten after mixing with asafoetida, clarified butter, oil, or any spice'. On other days, the monks might get different items: boiled barley and peas, baked 'cornflour', various roots, stalks, leaves, flowers, fruits or even meat—as long as the meat is not commissioned for them (it was okay to consume leftover meat that was donated to them, or came from an animal who died naturally or in an accident).* A complex taxonomy forbids certain foods to be mixed with others during a meal. Only the right hand is used for eating. Copper utensils are preferred but single-use earthenware utensils are also employed on special occasions, creating piles of discarded vessels similar to the piles of *kulhar* chai cups we associate with Indian train stations.

Each morning and after meals, monks chew on wood sticks called *dantkashtha*, extracted from certain stems or roots—such as from *Ficus indicus* or banyan tree—to clean their mouths and tongues. Though the wood stick is usually a bit astringent or pungent in taste, it apparently 'hardens the teeth, scents the mouth, helps to digest food, or relieves heart-burning'.

Clothes too, including undergarments, must follow certain rules for both monks and nuns: the material and length of the cloth and the waistband, their cut, stitch and colour, how much skin they can reveal and where, how the robe is pleated, wrapped and handled, say, while seated ('your knees are to be covered but your shanks may be bare'; with nuns, 'even in a urinal one must not have one's shoulders bare'), and so on. Yijing himself seems more than a little obsessed with such rules of hygiene, eating, bathing, dressing, worshipping, greeting, sleeping and many other aspects of personal conduct—even 'rules concerning evacuation', i.e., emptying the bowels—so it's not always easy to separate actual practices at Nalanda from Yijing's own obsessions and disciplinarian prescriptions for his audience. In a bid to ensure that his Chinese audience takes him seriously, he often adds that these rules were 'laid down by the Buddha himself'! I amuse myself trying to imagine the Buddha going on about 'rules concerning evacuation'.

At the end of summer comes a day of confession and 'atoning for faults'—faults that either one realizes in oneself, or are perhaps pointed

---

* European translators of Chinese texts use 'corn' and 'cornflour' to likely refer to another cereal like millet. Corn, a New World crop, came to India sometime after Columbus reached the Americas.

out by others. The idea of confession is to declare, 'with perfect sincerity', one's own offence and past faults in order to 'alter the past conduct and repair the future'. There were other ways to show errant monks their place too. 'In case a monk bragged and used other's belongings, he was teasingly called *Kulapati*', or a householder, an insult for a monk. Egregious violations of the code could even lead to expulsion from the monastery, though no examples are mentioned in the Chinese accounts.

When a monk or priest dies, his corpse is carried on a bier to the cremation ground. While the corpse burns, 'friends assemble and sit on one side', 'the Sutra of Impermanence is recited by a skilled man', and each man silently meditates on his own impermanence. After the ceremony, they bathe together in a pond, return to their rooms and 'cleanse the floor with powdered cow-dung'. If the dead person was especially revered or beloved, they build a small stupa, containing, as stupas tend to do, some of his cremated remains. Excavations have revealed a lot of miniature stone and brick stupas in at least one temple's courtyard.

A great many questions remain unanswered. It's not clear how many nuns were at Nalanda, and how they lived. Who provided all the basic services? Or as the scholar Frederick M. Asher asked, 'Who were the cooks and barbers, the sweepers and sculptors, the cloth-workers who prepared the monks' garments, if they were not monks? Did they remain within Nalanda's walls, or did they go home at night to a residence within an easy walking commute to the monastery?' It's also not clear whether the laity was allowed to visit the temples within Nalanda. The high wall around the Mahavihara suggests that public access was controlled. Perhaps the laity could only visit the few temples outside the wall. Perhaps they could visit the temples inside on selected festival days, but we can't be sure. What's also strikingly missing from the pilgrims' accounts is any sense of what these cloistered and bookish monks gave back to the villagers who in fact underwrote their lifestyle.

The monks' lives, it seems, weren't relentlessly austere. The discovery of dice suggests secular diversions. Perhaps there were physical games too. The canonical Cullavagga text cites monks in the early Buddhism of fourth century BCE as 'engaged in board games, parlor games, dicing, tumbling, shooting marbles, riding, and

Figure 6. Outer wall of a temple at Nalanda

swordsmanship'—so why not also at Nalanda?[13] Yijing also makes a
tantalizing reference to ceremonies where 'a band of girls plays music'.
But so much remains opaque. How many of the young monks, I wonder,
felt the stirrings of sexual desire after joining Nalanda and struggled
with it steeped in guilt; how many decided to quit the monastic life to
seek marital union or worldly riches? And we can only speculate about
the darker side of Nalanda's social life: sexual abuse, personal jealousies,
political rivalries and so on.

What the Monks Studied

An abiding interest in language and its relationship to reality was a
prominent feature of mid-first millennium scholastic Indian philosophy.
How does the structure of language impact our understanding of the
world? Does language correspond to an objective, mind-independent
reality? On what grounds can we establish the truth? Subjects of central
concern included linguistics and its various aspects—phonology (study

of speech sounds), morphology (study of words), semantics (study of meaning)—as well as epistemology, metaphysics, logic and ethics. However, the curriculum had little or no emphasis on politics, geometry, mathematics and physics, which may have opened up a different way of comprehending the nature of reality, as it did in ancient Greece. But many other sciences were pursued via the study of medicine, i.e., Ayurveda, which aggregated aspects of botany, zoology and chemistry in the service of a practical end: curing and sustaining the human body. Moreover, most of this philosophy occurred in implicitly atheistic frameworks, in a seemingly competitive and high-pressure environment. According to Xuanzang:

> The day is not sufficient for asking and answering profound questions. From morning till night they engage in discussion; the old and the young mutually help one another. Those who cannot discuss questions out of the Tripitaka [core scriptures] are little esteemed and are obliged to hide themselves for shame. Learned men from different cities, on this account, who desire to acquire quickly a renown in discussion, come here in multitudes to settle their doubts, and then the streams [of their wisdom] spread far and wide.[14]

According to Yijing, the main pillars of *vidya*, or knowledge, that Buddhists at the time had to acquire were: (1) *Sabdavidya*, grammar and lexicography, (2) *Silpasthanavidya*, the arts, (3) *Kikitsavidya*, medicine, (4) *Hetuvidya*, logic, and (5) *Adhyatmavidya*, 'science of the universal soul' or philosophy. Also included were readings in the Vedas and Samkhya. Yijing mentions many important texts and authors in each area, though it is by no means an exhaustive list. Since incoming monks at Nalanda had to be at least twenty years old, they had to have acquired enough foundational knowledge elsewhere.

'The Sutra [of Panini] is the foundation of all grammatical science,' writes Yijing. Sutra means 'short aphorism' and 'signifies that important principles are expounded in abridged form'. Panini, writes Yijing, was a scholar of old and a devotee of Shiva. His sutra 'contains 1,000 slokas' and children begin learning it at age eight. They also study *The Book of*

Dhatu and *The Book of Three Khilas*, focused on grammar and language. Next is a commentary on Panini's sutra, *The Vritti-sutra*, and *The Kurmi*, by 'the learned Patanjali'. 'Advanced scholars can learn this in three years,' writes Yijing. Next is *Bharatrihari-sastra*, by Bharatrihari, a famous thinker known for his frequent switches between monastic and worldly life. This work 'contains 25,000 slokas, and fully [discusses] the principles of human life as well as of grammatical science'. Another work by Bharatrihari follows, *The Vakya-discourse*, a treatise on inferential and inductive reasoning. *The Peina* is next, comprising 3000 slokas authored by Bharatrihari and a commentary by Dharmapala. It 'fathoms the deep secrets of heaven and earth, and treats of the philosophy of man'. Monks and laymen who have studied all of the above are said to have 'mastered grammatical science' and hence qualify to be 'well-informed'.

After outlining the grammatical sciences curriculum, Yijing names more authors whose works monks had to study.[15] As the brightest monks progress through their study, he adds, they aspire not only to master the topic but to advance it. For instance, 'when they have understood the arguments of *Hetuvidya* (logic), they aspire to be like Gina (the great reformer of logic) . . . When they discourse on the "non-existence" they cleverly imitate Nagarjuna', and so on.

What the monks studied at Nalanda included most flavours of Buddhism: two schools of Mahayana (Madhyamaka and Yogacara), eighteen schools of Theravada and later, during Pala times, Vajrayana, a Tantra-inflected form of Mahayana that lives on in Tibet. Though united by their goal of achieving liberation, or moksha, 'the Tripitakas of various sects differ from one another', writes Yijing, but they also had 'small points of difference such as where the skirt of the lower garments is cut straight in one, and irregular in another, and the folds of the upper robe are, in size, narrow in one and wide in another'. Some student monks went much farther than their peers and acquired commensurate fame and respect as Buddhist masters.

The Stars of Nalanda

Nalanda produced and advanced impressive new ideas and secular knowledge. The Buddha had himself upheld the value of scepticism and strongly advocated a rigorous testing of views to one's own satisfaction, rather than accepting them on authority. Nalanda became a scholastic institution par excellence, where philosophical ideas were deftly scrutinized, debated, refined, classified, recorded and taught. It was certainly a *universitas magistrorum et scholarium* (community of teachers and scholars, the Latin phrase from which the term 'university' is derived), though it was also different from what we understand as

Figure 7. Rooms inside a monastery

a university today. After all, it did not admit laymen, but only Buddhist monks who potentially came to stay for life, rather than graduate with degrees and return to public life (though they could return to the laity at any time, as many did after gaining an education; or go to another monastery; or strike out on their own as an ascetic or a teacher. Expectations also differed for visiting scholar monks). Admission was based on an applicant's knowledge of foundational Buddhist texts and readiness for celibacy and monastic life. Its pedagogy also hewed closer to the traditional *guru-shishya parampara* or master–disciple lineage. With these caveats, however, it's reasonable to regard Nalanda as the first great university of the world.[16]

Nalanda hosted many grand masters of Indian philosophy. Among them was Dignaga (480–540), who laid a new theoretical foundation for logic and epistemology, positing perception and inference as the only means of knowledge. His intellectual disciple at Nalanda, Dharmakirti (550–610), critiqued and advanced his ideas. Together, their work 'provoked the most sophisticated and most important philosophical debates with non-Buddhist rivals' and came to represent 'Buddhism in pan-Indian debates on problems of universals, philosophies of logic and language, and issues of justification'.[17] Indeed, many of their ideas even anticipated the work of modern European philosophers.

Another intellectual disciple of Dignaga was Dharmapala, associated with Yogacara, an idealist 'consciousness-only' Mahayana school (reminiscent of the work of Edmund Husserl and Maurice Merleau-Ponty). Only the mind is real, argued Dharmapala; consciousness alone is the ultimate source of all reality. This contrasted with the doctrine 'all is real' held by Sarvastivada, a leading Theravada school (reminiscent of Immanuel Kant's 'thing-in-itself').[18] In between these extremes—'only the mind is real' and 'all is real'—stood Madhyamaka, or 'Middle Way', the Mahayana school associated with Nagarjuna, who posited the idea of dependent origination, implying that things do not have a fixed or an innate essence, that all sensory phenomenon exists in relationship to others, and no objective, mind-independent reality is accessible to us (reminiscent of Ludwig Wittgenstein; for more on Nagarjuna, see the chapter 'The Void of Nagarjunakonda').

Santideva (c. late seventh–early eighth century), a votary of Madhyamaka, focused on ethics. He famously asked:

When fear and suffering are disliked
By me and others equally,
What is so special about me,
So that I protect myself and not others?

Santideva built an elaborate argument for impartial benevolence, so that 'each of us is rationally required to regard the welfare of anyone else as being just as important as our own welfare', a stance strikingly similar to the utilitarian ethics of Bentham, Mill and Singer. Animals, owing to their sentience, had prominence in Santideva's moral philosophy, and he urged everyone to be kind and compassionate to them. His radical stance nevertheless left a few blind spots in his own life—he failed to accord equal importance to the welfare of men and women.[19]

Santaraksita (c. 725–88), another interpreter of Madhyamaka, explored the thickets of the philosophy of mind, 'the relation between cognition and the body, and the role this relation plays in causal-explanatory accounts of consciousness and cognition'. He argued with the materialist Carvakas, whose physicalism held that consciousness was nothing but an emergent property of the material body, 'an expression of the body's functional organization and responsiveness to a world of objects, situations, and things'. Santaraksita defended the irreducibility of consciousness to the body's material processes with 'a different naturalistic account of cognition than the one put forth by the Carvaka'. Invited by the king of Tibet, where Buddhism had been introduced in the seventh century but had since floundered, Santaraksita also travelled to the country 'to establish the first monastic university, Samye, and served as its abbot'.[20] Indeed, he epitomized Nalanda's active outreach to foreign lands, which trained 'specialists in Tibetan and Chinese who prepared translations into these languages and who themselves went out as missionaries'.[21]

Other philosopher monks of renown associated with Nalanda include Kamalasila, Chandrapala, Gunamati, Sthiramati, Prabhamitra, Atisa Dipamkara and others, including many more named by Xuanzang. The Nalanda scholastics also esteemed Xuanzang. They beseeched him to stay and lured him with accolades and prestigious roles in their hierarchy. But he declined with this reply: 'The Buddha established his doctrine so that it might be diffused to all lands. Who would wish to enjoy it alone, and to forget those who are not yet enlightened?' Xuanzang's memory lived on in India for scores of years, and he was long accorded a place in Indian temple paintings with his 'hemp shoes, spoon and chop sticks mounted on multicolored clouds'.[22]

Xuanzang founded the Faxiang school of thought in China, whose ideas live on in Japanese Buddhism. Based on the Yogacara school, it focused on consciousness and posited that the world is only a representation of the mind. The Buddhist Tang emperor, Gaozong, supported Xuanzang's later enterprise and even built a pagoda—now the Big Goose Pagoda of Xian—to house his translations (many still in use) and display in a small museum on site. Outside the entrance is an elegant modern statue of the man. The emperor was so upset when he heard of the monk's death that he cancelled all audiences for three days.

The Decline of Buddhism in India

Buddhism had been receding in India since at least the seventh century, when Xuanzang saw abandoned and dilapidated monasteries. In the late eighth century, this decline accelerated with the rise of Adi Shankara, a votary of orthodox Brahminism and Advaita Vedanta, who also set up monastic educational institutions, or *mathas*, to rival Buddhist monasteries. He advocated the worship of Vishnu, Shiva, Shakti, Ganesh and Surya as 'different forms of the one *Brahman*, the invisible Supreme Being', deftly appropriating and uniting Puranic cults under Brahminism.[23] Other major new social forces included Bhakti, a mystical devotional movement, and various folk and Tantric cults whose origins mostly lay outside the Vedic–Brahminic fold. Buddhism's decline, writes Thapar, 'is partly linked to the popularity of religious devotionalism' and 'a variety of sects, such as the Tantric and Shakta'.

Many historians see this new religious profusion—of folk and Puranic deities, syncretic beliefs and devotionalism, yogic sexual practices and imagery of Tantra—as marking a shift from Brahminism to a new entity called Hinduism (a colonial-era label, retroactively applied).[24] This early Hinduism was fervent and unorthodox, and capacious enough to embrace many popular features of Buddhism— such as monastic orders, vegetarianism, prohibition of animal sacrifices, some resistance to caste—and even appropriated the Buddha as the ninth avatar of Vishnu.

One could say that the religious market was shifting to more user-friendly products in which Buddhism began losing lay followers, owing to its relatively sober and austere practices and the alienating monastic-scholastic focus of its priestly class. The popular new Hindu sects, cults and devotional movements combined so much fusion and appropriation of practices that it may not have seemed like a big shift to lay Buddhists. From Yijing's account, even their rituals were quite similar, and likely became more so. Dharmasvamin (1197–1264), a Tibetan monk pilgrim to Nalanda, saw both Hindus and Buddhists bathe their deities in curd, milk, honey, sugar and ghee. The real but complex theological and philosophical differences perhaps didn't matter much to lay Buddhists. Over multiple generations, they began to flock to specialized Hindu gods that were seen as responding to their mundane woes and misfortunes and presiding over their rites of passage. With this shift among the populace, the royal patronage for Buddhism began drying up too.

Some scholars also blame the lavish land endowments that Nalanda and other monasteries had accrued since the Guptas, including tax revenues in perpetuity from villages on that land. This practice produced its own collateral damage: a slow rot that undermined the monasteries. As they gained economic self-sufficiency, they did so at the cost of forgetting their central mission of alleviating suffering in the world. They grew 'largely divorced from day-to-day interaction with the laity, and instead became landlords over growing monastic properties'.[25] They isolated themselves and retreated into private courtyards, often by erecting physical barriers. Their thick boundary walls and gated living became more than just metaphors for self-absorbed seclusion.

This was in fact a profound shift from the earliest monasteries, where the laity visited temples that were adjacent to the monks' residential quarters—as in the Dalai Lama's complex in Dharamshala today. This fostered trust, community and mutual dependence— the monks provided worship and other valued services,

Figure 8. A large room in a monastery, perhaps a senior teacher's

especially at major Buddhist pilgrimage sites where the early monasteries were located and in return received alms that sustained them. Monks balanced their individualistic quests with community obligations. Excavated inscriptions show, for instance, that after Ashoka's demise, monastic life at Sanchi was sustained much less by royal patronage and far more by lay donors, including many women.[26] According to archaeologist scholar Lars Fogelin:

As the [monastic] *sangha* progressively withdrew from regular contact with the laity in the first millennium CE, the laity returned the favor, shifting their devotions to rival religious orders. This shift was facilitated by the incorporation of Buddhist architectural, ritual, and doctrinal elements by rival religious sects . . . the laity increasingly found the rites and rituals of nascent Hinduism and other sects more satisfying . . . By the end of the first millennium CE the laity had abandoned Buddhism throughout most of India.[27]

'The decline of Buddhism in the Ganges heartland and the peninsula occurred before the Turkish conquest,' writes Thapar.[28] Both Buddhism and Brahminism required royal patronage, but kings were shifting to an exclusively Brahminical ideology. Excluding the Palas, the new dynasties that arose in the last quarter of the first millennium—such as the Karkotas, Pratiharas, Chandelas, Rashtrakutas, Pandyas and Pallavas—were all Brahminical with little or no affinity for Buddhism. In the central Indian region that became the realm of the Chandelas (831–1308), Buddhism and its monastic orders had almost entirely disappeared—after once thriving there under the Mauryas (builders of Sanchi and Bharhut), the Guptas and Harsha.[29]

The Palas were the last major Buddhist dynasty in India, but they'd been gone for nearly a century when the Turkish conquerors arrived, c. 1200 CE. Bengal and Bihar were then ruled by the orthodox Brahminical Sena Dynasty, which had introduced Kulinism, or supremacist caste rules in society, and had begun persecuting Buddhists, causing many of them to flee Bengal.[30] 'When the Muslim invasions came,' writes scholar Gail Omvedt, 'the final blow was dealt to this nearly vanished Buddhism, vulnerable because of its lack of support in the life of the people and its centralization in the monasteries.'[31]

In time, without followers or patrons, Buddhist sites in eastern India too fell into ruin or were occupied by other religious orders. For instance, the Mahabodhi Temple at Bodh Gaya was turned into a Shiva temple; the bricks of Uddandapura were recycled for an Islamic mausoleum. By the mid-second millennium, Fogelin writes, 'only vestiges of Buddhism remained in the practices of rival religious orders'. In the 1660s, Frenchman François Bernier knew nothing about Buddhism even after spending a decade in India. He called it 'a seventh sect' of Hinduism, whose few 'adherents are despised and hated, censured as irreligious and atheistical, and lead a life peculiar to themselves'. In the next two centuries, even these few adherents would disappear.

It is often said that ancient Indians were not interested in history, that their accounts of the past are inseparable from myth. Such accounts are indeed common but they're not the whole story. Early Pali texts, especially from Sri Lanka, suggest that Indian Buddhism too had fostered a sober chronicling of the past. This is a lot closer to 'proper history' than the Brahminical chronicles. 'The disappearance of Buddhism from

India,' writes Omvedt, also led to 'the disappearance of some of the most valuable Indian historiography, and a deep Brahmanic bias in the existing records'.[32]

The Demise of Nalanda

Many history books and Internet sites today confidently state that c. 1200 CE, Nalanda was put to a brutal and decisive end by Bakhtiyar Khilji (not to be confused with Alauddin Khilji who lived a hundred years later and was caricatured in the 2018 film *Padmaavat*). Bakhtiyar Khilji (d. 1206) was a Turkic commander in the army of Qutb-ud-din Aibak (1150–1210), and was sent to conquer Bihar and Bengal.[33] He allegedly looted and burned Nalanda Mahavihara and killed hundreds or even thousands of its monks. 'Official guides' offer this story to visitors with lurid accounts of how Nalanda's great library smouldered for six long months. Unfortunately, this story is based on very little evidence.

That Khilji sacked Nalanda is inferred mainly from three sources. The first is sections of a few walls in a couple of monasteries where the bricks show fire damage; in other areas and in one monastery's courtyard, archaeologists have also found ash and charcoal. Fire was then commonly used for cooking, heating and lighting. The said damages could've been caused, before or after Khilji, by accidental fires that historians believe have occurred at various times in Nalanda's long history. For example, a stone inscription 'of the eleventh year of Mahapala I [c. 999 CE] refers to the destruction of Nalanda by fire and its subsequent restoration'.[34]

The second source is the account of Persian historian Minhaj al-Siraj, who was a child at the time of the alleged invasion and wrote from second-hand accounts he gathered forty years later. Al-Siraj, however, does not mention Nalanda at all; only that Khilji attacked and captured 'the fortified city of Bihar' and 'acquired great booty'. Inside the city was a college 'with a great number of books' and an unspecified number of 'Brahmans' with 'their heads shaven', who 'were all slain' by Khilji's army. Going by this clue, as some scholars have argued, it was the monastery of Uddandapura (aka Odantapuri), located on a hill within the fortified town of Bihar Sharif (Khilji and his men likely conflated that Buddhist monastery with a Brahminical 'college'; Buddhism had nearly vanished by then in the north-western regions from where Khilji came).[35]

The town of Bihar Sharif was then a political and economic centre, presiding over a fertile hinterland fed by several rivers. When I visited Uddandapura during my stay in Bihar Sharif, I was struck by the lure of riches and power that its hill fort must have held to an expansionist army. Excavations show that its fort and monastery were remodelled and used by later Muslim rulers. Unlike Bihar Sharif, Nalanda had little political or economic allure, and it wasn't a thriving centre of religion patronized by rival kings. On the contrary, it was struggling for survival under the hostile Sena Dynasty.[36] Nalanda was perhaps also lucky because, as a scholar claims, it 'lay not on the main route from Delhi to Bengal, but required a special expedition'.[37] Though a direct distance of 12–15 km isn't prohibitive, there may also have been a forest then—with snakes, tigers and black bears—between Nalanda and the army's main route to Bengal via Bihar Sharif, implying a longer detour.

The third source is a biography of Dharmasvamin. After returning to Tibet, he described his two years of study at Nalanda, c. 1234–36, to his biographer, who wrote a third-person account of the journey, partly in his own words.[38] Though much diminished, Nalanda was still operating during Dharmasvamin's visit. His account doesn't mention Khilji, only that many monasteries at Nalanda had been 'damaged by the Turks and there was absolutely no one to look after them, or to make offerings . . . many [monasteries] were left undamaged'. Nalanda was then patronized by the Buddhist king of Magadh. He ruled from his capital at Bodh Gaya and had apparently survived the Turks' onslaught and regional hegemony. (Generations of these new arrivals and their descendants were seen primarily in ethnic terms as *Turushka*s, or Turks, and secondarily as Muslims.)

Rather than a dramatic final end, Dharmasvamin's biography and other historical sources suggest a drawn-out phase of decay and depopulation of Nalanda. This was driven by many factors, including: (1) sharp funding cuts under the Palas and from other donors; (2) the Sena Dynasty's persecution of monks over many decades; (3) sporadic attacks over many decades by roving bands of soldiers in the army of Bakhtiar Khilji's descendants, who, in their bid for independence, were themselves often at war with Iltumish and others of the Delhi Sultanate (when they were finally reined in, Nalanda and Bihar fell back under the Delhi Sultanate, c. 1250).

North gate of the 'citadel' of Dholavira where the famous signboard was found. The ground visible on the top left is part of the 'stadium' or ceremonial ground.

View of Dholavira's 'citadel' from the middle town, with the 'stadium' in the middle

A post-Harappan home (*bhunga*) atop the 'citadel' of Dholavira

A Buddhist monastery of Vijayapuri at Nagarjunakonda, with a giant statue of the Buddha in an apsidal temple.

The bathing ghat of Vijayapuri, now on Nagarjunakonda Island

The only amphitheatre discovered in ancient India, at Vijayapuri

Monks' cells around a courtyard in a monastery at Nalanda Mahavihara

Stairs leading to an upper floor in a monastery at Nalanda

A section of the Western Group of temples, Khajuraho

Lovers on Lakshmana Temple

Lovers on Devi Jagdambi Temple

Remains of a market street in front of Vittala Temple, Vijayanagar (Hampi)

A temple tank near Krishna Temple, Vijayanagar (Hampi)

Achyutaraya Temple gopuram (from inside the complex), Vijayanagar (Hampi)

A Baul singer by the Ganga in Varanasi

The narrow lanes of Varanasi's old town

Funeral pyres on Manikarnika Ghat, Varanasi

But Nalanda's story doesn't end there. An early eighteenth-century Tibetan history of Buddhism claims that Nalanda was repaired after the Turkish raids and continued at least until a conflict (no date given) erupted with some Brahmin mendicants, who caused a 'great conflagration which consumed Ratnadodhi, one of the [three] libraries of Nalanda'.[39] True or not, this is apparently the last mention of Nalanda in our historical sources.

What, then, is the truth of Nalanda's demise? While these historical sources don't rule out a devastating attack on Nalanda by Bakhtiar Khilji, they don't provide clear evidence for it either. Why then do so many claim that Khilji ravaged Nalanda—and the Turks destroyed Buddhism in India—when there's a far more persuasive web of reasons for their demise? Historian Johan Elverskog blames it on the seduction of 'a clear-cut narrative with good guys and bad', one that 'avoids entirely the complex shades of gray that most often color the messy fabric of history'.[40]

Another complicating factor was British Indology. Building on a long-standing European antipathy towards Islam, the British emphasized 'Muslim barbarity and misrule in order to justify the introduction of their supposedly more humane and rational form of colonial rule'.[41] The British contrasted the darkness of Muslim rule with their own, 'when the full light of European truth and discernment begins to shed its beams upon the obscurity of the past'.[42] The emerging Hindu nationalists were only too happy to accept the British view of Muslims. Consequently, in most 'British colonial and Hindu nationalist histories', writes Fogelin, 'the Muslim invaders are credited with destroying Buddhism—with [Khilji's] act serving as an example of Muslim depravity'.[43] B.R. Ambedkar, who became a Buddhist months before his death, also blamed the fall of Buddhism (and Nalanda in particular) on Muslim invasions and Islam.[44] As Omvedt noted, 'Ambedkar as well as distinguished historians like [AL] Basham fell into a Hindutva conceptual trap in blaming Islam.'[45] Contemporary prejudices and stereotypes about Buddhism and Islam—one now 'synonymous with peace, tranquility, and introspection, the other with violence, chaos, and blind faith'[46]—further complicate historical revisions.

A naïve visitor might think that the psychic shock of Nalanda's plunder was so great that it lives on in local cultural memory. But even if Khilji had plundered Nalanda himself, it is highly unlikely that any memory of it would have survived in modern Bihar. Buddhism was entirely ousted in Bihar and the rest of India, its monuments physically buried, and the Buddha's historicity forgotten (except in the western Himalayan regions close to Tibet, in Ladakh, Lahaul and Spiti). Buddhism prospered outside India, writes scholar Jawhar Sircar, 'but in its cradle and nursery its existence was snuffed out: not only physically but in terms of history, education and popular memory'.[47] Generations of villagers, at times raiding Nalanda's exposed red bricks, had no idea what the ruins represented. Rather, what animates the melancholy lamentations of the 'official guides' and others today is a case of what Thapar has called 'the construction of social memory', led by the sectarian eye and agendas of twentieth-century Hindu nationalism.[48]

A Modern Revival?

An ambitious new project is underway for an international university at Rajgir, about 15 km from Nalanda. A consortium led by Singapore, Japan, China and India has endowed it with a pot of riches, as royal patrons once did for Nalanda. In 2010, the Indian Parliament passed the Nalanda Bill, bringing the university into legal existence.

A brand-new campus with an innovative pedagogy and architectural motifs inspired by Nalanda Mahavihara is being built with eco-friendly features like recycled waste and water, renewable energy self-sufficiency, walking and biking paths, electric shuttles, ponds, etc.[49] However, from what I see during my visit to the construction site in mid-2018, it'll need much luck to become operational before 2025. Mainly a residential postgraduate institute, it'll have schools of Buddhist studies, philosophy and comparative religion; historical studies; international relations and peace; languages and literature; ecology and environmental studies; and more.

Will the new university attract students and faculty despite its backwater location?[50] Will it distinguish itself as did Nalanda Mahavihara, while avoiding the latter's costly mistakes? Will the budding university, now in an interim location a mile away, survive the politics of Hindutva nationalism that's already interfering with its mission?[51] At least going by its foundational goals, the new Nalanda University is explicitly 'aimed at advancing the concept of an Asian community . . . and rediscovering old relationships'.[52] Xuanzang and Yijing would surely have approved.

Alberuni's India
(1017–30 CE)

On the new moon day in the month of Kartika, the Hindus celebrate a festival called Dibali, wrote the Persian traveller Alberuni in 1030 CE. People 'bathe, dress festively, make presents to each other of betel-leaves and areca-nuts; they ride to the temples to give alms and play merrily with each other till noon. In the night they light a great number of lamps in every place'.[1]

'The cause of this festival,' writes Alberuni, 'is that Lakshmi, the wife of Vasudeva, once a year on this day liberates Bali, the son of Virocana, who is a prisoner in the seventh earth.' Bali comes out into the world. 'The Hindus maintain that this time was a time of luck in the Kritayuga [Satyuga], and they are happy' that this feast-day resembles that time. In Alberuni's day, the festival of lights seems not to have been associated with a man liberating his imprisoned wife but with a woman liberating an imprisoned man—a story that appears in the Chandogya Upanishad.

Alberuni also writes about a festival called Shivratri, when 'they worship Mahadeva during the whole night; they remain awake, and do not lie down to sleep, and offer to him perfumes and flowers'. At pilgrimage sites, Alberuni is impressed by the tanks and step wells that the Hindus construct for their ablutions. 'In this they have attained to a very high degree of art, so that our people (the Muslims), when they see them, wonder at them, and are unable to describe them, much less to construct anything like them.' Alberuni wrote a thick tome on India full of fascinating insights and opinions on Indian culture and society.

The Life of Alberuni

In 1017 CE, a king of the Mamuni Dynasty ruled in Khiva (Uzbekistan). In his court was a forty-four-year-old Persian scholar and polymath named Alberuni. A native of the region, he served as a political adviser and astronomer-astrologer. 'Possessing a profound and original mind of encyclopaedia scope', Alberuni was fluent in five languages and excelled in mathematics, physics, mineralogy, medicine, philosophy, history, geography and many more disciplines.[2]

Alberuni's life would change dramatically that year. A thousand miles away in Ghazni (Afghanistan), a warrior-king named Mahmud, a relative of the Mamuni king, was plotting against Khiva. Mahmud belonged to the Ghaznavid Dynasty of Sunni Turks in a largely Persianate culture. They had emerged from the military ethos of the ghazis—a dedicated warrior class raised to guard the north-eastern frontiers of the Abbasid Caliphate. In the summer of 1017, Mahmud of Ghazni invaded and plundered Khiva and returned home with much booty and 'the leading men of the country as prisoners of war or as hostages'.[3] Among the latter was Alberuni himself.

By then, Mahmud was already infamous. Since 1001 CE, he had been raiding India almost annually. His 'targets were the richest temples', writes Romila Thapar, which hoarded gold and revenue from their lands, endowments and pilgrim donations. 'The destruction of temples even by Hindu rulers was not unknown, but [Mahmud] inaugurated an increase in temple destruction compared to earlier times.' He was also a religious fanatic. He raided temple towns like Mathura, Thanesar, Kannauj and Somnath. Twice, Mahmud also 'waged hostilities against Multan, whose ruler, Daud, was an Ismaili' and so the 'wrong' kind of Muslim.[4] Mahmud even desecrated a Shia mosque in Multan and killed many Muslim 'heretics'.[5] He was bad news not just for the Hindus.

In the ensuing years, Alberuni, though he despised Mahmud, remained loosely attached to his court as a resident scholar. The court had other poets and scholars too, including at one time the great Persian poet Firdausi, making Mahmud a kind of patron of the arts (Firdausi, however, had had a falling out with Mahmud and had fled for his life years before Alberuni's involuntary arrival).

The details are murky but Mahmud's raids created opportunities for Alberuni to travel to India, perhaps accompanying a prince of Khiva now serving Mahmud.[6] Until then, everything known in the Turko-Persian-Arabic world about the Hindus, claims Alberuni, was 'second-hand information . . . a farrago of materials never sifted by the sieve of critical examination'. Thereafter, led by his curiosity and with no hope of reward from Mahmud, Alberuni learnt Sanskrit, travelled to many parts of India during his visits, met learned men and spent most of the next thirteen years observing, questioning and studying Indian thought and society.

Around 1030, Alberuni recorded his findings in a monumental work with an arresting title, *Taḥqīq mā li-l-hind min maqūlah maqbūlah fī al-'aql aw mardhūlah* or 'Verifying All That the Indians Recount, the Reasonable and the Unreasonable'.[7] Alberuni wrote this work to provide, in his own words, 'the essential facts for any Muslim who wanted to converse with Hindus and to discuss with them questions of religion, science, or literature'. It was translated from Arabic to English as *Alberuni's India* by Edward C. Sachau in 1888, still the only translation available.

Alberuni was a mildly devout Muslim, likely Shia, with modest pride in the Persian culture of Islam. He was remarkably open-minded, well informed, and a big believer in science, reason and evidence. He couldn't stand humbug, writes Sachau, claiming that on 'the horrid practices of Rasayana, i.e. the art of making gold, of making old people young, etc., he bursts out into sarcastic words which are more coarse in the original than in my translation'.

We know almost nothing about Alberuni's early life or family. He grew up without a father and was likely a bachelor all his life. He was a child of the so-called Golden Age of Islam, when science and cosmopolitan culture thrived in Baghdad and other cities of Western Asia. His other eminent near-contemporaries were Avicenna, Alhazen and Omar Khayyam.[8] A prolific writer, Alberuni compiled a list of his own works when he was sixty. He continued to write after that (he died in 1048 CE at the age of seventy-five), but his surviving list has 146 titles averaging ninety pages each. Nearly half of these works are on astronomy and mathematics, writes scholar George Saliba. Only twenty-two have survived, about half of which have been published.

Besides his work on India, Alberuni wrote another encyclopaedic work, *The Chronology of Ancient Nations*, containing an 'anthropological account of various cultures', both dead and living. It includes, for instance, the most detailed, 'scientifically reasoned' analysis of the Jewish calendar till then. As a set, writes Saliba, 'these two works preserve the best premodern description of the cultures Alberuni came to know'. In his other works, Alberuni 'developed new algebraic techniques for the solution of third-degree equations'. He defended 'the mathematical sciences against the attacks of religious scholars' by showing them how spherical trigonometry could accurately find the direction of Mecca.[9] Though Alberuni was an ace astronomer, he was often paid to be an astrologer. He seems to have played along reluctantly; in his own words, his faith in astrology was 'as weak as that of its least adherents'. His accomplishments include the following:

> In his works on astronomy, he discussed with approval the theory of the Earth's rotation on its axis and made accurate calculations of latitude and longitude. In those on physics, he explained natural springs by the laws of hydrostatics and determined with remarkable accuracy the specific weight of 18 precious stones and metals. In his works on geography, he advanced the daring view that the valley of the Indus had once been a sea basin.[10]

Alberuni published *India* after Mahmud died in 1030 and his son became king. With this change of despots, Alberuni's fortunes suddenly improved a lot. He now described Mahmud as 'having failed in the duties of a protector of art and science' at home.[11] He decried Mahmud's raids in *India*, especially in Mathura and Somnath, claiming that 'Mahmud utterly ruined the prosperity' of the regions he raided, created a hatred of the Muslims among the locals, and caused the Hindu sciences to retreat 'far away from those parts of the country conquered by us' to places 'where our hands cannot yet reach, to Kashmir, Benaras, and other places'. He was clearly not fond of his ex-boss.

Mahmud hadn't attempted to establish an empire in India. His Indian raids had mainly funded his Central Asian campaigns and turned Ghazni into a fine city, with a grand mosque and a library full of looted books.[12] After his death, the Ghaznavid raids ceased. Our knowledge of these raids comes entirely from Turko-Persian sources, including Alberuni. Curiously, writes Thapar, even for the worst of the raids, at Somnath Temple in 1025, local Hindu textual sources of the day neither mention it, nor suggest a sense of continuing social trauma.[13] If it were part of Hindu memory (as claimed by Hindu nationalists), it would have appeared recurringly. Instead, local textual sources suggest that socio-economic life bounced back and the raid was forgotten by the Indians.[14] Twelve years after the attack, a king from the Goa region recorded performing a pilgrimage to the temple, but he failed to mention Mahmud's raid.[15]

Thapar calls the 'unbroken silence' of the Hindu texts about Mahmud's raid on Somnath Temple 'an enigma'. Somnath was next to the major port of Veraval, and within two centuries, Persians and Arab merchants were actively trading with the local Hindu king. They were granted land to build a mosque in the vicinity of Somnath Temple and 'received assistance' from the temple priests.[16] Perhaps trading was more lucrative than preserving bad memories! Only after British scholars discovered the raids in the Turko-Persian sources in the nineteenth century—and used it to develop a narrative about Hindus and Muslims—was the social memory of the trauma 'reconstructed' by Hindu nationalists for their own purposes, writes Thapar.[17]

> Interestingly, the earliest claim that the raid resulted in something akin to a trauma for the Hindus was made not in India but in Britain, during a debate in the House of Commons in 1843, when members of the British parliament stated that Mahmud's attack on Somanatha had created painful feelings and had been hurtful to the Hindus for *nearly a thousand years*. Subsequent to this, references began to be made to the Hindu trauma. [emphasis mine]

Mahmud inflicted much suffering on the world, but he also accidentally paved the way for Alberuni to write his magnum opus. Alberuni's 'observations on Indian conditions, systems of knowledge, social norms and religion', writes Thapar, 'are probably the most incisive made by any visitor to India'.[18] Notably, in his thirteen years in the north, west and central India, Alberuni never came across Buddhism, which had by then receded to the east. 'India, as far as known to Alberuni, was Brahmanic, not Buddhistic,' writes Sachau. He 'knew scarcely anything at all about Buddhism, nor had any means for procuring information on the subject'.[19] Clearly, Buddhism's demise from much of India predated the Turko-Persian invasions, as discussed in the previous chapter on Nalanda.

India According to Alberuni

Central to 'the Hindu world of thought', writes Alberuni, 'is that which the Brahmins think and believe, for they are specially trained for preserving and maintaining their religion. And this it is which we shall explain, viz the belief of the Brahmins'. This declaration makes it clear which section of Indian society—and its ideas, beliefs and values—is the one Alberuni mostly describes in *India.*

'The Hindus have numerous books about all the branches of science,' he writes. They 'have books about the jurisprudence of their religion, on theosophy, on ascetics, on the process of becoming god and seeking liberation from the world', on various schools of thought like Samkhya, Mimamsa, Nyaya, Yoga, Lokayata and many more. He feels overwhelmed at first, 'How could anybody know the titles of all of them, more especially if he is not a Hindu, but a foreigner?'

But Alberuni rolls up his sleeves and dives right in. 'I do not spare either trouble or money in collecting Sanskrit books . . . and in procuring for myself, even from very remote places, Hindu scholars who understand them and are able to teach me.' He learns Sanskrit, finding it a difficult language due to its range and complexity, much like Arabic. He observes that the Hindus of north India speak Sanskrit in two registers, a 'vernacular one . . . and a classical one'. He feels lucky to be able to undertake all this learning so freely, and thanks God for the opportunity.

In time, Alberuni reads a large number of Hindu religious, philosophical and astronomical texts. Much of *India* consists of his expositions of Brahminical texts and practices. He highlights choice parts from the Gita, the Upanishads, Patanjali, Puranas, the four Vedas and scientific texts by Aryabhata, Brahmagupta, Varahamihira and others. He relates stories from the two epics and other mythologies. He presents the Hindu science of grammar and metrical composition. He describes their social customs and hierarchies. He also compares Hindu thought to the Greek thought of Socrates, Pythagoras, Plato, Aristotle, Galen and others, and at times with Sufi teaching.

'The Hindus use the numeral signs in arithmetic in the same way as we do,' he writes (a couple hundred years earlier, zero and the decimal system had been adopted by the Muslim world, and were then transmitted to Europe as Arabic numerals[20]). 'I have composed a treatise showing how far, possibly, the Hindus are ahead of us in this subject.' He also translated two books into Arabic 'one about the *origines* and a description of all created beings, called *Samkhya*, and another about the emancipation of the soul from the fetters of the body, called *Patanjali*'.

After this deep immersion in Brahminical texts and society, Alberuni begins *India* with several general remarks about the Hindus and their society. He explains that just as the 'confession, "There is no god but God, Muḥammad is his prophet", is the shibboleth of Islam, the Trinity that of Christianity, and the institute of the Sabbath that of Judaism, so metempsychosis [reincarnation] is the shibboleth of the Hindu religion. Therefore, he who does not believe in it does not belong to them, and is not reckoned as one of them'.

Muslim and Hindu religions are poles apart, he writes. But while Hindus argue internally, they never physically fight over theological disputes. Instead, 'their fanaticism is directed against . . . all foreigners. They call them *mleccha*, i.e., impure, and forbid having any connection with them [via a] relationship, or by sitting, eating, and drinking with them, because thereby, they think, they would be polluted'. This, he thinks, 'constitutes the widest gulf between us and them'.

Alberuni gives the Hindus a wide berth as he considers that 'the repugnance of the Hindus against foreigners increased' after 'the Muslims began to make inroads into their country'. But this isn't the only reason for the barriers he senses between the Muslims and the Hindus. The barriers are also caused by other 'peculiarities of their national character, deeply rooted in them, but manifest to everybody'. Mentioning them, he feels, 'sounds like a satire'. For instance:

The Hindus believe that there is no country but theirs, no
nation like theirs, no kings like theirs, no religion like theirs,
no science like theirs. They are haughty, foolishly vain,
self-conceited, and stolid. They are by nature niggardly in
communicating that which they know, and they take the
greatest possible care to withhold it from men of another caste
among their own people, still much more, of course, from
any foreigner.

Alberuni had, however, begun humbly. 'At first I stood to their
astronomers in the relation of a pupil to his master,' he writes. But soon,
'I began to show them the elements on which this science rests, to point
out to them some rules of logical deduction and the scientific methods
of all mathematics, and then they flocked together round me from all
parts, wondering, and most eager to learn from me, asking me at the
same time from what Hindu master I had learnt those things'. This
really got his goat, and seemed to him illustrative of a broader attitude
among the Hindus:

> According to their belief . . . no created beings besides them
> have any knowledge or science whatsoever. Their haughtiness is
> such that, if you tell them of any science or scholar in Khorasan
> and Persis, they will think you to be both an ignoramus and a
> liar. If they traveled and mixed with other nations, they would
> soon change their mind, for their ancestors were not as narrow-
> minded as the present generation is.

Such 'is the state of things in India', he laments, that Brahmins attempt
to combine ideas of purity with the pursuit of science. 'I showed them
what they were worth,' he huffs, 'and thought myself a great deal
superior to them.' They're 'devoid of training in astronomy, and have
no correct astronomical notions. In consequence, they believe that
the earth is at rest' (Aryabhata, 500 years earlier, had argued that the
earth rotates on its axis daily, a view that had travelled west and had
been embraced by Muslim astronomers; smart global opinion posited
a spherical earth rotating on its axis in a geocentric universe; however,

most Indian astronomers after Aryabhata, including Varahamihira and Brahmagupta, had rejected this theory, and so Indian astronomy had regressed on this major issue).[21] Alberuni translated for them the books of Euclid and Ptolemy's *Almagest* into Sanskrit, and explained how to construct an astrolabe to understand the rotation of the earth. In doing this, he says disarmingly, he was guided only 'by the desire of spreading science'. (Modern scholars too have noted 'the smugly insular stance of Sanskrit scientific literature which, refusing to recognize the authority of non-Indian science, remained for centuries willfully ignorant of its competitors'. This changed after Persian culture and language began spreading in India.[22])

'The Brahmins recite the Veda without understanding its meaning,' writes Alberuni. 'Only few of them learn its explanation, and still less is the number of those who master [it well enough] to hold a theological disputation.' They don't 'allow the Veda to be committed to writing' because it must be 'recited according to certain modulations'. They teach it to the Kshatriyas, but the Vaishyas, Shudras and the outcastes 'are not allowed to hear it, much less to pronounce and recite it. If such a thing can be proved against one of them, the Brahmins drag him before the magistrate, and he is punished by having his tongue cut off'. The Brahmins maintain that 'certain passages in the Veda . . . must not be recited within dwellings, since they fear that they would cause an abortion both to women and the cattle. Therefore, they step out into the open field to recite them. There is hardly a single verse free from such and similar minatory injunctions', writes Alberuni, before providing an overview of each of the four Vedas and how they are recited. The *Samaveda*, for instance, 'treats of the sacrifices, commandments, and prohibitions. It is recited in a tone like a chant, and hence its name is derived, because *sâman* means *the sweetness of recitation*'. He goes on to explain the 'cause of this kind of recital' by relating a mythological story behind it.

The four-fold varna system made a deep impression on Alberuni. He notes that members of each varna are forbidden to dine with members of other varnas. Below them are 'people called *Antyaja*, who render various kinds of services' and live outside the towns and villages of the four varnas. Then there are people called Hadi, Doma, Chandala and Badhatau, who 'are not reckoned amongst any caste [and] are occupied with dirty work, like the cleansing of the villages and other services . . . In fact, they are considered like illegitimate children; for according to general opinion they descend from a Shudra father and a Brahmin mother as the children of fornication; therefore, they are degraded outcasts'.

Alberuni quotes Krishna from the Bhagavad Gita as affirming this varna order: 'If anybody wants to quit the works and duties of his caste and adopt those of another caste, even if it would bring a certain honour to the latter, it is a sin, because it is a transgression of the rule.' Alberuni despises social institutions that cannot 'be broken through by the special merits of any individual', and yet such institutions, he says, abound among the Hindus. 'We Muslims,' he writes, 'of course, stand entirely on the other side of the question, considering all men as equal, except in piety; and this is the greatest obstacle which prevents any approach or understanding between Hindus and Muslims.'

Alberuni notices the Hindu penchant for classifying things and making all kinds of random lists, like dividing all living beings into three classes and fourteen species. Declaring the number of hells to be 88,000. In the Hindu 'enumeration of things there is much that is arbitrary,' he writes. 'They use or invent numbers of names, and who is to hinder or to control them?'

He notes that in their schools, children use black tablets on which they write 'with a white material from the left to the right'. Adults write letters and books on the bark of the tuz tree after oiling and polishing it. 'The whole book is wrapped up in a piece of cloth and fastened between two tablets of the same size. Such a book is called puthi (cf. pusta, pustaka).' For the Sanskrit texts he reads, he observes that 'Indian scribes are careless, and do not take pains to produce correct and well-collated copies', due to which an author's work often becomes incomprehensible over time. He describes many of their board games too. At times, he resorts to stories to make his point. One such goes as follows: 'Once a sage was asked why scholars always flock to the doors of the rich, whilst the rich are not inclined to call at the doors of scholars. "The scholars," he answered, "are well aware of the use of money, but the rich are ignorant of the nobility of science."'

Farmers and herders pay an unspecified land use tax to the king. Then they pay one-sixth of their income in taxes to the king for protecting their 'property, and their families. The same obligation rests also on the common people, but they will always lie and cheat in the declarations about their property'. Trading businesses, too, pay tax to the state. 'Only the Brahmins are exempt from all these taxes.' Alberuni's account makes it clear that as usual, the Brahmins had a pretty sweet deal. Even the law of the land treated them leniently. They literally got away with murder, asked only to atone for the crime by 'fasting, prayers, and almsgiving'. Members of other castes got stiffer penalties for the same crime. Interestingly, the Brahmins were punished more for flouting the caste order. Alberuni writes, 'If a Brahman eats in the house of a Shudra for sundry days, he is expelled from his caste and can never regain it.'

Alberuni reports that 'the Hindus, are not very severe in punishing whoredom'. Some of these 'whores' even 'sing, dance, and play' in their temples (this must be in reference to devadasis). Alberuni calls this a fault of the kings, who make prostitutes 'an attraction for their cities, a bait of pleasure for their subjects, for no other but financial reasons'. The kings use the revenues from the business of prostitution, 'both as fines and taxes', to offset their military expenses.

'As regards charms and incantations,' writes Alberuni, 'the Hindus have a firm belief in them, and they, as a rule, are much inclined towards them.' Hindu men also fast in various ways and for different objectives, such as to vanquish enemies, to gain wealth, wisdom or health or to be a favourite of the women. On one particular fasting day of the year, 'they soil themselves with the dung of cows, and break fasting by feeding upon a mixture of cow's milk, urine, and dung'. Giving alms is considered meritorious, and many donate up to 10 per cent of their income.

'The Hindus marry at a very young age; therefore, the parents arrange the marriage' of their children, writes Alberuni. No gifts are exchanged, but the husband gives a gift to his new wife, which becomes her personal wealth on which he has no claim. 'Husband and wife can only be separated by death, as they have no divorce.' During a woman's menstrual cycle, 'the husband is not allowed to cohabit with his wife, nor even to come near her in the house, because during this time she is impure'. 'A man may marry one to four wives,' writes Alberuni. The number allowed 'depends upon the caste'. A Brahmin 'may take four, a Kshatriya three, a Vaisya two wives, and a Shudra one. Every man of a caste may marry a woman of his own caste or one of the castes or caste below his; but nobody is allowed to marry a woman of a caste superior to his own'. For a man, 'if one of his wives die, he may take another one to complete the legitimate number'. If the husband dies, however,

> [the wife] cannot marry another man. She has only to choose between two things—either to remain a widow as long as she lives or to burn herself; and the latter eventuality is considered the preferable, because as a widow she is ill-treated as long as she lives. As regards the wives of the kings, they are in the habit of burning them, whether they wish it or not, by which they desire to prevent any of them by chance committing something unworthy of the illustrious husband. They make an exception only for women of advanced years and for those who have children; for the son is the responsible protector of his mother.

When a person dies, the surviving heirs 'are to wash, embalm, wrap [the body] in a shroud, and then to burn it with as much sandal and other wood as they can get'. After the cremation, the attendees all 'wash themselves as well as their dresses during two days, because they have become unclean by touching the dead'. If the ashes can't be consigned to the Ganga, a nearby brook is chosen. 'If the heir is a son, he must during the whole year wear mourning dress; he must mourn and have no intercourse with women'. Inheritance follows patriarchal norms; the daughter gets a quarter of the son's inheritance. A wildcard clause could make things unpleasant for the heirs: 'The debts of the deceased must be paid by his heir', whether or not the deceased has left any inheritance. The widow inherits nothing. If she 'does not burn herself, but prefers to remain alive, the [male] heir of her deceased husband has to provide her with nourishment and clothing as long as she lives'. If she doesn't have a son, she is at the mercy of other male relatives.

Alberuni approached India like a scholarly journalist. We could as well call him the first Indologist. As with so many early travellers, he didn't speak about his own life and mainly aspired to 'place before the reader the theories of the Hindus exactly as they are'. *India* is the work of a deeply intelligent, curious and decent mind. Alberuni ends *India* with a simple prayer: 'We ask God to pardon us for every statement of ours which is not true.'

The Enigma of **Khajuraho**
(c. 950–c. 1250 CE)

It is February and I'm in Khajuraho to see its thousand-year-old temples, famed for their explicit and finely carved erotica. I arrived here by train just ahead of the annual Shivratri festival, expected to draw thousands from nearby villages. On the day, the visitors first attend an annual mela—full of shops, eateries, home remedies, games, a Ferris wheel and more—before the big evening event: the wedding procession of Shiva and Parvati. Led by drummers, the procession grows as it snakes around town towards the thousand-year-old Matangeshwara Shiva Temple, where the divine wedding is enacted, ensuring the procreative continuity of the universe.

The procession features multiple floats that, bizarrely enough, have refrigerator-sized loudspeakers blasting techno rave and Bollywood dance music. Each float is followed by wildly dancing young men and boys—but no dancing women or girls—as if their own bosom pal were getting hitched. The cacophony is amplified by other street music, honking vehicles, religious chants like *bum bum bhole*, firecrackers, and agitated dogs, donkeys and cattle.

On a float near the back of the parade are two bored-looking kids dressed as Shiva and Parvati, with other gods in ancillary floats bringing up the rear. Their costumes and make-up are comically inept, but in such popular festivals, isn't it always the spirit that counts? And this festival and mela go back a ways. British archaeologist Sir Alexander

Cunningham recorded the event in 1865. Shobita Punja, a writer on Khajuraho, has claimed, though based on little evidence, that even a thousand years ago—in Khajuraho's prime when these temples were built—people celebrated Shivratri and hosted a divine wedding.

However, few would disagree that the most amazing and captivating aspect of these temples is their fine erotic art. Every modern visitor likely

Figure 1. Amorous couple, Lakshmana Temple

wonders: What does this art actually *mean*? What kind of people built this? Why did they depict sex so vividly on their temple walls, right next to their gods? Or as Devangana Desai, a noted scholar of the erotic temple sculpture of India, asked while pursuing her PhD in late 1960s Bombay: What explains 'the enigmatic presence of sex in the religious art of a culture that glorified austerity, penance and renunciation'?[1] These are also the questions that have brought me to Khajuraho. Their answers, as I have learnt, are neither as clear-cut nor as well-known—even among our scholarly literary elites—as one might imagine for such a major tourist spot and UNESCO World Heritage Site. I simply have to find out for myself.

More certain than the age of the Shivratri festival are the much older references to the sacred geography of the region in Vedic texts, the Ramayana and the Mahabharata. The Pandavas apparently began their last, concealed year of exile in a forest nearby. The Vindhya Range, where Khajuraho lies, was once the southern extent of Aryavarta, marking north and south Indian cultures. To its south, the dominant Indo-Aryan cultural elites of the north imagined forests sheltering Mleccha tribes, rakshasas and fierce deities like Kali. Also ancient is Shiva's presence in the region. While Shiva's origins remain contested, he's clearly a composite god with features of many indigenous folk deities, one of whom may well have been from the Vindhyas. He retains many non-Aryan attributes, such as being a dark-skinned forest dweller, a healer, lord of animals (*pashupati*), a dancer and player of drums, wearing long matted hair, tiger skin and a garland of snakes. The Shiva that emerged later had these and additional attributes, such as a Himalayan abode, a third eye, the powers of a creative destroyer and much more. As with the Buddha, Brahminical Hinduism later appropriated both Shiva and Kali.

The forests mentioned in the legends are long gone. My train from Jhansi to Khajuraho went across an arid scrubland broken up by irrigated farmland and village homes. Pastoralists abounded, raising goats, cattle and chickens. I saw green fields with crops of lentils, wheat, mustard and sugarcane, fed almost entirely by groundwater. The region's chronically low land productivity has been worsened in recent years by erratic rainfall and droughts, raising poverty rates and driving more of the young villagers to big cities.

The Rediscovery of Khajuraho

The first Britisher to stumble upon the ruined temples of Khajuraho and their sexually explicit sculptures was Captain T.S. Burt of Bengal Engineers. Burt was passing through the region in 1838. Intrigued by the stories he had heard about provocative ruins half-buried in the jungle, he got a few strong men to carry him in a palanquin for 44 kilometres to reach Khajuraho. A dense forest had long engulfed the temples. Pushing through the undergrowth, he was 'much delighted at the venerable, and picturesque appearance these several old temples presented'. The unintentionally amusing account below was part of what Burt recorded that day:

> I found in the ruins of Khajuraho seven large Hindoo temples, most beautifully and exquisitely carved as to workmanship, but the sculptor had at times allowed his subject to grow rather warmer than there was any absolute necessity for his doing; indeed, some of the sculptures here were extremely indecent and offensive; which I was at first much surprised to find in temples that are professed to be erected for good purposes, and on account of religion. But the religion of the Hindoos could not have been very chaste if it induced people under the

cloak of religion, to design the most disgraceful representation to desecrate their ecclesiastical erections. The palky bearers, however, appeared to take great delight at the sight of those to them very agreeable novelties, which they took good care to point out to all present.[2]

In the 1850s, archaeologist Alexander Cunningham documented the site more formally but he too was scandalized by the sculptures, finding them 'highly indecent', 'disgustingly obscene' and 'highly indelicate'. He wrote, 'everywhere there are number of female figures who are represented dropping their clothes, and thus purposely exposing their persons'.

Figure 2. Vishwanath Temple panel

The quaint mix of restraint and horror in the accounts of Burt and Cunningham might seem very Victorian to us today, but it is of a piece with modern Indian prudishness. Hindu conservatives mostly favour a sanitized, delimited and 'respectable' view of Hinduism without this 'shameful sex', which stains their idea of ancient Hindu glory. On Valentine's Day last year, the Hindu right group Bajrang Dal raged against even modest public displays of affection between couples—ironically in the name of tradition! In previous years, they've even protested the sale of the *Kamasutra* outside these temples. Some attribute this modern shift in attitudes towards sexuality to Hindu India's encounter with Muslims or Europeans. But as I'll argue, it has more to do with ideological fault lines within Hinduism itself. Suffice to say that Khajuraho's temple art sits uncomfortably in the modern Hindu imagination.

The temple art of Khajuraho, however, challenges and unsettles more than just the sexual prudes in modern culture, Victorian or Indian. It confronts our fundamental ideas and assumptions about art, aesthetics and 'proper' religious moods and sentiments. It challenges us to make sense of religious art that depicts not just heterosexual sex but also bestiality, masturbation, orgies, gang bangs, oral sex, lesbian and gay sex, exhibitionism and possibly even non-consensual or exploitative sex (one panel shows multiple men bearing weapons while having sex with a woman). The panels often depict aristocratic and royal men and women, as well as ascetics—bearded and clean-shaven, sometimes pot-bellied, wearing *rudraksha* beads and *kundala*s in their ears—participating, or just 'assisting', in these sexual acts. This is a far cry from the modern Hindu idea of moksha-pursuing ascetics. At times, even dancers and musicians turn up to heighten the erotic experience. Athletic poses are common and idealized youthful bodies are the norm.[3]

The walls of Khajuraho of course feature a lot more than erotic art, which accounts for less than 10 per cent of all sculptures. There are major and minor gods, often enacting scenes from various stories, in conventional roles or in amorous pairs. Mundane and secular subject matter abounds, such as *surasundari*s, or graceful young maidens, depicting 'common human moods, emotions and activities' like 'disrobing, yawning, scratching the back, touching the breasts, rinsing water from the wet plaits of hair, removing thorns, fondling a baby, playing with pets like parrots and monkeys, writing a letter, playing on a flute or vina, painting designs on the wall or bedecking themselves in various ways by painting the feet, applying collyrium',[4] gazing in the mirror, carrying a lotus or a water jar, dancing, playfully tugging at an ascetic's beard, holding a manuscript, etc. Other secular sculptures include 'domestic life scenes, teachers and disciples, dancers and musicians', ascetics, royal hunts, marching armies, battle scenes, animals like elephants, parrots, boars, snakes, a 'lion with an armed human rider on the back and a warrior counter-player attacking it from behind', and some mythical animals.[5] There are also many scenes where it's hard to say what's going on.

It helped that the region was blessed with high-quality sandstone, which allowed the carving of fine sculptural details like ornamental jewellery, delicate nails and strands of hair, sheer robes clinging to the skin and a wide palette of moods: delight, serenity, playfulness. In large workshops, amid the sounds of hammers and chisels, master artisans conceived and carved their artwork and taught apprentices. 'A panel kept in the Khajuraho museum depicts a large number of labourers carrying stones with the help of long wooden poles.'6 Copperplate inscriptions have revealed that artisans got new titles as they acquired greater skill. A skilled artisan was called a *Silpin*, and many an image is inscribed with the names of Silpins. With higher skill, he became a *Vijananin*. A few became adept enough to be called *Vaidagdhi Visvakarman*, who went beyond mere technicalities of craft to the aesthetics of art.[7] Scholars have also identified a sophisticated language of playful puns, allegories, metaphors, hidden meanings and double entendres (*ślesha*) employed by the sculptors in their statues and inscriptions, a custom that also flourished in the poetry of Chandela times.

The Mysteries of Khajuraho's Art

Indeed, what sort of cultural milieu could have produced such explicit depictions that most people today would consider hardcore porn? Did they also make the men and women of ancient Khajuraho blush? Do these erotic sculptures depict the actual sexual tastes and mores of the patrons and the public, or were they mere decorative motifs and conventions detached from real life (akin to how we Indians expect our movie stars on screen to break out in choreographed song and dance, while never doing so in our own lives)?

The few texts that survive from the Chandela realm shed little light on their artistic motivations. All we have are clues from a few Sanskrit inscriptions, a philosophical court play titled *Prabodhachandrodaya* (more on this later) and other data from elsewhere in India. Over the decades, many theories have tried to explain the purpose and meaning of the explicit erotica on temple walls, such as: (1) the sculptures show what the townsfolk were doing when the celestial wedding pageant rolled by their city, and the erotica represents the consummation of the divine marriage;[8] (2) the erotic sculptures were designed to impart sex education to the Chandela public; (3) they celebrate the male–female creative union; (4) they are a visual rendition of the *Kamasutra*; (5) they were driven by the sexually liberal and reformist agenda of a royal family; (6) they show the rampant hedonism or cultural decadence of the Chandela society; and so on.

But these theories don't survive the most basic questions one might ask. What explains the wide range of sexual acts on the panels? Why did the sculptors express the idea of male–female creative union in such explicit, rather than figurative, ways? What about the panels on homosexuality that have nothing to do with fertility or male–female union? Desai has also persuasively argued that Khajuraho's erotica should not be seen as 'illustrated *Kamasutra*', as it is often sold to gullible tourists.[9] The *Kamasutra* is a secular treatise on the 'techniques' of love and courtship (more on this soon), 'whereas the erotic figures of Khajuraho, as also of Bhubaneshwar, Konarak and other Indian temples, belong to a different tradition, where both religious (Tantric) and worldly interest could merge'.[10] It is also not easy to reconcile the theory

of rampant hedonism and cultural decadence with what we know of the feudal order and religious orientation of the royals and the temple-going public in the Chandela realm. After all, even if this was the work of mere voluptuaries, why didn't they restrict all erotic depictions

Figure 3. Lakshman Temple panel

to their private living spaces and pleasure palaces? Why did they feel the need to so prominently stamp their temples with erotica? And why did these depictions vanish a few centuries later?

Among the worst sources to learn from are the 'official guides' outside Khajuraho. They mostly peddle silly or half-baked stories about the erotica. The most ludicrous—and perhaps why the most common— story goes like this: It was an age of war and a lot of men had died. The rest were turning in droves to *sanyaas*, or asceticism, and a life in the forest (in another variant, the men were turning in droves to Buddhist monasticism, never mind that Buddhism was practically non-existent in the Chandela realm and that Hinduism's own Adi Shankara and his mathas were driving much of the renunciatory monasticism across India at this time). This mortified the Chandelas—if people stopped procreating, society would collapse. 'Big problem!' exclaims one guide.

So the wise Chandela kings hatched an ingenious plan to ambush these unsuspecting men with erotica when they piously came to visit the temples. The titillation would raise their interest in sex and save society; and, a beaming guide reveals, the ploy evidently worked!

Another common story, a guide relates, is that the sculptors, as an act of artistic freedom, imagined the temple as the world and depicted all of life on its walls—the good, the bad and the ugly—leaving it to the discerning public to know the difference. When I ask him how bestiality fits into this view, he claims it was a subliminal 'warning to the public' to not indulge in 'dirty things'! A blander third story is that the temples variously depict the four aims of life: *artha*, kama, dharma, moksha. But the guides simply regurgitate these words, failing to explain why depictions of kama had to be so explicit, rather than figurative.

Sadly, the ignorance peddled by the guides goes even further. For example, when Burt 'rediscovered' these temples, many had been badly damaged by vandals, lightening, trees and age-related decay (considerable restoration work has since been undertaken). Yet one guide blames the damaged state of the temples on Aurangzeb! Never mind that the temples already lay deeply buried in the jungle by Aurangzeb's time. When I point this out, he seeks to correct me: 'No, no, Sirji! The temples were *active* then!' Most guides seem to also make things up as they go along, confidently expounding on sculptural scenes about which even scholars are divided or silent. No self-respecting guide here ever says, 'I'm not sure.'

After talking to several guides one afternoon, I amble through town to the eastern group of temples, from where I can see the low, white-edged Dantla Hills, so named for resembling the worn-out teeth (*danth*) of old men. These hills and Khajuraho lie atop the Bundelkhand gneiss, the oldest rock bed in India. It is early February; the days are getting longer and warmer and the air less polluted. At night the moon isn't orange-yellow but white, and the sky has far more stars than I ever see in Delhi NCR.

A local boy soon falls in step with me, a self-appointed guide angling for a tip. He points out two flowering trees: flame of the forest, with bright orange-red flowers used in temple rituals, and mahua, whose flowers taste like figs when dried and make a potent hooch when fermented.

Even animals are said to be drawn to the fragrance of its rotting flowers, and funny stories of drunk animals, such as deer, monkeys, bears and elephants appear in local folk tales.[11]

During dinner I think again of my encounter with the guides. I feel a rush of anger at first, then of sadness, at all the hokum they spread and their lack of intellectual curiosity and reasoning skills. Back in the room, my mind drifts to the larger malaise in Indian education, its deficits of critical thinking and historical imagination, until I fall asleep listening to a wedding band at a dharmashala across the street playing nostalgic Bollywood golden oldies from my youth.

The Realm of the Chandelas

The origins of the Chandela Dynasty (831–1308 CE) remain obscure. Some historians have noted their early tribal associations, their worship of a tribal deity, Maniya Devi, and 'connections with the tribal Gonds and Bhars, [including] family ties with the Gonds'.[12] If the Chandelas had the subaltern social lineage this suggests, it likely made them insecure in their claims of royal entitlements, which may be why they tried so hard to invent a 'more respectable' Kshatriya genealogy. In due course, they were able to morph their identity into Rajputs of the lunar line, i.e, *Chandravanshis*, through myth-making. One of their founding myths, recorded on an inscription, traces their descent and name to sage Chandratreya, son of the Vedic sage Atri, who was born from a one-night stand between—you guessed it—a Brahmin's ravishing daughter, Hemavati, and the moon god!

Until the early seventh century, the region had been part of the Gupta Empire (319–605 CE). New styles of temple art, architecture, engineering, governance, as well as religious and secular culture patronized by the Guptas entered the region, which the Chandelas later inherited.[13] After the Guptas, the control of the region passed to Harsha of Kannauj (ruled 606–47 CE), then to the Gurjara-Pratiharas. Early Chandela chiefs, based in Khajuraho, were mere vassals of the Gurjara-Pratiharas until their seventh in line, Yashovarman, broke free in the mid-tenth century and declared a sovereign state. To commemorate his victory, he stole a prized statue of Vaikunth-Vishnu from a Gurjara-

Pratihara temple and installed it in a grand new temple he built at Khajuraho. The Chandela realm, Jejakabhukti, now extended 700 km from Varanasi to Vidisha, and was bounded by four rivers: Yamuna, Narmada, Chambal and Tons.

Yashovarman is said to have inaugurated a 'golden age' that lasted about a hundred years, with relative peace and prosperity, stable administration and where sculptural art, architecture, literature, theatre, dance and music flourished, all actively patronized by him and many successors. Of the twenty-odd Chandela rulers, none were women.

'Golden age' is of course relative. Golden for whom? Starting from the Gupta age in the fourth century CE, most peasants in northern India lived in a feudal order, toiling to pay taxes to their overlords—from the village thakur to the king—in the *samanta* system. This hierarchy of landed feudatories was obsessed with territorial control and expansion, as well as 'maintenance of a high social status in Hindu caste hierarchy', producing a culture of *dana* (religious donation) and temple-building. It was in this social context that the Chandela Rajputs too tried to raise and 'legitimize their social status by building temples, tanks, and by giving gifts to priestly Brahmins', which, going by Puranic texts, brought fame and merit to the royals.[14] Historical sources suggest that the elites of Chandela society followed the social conventions typical of other Indian elites of the age. They 'believed in magic and supernaturalism', and kept priests and temples happy with gifts of land, the revenue from which was usually tax free. In time, temple officials became landlords, and temples here, as across India, became rich and powerful feudal institutions, acting as 'landholder, employer, consumer of goods and services, bank, school, museum, hospital and theater'.[15] The upper classes also indulged in ostentation and self-praise and were competitive about acquiring fame and merit (*punya*) through religious works, always aiming to outdo their peers and ancestors.[16]

Most of the twenty-five rediscovered and restored temples in Khajuraho date from this 'golden age' starting around 950 CE, though as many as eighty-five temples were built over 250 years, from 900–1150 CE. They were commissioned not just by kings, but also by queens, chieftains in the court and Jain merchants. Scholars aren't certain what this temple town was called back then, which had many beautiful lakes.

Figure 4. Kandariya Mahadev Temple

Just one inscription offers a clue: Khajuravahaka, or the district of khajura ('date palm tree', plentiful in the region). The Persian traveller Alberuni wrote in 1030 CE that the capital of 'the realm of Jajahuti' was Kajuraha, but he left no further details.

Generally speaking, the earlier Chandelas were Vaishnavites, the later ones Shaivites. Ten of the extant temples at Khajuraho are dedicated to Vishnu and his incarnations (Varaha, Vamana, Vaikunth), eight to Shiva, one each to Surya and sixty-four yoginis (i.e., Tantric goddesses and assistants to Shakti or Kali) and five to Jain tirthankars. Buddhism is conspicuously missing, save for a solitary image of the Buddha. Other gods, heroes, sages and religious beings that appear often include Rama, Sita, Krishna, Balarama, Parvati, Lakshmi, Saraswati, Brahma, Narasimha, Ardhnarisvara, Matsya, Nandi, Bhairava, Sadasiva, Hanuman, Parasurama, Kalki, Kama, Rati, Ganesh, Indra, Agni, Kuber, Vishvakarma, Tantric goddesses like Chamunda, Matrikas and others, as well as many lesser divine beings in supporting roles—incarnations or animal vehicles.

In their temple designs, the architects sought to integrate a complex cosmic vision with ideas of a sacred geography—the temple as the cosmos—involving 'directional alignment and geometrical and astronomical coordinates',[17] as well as the dictates of *Vastu Shastra*. They exemplified the Nagara style—tall shikhara towers and other spirals atop inner sanctums evoke the Himalayan abode of the gods. People from all walks of life visited them not just to worship but to also partake in cultural events and to enjoy the bustling life of their capital. 'In the halls of temples, religious texts were recited, and dance and music was performed,' writes Desai. 'The Chandella dramatists composed plays, both mythical and farcical, to be staged during temple festivals.'

Across India, the later centuries of the first millennium CE were an age of new popular-mystical faiths and sects that were distinct from Brahminism. Their roots often lay in the folk beliefs, animistic cults and rituals of peoples either outside or at the margins of the Vedic fold (which may have included the subaltern forebears of the Chandela kings). Mostly disinterested in the Vedic corpus and its sacrificial rituals, these sects emphasized devotion to a personal god, worshipped idols and a vast range of non-Vedic deities, and drew upon stories from texts known as Puranas and *Agamas*. As these folk beliefs coalesced, the adherents clustered into three broad sects—Shaiva, Vaishnava, Shakta-Tantra—and even gained upper-class disciples and patrons who were perhaps breaking away from Buddhism or Vedic Brahminism.

This emerging religiosity, often called Puranic Hinduism, was flexible enough to absorb multiple local deities as forms (or avatars) of their primary gods. While each sect imparted an identity to its members, their actual beliefs and practices displayed much fusion and plurality. The later Chandelas, for instance, subscribed to a faith that fused worship of Shiva with Tantric ideas. These Puranic sects also variously absorbed Vedantic Brahminism—its rituals, texts, caste rules, Advaita thought, etc.—to give rise to what scholars would later call Hinduism. It was this Hinduism, plus some Jainism, that made up the religious landscape of Khajuraho.[18] There was virtually no Buddhism, which by now had receded mostly to eastern India.

The Chandelas suffered the vicissitudes of war often enough, whether against the Chedis of Jabalpur, the Chalukyas of Gujarat or the Rajput king Prithviraj Chauhan of Ajmer. In 1022, the Chandelas successfully rebuffed the formidable raider Mahmud of Ghazni, an event they apparently celebrated by commissioning the grandest Chandela temple of all, the Kandariya Mahadeva. However, nearly two centuries later, in 1202, the Chandelas fell to Qutbuddin Aibak of the Delhi Sultanate and became a vassal state. Thereafter, Chandela power continued to decline and they largely abandoned Khajuraho in the thirteenth century, retreating to their distant and formidable hill fort of Kalinjar, long associated with Shiva in mythology.

The ensuing political irrelevance of Khajuraho may be why its temples were largely ignored by the Turko-Afghan and later the Indo-Muslim kings of the Delhi Sultanate (1206–1526).[19] In 1335, however, the Moroccan traveller Ibn Battuta, who may or may not have visited Khajuraho, wrote about it and mentioned 'temples containing idols which the Muslims have mutilated', though, curiously, no such mutilation is evident in the extant temples. Battuta also mentioned yogis and healers with long clotted hair who apparently cured diseases like leprosy and elephantiasis. Within hundred years or so, long before the Mughals arrived, the great temple town of Khajuraho would drop out of history and memory to be mostly consumed by the forest.

Today, no trace remains of the dense jungle that had enveloped the temples. They've long been replaced by scrubland and agricultural villages, and more distantly, the arid forest of Panna National Park (which I visited one day from Khajuraho and was lucky to spot three tigers and a leopard). Khajuraho seems little changed from my previous visit thirteen years ago. Its population has risen a bit to 28,000, but its child sex ratio (0–6 age) declined from 91 to 89 per cent females between 2001 and 2011. It is rustic as ever: dogs and cattle roam the streets; traffic laws are rarely followed; people honk needlessly and blast loud music at odd hours; men pee on walls all over town; feral pigs rummage piles of refuse. Not a pretty place, but as I stoically remind myself, at least the people are hospitable, seem gainfully employed and the town feels safe for tourists. There are few decent eateries in town and no bars outside the luxury hotels, but nearly every eatery can arrange a quarter or half bottle of any IMFL upon request. One waiter cheerfully tells me, 'No problem sir, this is India!' I nod in happy agreement.

International tourism and globalization have certainly brought about changes. The walls of the hotel where I'm staying are adorned with backpacker-chic images of Che Guevara and Bob Marley. On the roof deck, they play the kind of music I can only call 'Western yoga pop'. I'm tickled to see a cannabis shoot growing in a plant pot. The hotel's young owner and manager, a local man of Thakur descent, met a young Russian tourist seven years ago and married her the previous year. He says with a chuckle that his family went along on the condition that they never get divorced. Both now live in town but spend their summers in Russia. He tells me that his sister's recent marriage set him back by Rs 35 lakh (US $55K), the majority of it being dowry; he disapproves of dowry but yielded after recognizing its entrenched reality in his orthodox Thakur community. He's surprised when I tell him that had they lived in Chandela times, his family may well have received a bride price instead.

The state of Madhya Pradesh has tried to revive some traditions with the annual week-long Khajuraho Dance Festival, whose forty-fourth edition falls during my visit. It is inaugurated by Anandiben Patel, the state governor and former chief minister of Gujarat. Her entourage mercifully arrives only an hour late. The audience waits under a darkening sky, resenting this display of self-importance that seems to me more befitting a Chandela king. Another evening I attend a *Hasya Kavi Sammelan* ('comic poets conference'), which uses both 'standard' and Bundelkhandi Hindi, the latter of which I often miss. Listening to them I wonder about the Chandela sense of humour. Would they have laughed at these jokes?

The Roots of Erotica in Religious Art

The basic idea of fusing sexual and religious imagery has appeared in many parts of the world. Folk religions often evoke new life and rejuvenation through magico-religious symbols and acts. In India, the earliest such surviving imagery dates from the Harappan times, such as the phallic statues of Dholavira.[20] The Mauryan period has turned up many small terracotta plaques, likely used as votive offerings to popular fertility goddesses like Sri. These plaques have symbolic—non-erotic and non-amorous—depictions of male–female unions, believed to be auspicious for fertility and abundance (a similar idea inspires the likely even older iconography of yoni–lingams). But by the start of the Common Era, such plaques had evolved so that they started carrying realistic sensual images, including plainly carved amorous and copulating couples. It's likely that they still served the same votive purposes, perhaps in addition to being decorative objets d'art.

The earliest known fusion of sexual and religious imagery *in stone* in the subcontinent is on Buddhist monuments at Sanchi and Bharhut (second century BCE). Even though these earliest depictions were tame— non-erotic and non-amorous—it's safe to say that the inspiration for them did not come from the sex-negative Buddha. Rather, it arose from the syncretic milieu of the builders and their simultaneous embrace of many folk cults, including of yakshis and Sri, alongside the teachings of the Buddha.

In ensuing centuries, partly influenced by Graeco-Gandharan art, a greater sense of realism and sensualism became more common in monumental stone art. Seemingly secular and worldly themes—such as bacchanalian scenes with drinking, dance and music—began appearing on panels next to evidently religious images. The fertility theme was now evoked using heterosexual couples 'kissing, embracing and [indulging in] other precoital activities'[21]. They also symbolized kama, or desire, which sustains the world. Incrementally, the 'cultic function was superseded by the aesthetic and the sensual'.[22] In the early centuries of the first millennium CE, amorous (but non-coital) couples became an auspicious and decorative motif (*alankara*) on entrances of temples and monasteries of all major religious sects across India.

Clearly, as Desai writes, 'the social climate of the time' must have 'encouraged the use of the erotic motif as a form of embellishment in religious art'.[23] The tastes of the elites shaped this art, but it must also have been continuous with earlier symbols to have resonated with the townsfolk and the peasants who visited these temples. Even as the motif of amorous couples grew more realistic, it would still have signalled to the average visitor a sense of beauty, divine order, abundance, auspiciousness, fertility and propitiatory power. In other words, the sensual images were meant to comfort—not offend or challenge—the sensibilities of the temple-goer. (Curiously, some images we might associate with fertility are rare or non-existent on these temple walls, such as pregnant women, women giving birth or women with babies.)

The earliest sculptures of *copulating* couples appeared on religious monuments in mid-first millennium CE. Though initially small and discreetly placed, they appeared on temples across India, including in Mathura, Gujarat, Mysore, Ajanta, Ellora, Badami, Aihole, Pattadakal, Bhubaneshwar and many other sites. But the size, finesse and centrality of erotic art on temple walls kept growing until it became a wider artistic convention that, not surprisingly, paralleled the rise of Tantrism. All across India after the mid-first millennium, writes Thapar, 'articulation of the erotic is evident in poetry and temple sculpture, perhaps released by the rituals and ideas current in Tantric belief and practice which were being assimilated among the elite.' Representations of these erotic themes are 'striking, whether in the *Gita Govinda* or in the sculptures at Khajuraho'.[24]

According to Desai, the first-known cunnilingus scene on temple art appeared in Aihole in the sixth century; the first bestiality scene in Bhubaneshwar in the eighth century; the first orgiastic scene in Pattadakal in the eighth century. What's striking about Khajuraho's erotic temple art is therefore not the uniqueness of any one of its depictions but their impressive range, number and size, as well as their sensual boldness, artistic finesse, thematic diversity and visual prominence on both outside walls *and* the walls of inner sanctums, the *garbhagriha*. But how did Tantrism impact such depictions of the erotic on temple walls?

To understand what all this explicit sex on temples meant to their creators, we must try and enter their world and imagine it from within. To do this, let's begin with three fairly simple and uncontroversial premises. *First*, the sponsors of explicit erotica on temple walls clearly saw it as compatible with depictions of the divine. *Second*, these temples

Figure 5. Chitragupta Temple panels

were public monuments and places of worship, commissioned by the royals not to shock, outrage or confuse people but to communicate a stable vision of life and to acquire merit, fame and legitimacy. *Third*, since the temples were built over 250 years by multiple kings, this vision wasn't just driven by a small coterie of reformist royals—a revolutionary vanguard determined to broaden people's sexual horizons. Rather, it's safe to assume that the art was an expression of an aesthetic that was already common in the realm and was broadly shared with the legions of sculptors and the wider public. The scale of these monuments meant that vast resources of Chandela society were marshalled for it, involving many classes of people, whose enthusiasm was essential for success.

If we accept these three premises, we can then ask: What were the shared foundations and pillars of this aesthetic? What was the world view that gave rise to these 'ecclesiastical erections', in the memorable words of T.S. Burt?

Sex and the City from Gupta to Chandela Times

Khajuraho's erotica may jive with modern liberal ideas that celebrate sensual desire and youthful bodies, but the cultural milieu of Khajuraho was quite different from our own. To assess its moral qualities, we ought to understand its social and power relationships and the status it afforded its women. While the historical data is patchy and ambiguous, we do have a host of suggestive details.

Khajuraho's culture was evidently sex-positive, certainly among its elites and aristocrats, who were part of a class of Indians that had actively cultivated the art of sex and the sexual escapade since at least Vatsayayana, author of the *Kamasutra*, the most famous of the many treatises on kama, or *ars erotica*, in ancient India. Largely a secular work written centuries before Khajuravahaka, at the start of the Gupta Empire, the *Kamasutra* remained a popular and influential text for a millennium, especially with the urban upper crust. It defends the pursuit of erotic pleasure as a goal in itself, apart from the reproductive purpose of sex. Part Epicurean, write scholars Wendy Doniger and Sudhir Kakar in the introduction to their translation, the *Kamasutra* is about 'the art of living—about finding a partner, maintaining power in a marriage, committing adultery, living as or with a courtesan, using drugs—and also about the positions in sexual intercourse'.[25] It posits 'that pleasure needs to be cultivated, that in the realm of sex, nature requires culture'. It emphasizes grooming, etiquette, diplomacy and even post-coital conversation.

The *Kamasutra* does have a distinctly patriarchal script and many of its suggestions strike modern readers as cringe-inducing, manipulative and retrograde. But it also defends choice, agency and self-cultivation for at least a certain class of women—and a woman as a 'full participant in sexual life, very much a subject in the erotic realm, not a passive recipient of the man's lust'. Not just a manual for men, it also offers advice to maidens, courtesans, wives and mistresses, and sees women as individuals in an exciting social game. 'It is surprisingly sympathetic to women,' write Doniger and Kakar, 'particularly to what they suffer from inadequate husbands.' It is attentive to a woman's 'feelings and emotions that a man needs to understand for the full enjoyment of erotic pleasure', and argues 'that a woman who actively enjoys sex will make it much more enjoyable for him'. Though it's now all but ignored in India, and not seen as an ancient Sanskrit text worth celebrating, write Doniger and Kakar, 'there is nothing remotely like it even today, and for its time, it was astonishingly sophisticated'. Vatsyayana even advances 'the radical notion that the ultimate goal of marriage is to develop love between the couple and thus considers the love-marriage to be the pre-eminent form of marriage'.[26]

Polygamy and adultery had been common in high society across India during the half millennium preceding the Chandelas. 'Kings, noblemen and the wealthy had as many wives as they could afford' and as per their social status, writes Desai. Their wives too had lots of affairs, if on the sly. During royal parties, 'city women and wives of chiefs took [alcoholic] drinks in the company of men and mixed freely with them'. Prostitution was legal and taxed, and the women had 'some legal protection'.[27] The state apparently stipulated 'punishments for various categories of rape', including 'physically branding the rapist'.[28]

Rich, powerful men sought the company of courtesans, who were educated, cultured, upper-class women proficient in the 'sixty-four arts' of refinement, such as music, dance and *ars erotica*. They could choose their clients and apparently 'lived in a special quarter of the city, either independently or financed by the king'—an upscale area visited by the elite, rather than a seedy red-light district. 'Although roundly condemned by the clergy, courtesans were immensely popular and admired, just like modern celebrities.'[29] Many kings and aristocrats kept concubines and took them on 'hunting expeditions, picnics to gardens, water-sports, summer resorts and also to battles'.[30] A man's concubines were sometimes even expected to regale his honoured guests.

Figure 6. Vamana Temple panel

Some aristocrats secretly had sex with maidservants and lusted after other men's wives. Among the Indian male elites in Chandela times, 'extramarital love with a married woman was considered the highest experience of life'. The *Kamasutra*, despite a standard disclaimer to 'never seduce other men's wives' and to guard one's own wives, dedicates one of its seven sections to the artful seduction of other men's wives, using a spectrum of tactics ranging from gentlemanly to thuggish. Desai cites sources to show that kings and feudal chiefs could 'take liberty with wives of subordinates'. In a west Indian province, a man apparently presented his beautiful wives to the king and his ministers as a 'love-gift'.[31]

Kings were often 'described in eulogies and inscriptions as great lovers'. Vatsyayana mentions a kingdom in Gujarat where women apparently turned up at the royal harem on their own, singly or in groups, to volunteer their services to the king. Royal and aristocratic harems often had women from all over India and even Africa and Arabia. 'Sanskrit poets and *Kamashastra* ["science of erotica"] writers take delight in describing the peculiarities of the amorous pleasures of women of different regions.' Lonely women in the harem used sex toys, and in desperate times seduced guards, servants, artisans and men who were sneaked in disguised as women. Just south of Khajuravahaka, in Vidarbha, 'women in the royal harem allowed beautiful village women to enter and stay with them for a fortnight or a month'. The princes of Vidarbha even 'had access to the harems and mated with all wives of their father except their own mother'. In eastern India, Brahmins 'obtained permission to enter the harem with the excuse of offering flowers'. In some cases, even the 'wives of the king helped him in his affairs'. Aphrodisiacs and sex potions were much in demand.[32]

No wonder, adds Desai, 'the art of this sensuous society was suffused with eroticism'. Erotica also appeared on secular objets d'art in their living spaces: on combs, toilet trays, paintings and furniture.[33] Literary poetic works from the second half of the first millennium also abound with sensual love play. Even the non-elites, who subscribed of the new Tantra-infused sects, likely had fewer hang-ups about sex and courtship when compared to their counterparts today. Desai writes that during certain revelries and festivals of fertility, amid wine, song and dance, a wider cross-section of people let their hair down and ignored many traditional restraints on sexual morality.[34] Married women on such occasions were said to pursue opportunities for hanky-panky with strangers, though its actual incidence is uncertain.

Across India and in Khajuraho, big temples kept devadasis ('female servants of god'). A Chandela queen is on record for offering devadasis to a Vishnu temple, though it's not clear how common this was. 'Married' as young girls to specific gods, devadasis learnt the high arts of dancing, singing, music and theatre performed publicly at the temples. They pioneered and innovated many forms of art, such as the dance form Sadir (a precursor to Bharatanatyam). They didn't need to honour caste boundaries, writes Thapar. 'As women they could deny the centrality of procreation, not observe monogamy and have an independent income. Thus they opposed Manu's rules regarding the subservience of women to fathers, husbands and sons.'[35]

Many devadasis however also served as cultured prostitutes to temple priests, officials, pilgrims, patrons and royals. Some inscriptions and texts from across India luridly remark on the sexual charms of devadasis. Could it be, as some scholars have argued, that there was once less public shame, stigma and exploitation associated with this profession than in the centuries closer to us? Many upper-class women were devadasis. If a king desired a married woman, he could work out a deal whereby she would sign up as a temporary devadasi, and he would then enjoy access to her without social disapproval. Some devadasis took long-term partners or said no to prostitution. Some of them even gained wealth and status, though many more surely dealt with sexual predators and lived lives of quiet desperation. Clearly, mere worship wasn't top of mind for everyone associated with temples. Some of the surasundaris on Khajuraho's temple walls are arguably devadasis, sometimes paired with ascetics and royal men and women.

At a macro level, then, Indian high society in the late first millennium CE, including in the Chandela realm, seems built by elite men for elite men. Its most remarkable feature was its immensely sex-positive culture. Women enjoyed a measure of sexual and intellectual freedom—at least enough to pursue whatever it took to be more alluring to elite men, and to use their sensual charms to get ahead in what was still predominantly a feudal patriarchy framed by caste rules.

Chandela Religion and Its Tantric Substrate

The religion that emerged at Khajuraho, writes Desai, was 'a synthesis of two religious orders, Tantric and Puranic, resulting in a Miśra (mixed or composite) religion', which included 'Vedic mantras and caste-order along with the Tantric mode of worship'.[36]

Tantrism started acquiring prominence in north India in mid-first millennium CE, though its roots go back to 'prehistoric concepts of a fertile mother goddess and ancient systems for her worship'. It resisted a precise definition because it never became 'a coherent system' and remained a cluster of ideas and practices with a family resemblance. 'Tantrism' itself is a modern Western term that, like 'Hinduism', is not indigenous to the tradition.

In the late twentieth century, Tantrism entered the New Age culture in the West and got a boost from gurus like Osho. Alas, the dominant idea of Tantrism in the West today—packaged as an exotic regimen to heighten sexual pleasure—is quite reductive. It's a pale shadow of its full expression in ancient India, when it was a lot more than exotic sexual practices.

Most ancient practitioners of Tantra likely recognized what they did 'as different from the Vedic tradition'.[37] But while it was mainly a heterodox system, it fused and coexisted with older norms and beliefs in many Vedic and non-Vedic faiths, such as Shaivism, Vaishnavism, Shaktism, Buddhism and Jainism. In other words, between 500 and 1300 CE, most self-professed Vaishnavites and Shaivites, alongside pursuing many orthodox Brahminical and mystical–devotional practices, also pursued, *along a spectrum*, various Tantric practices. As usual, folk religiosity cared little for the neat boundaries and fine distinctions of theologians. It freely mixed ideas, practices and rituals based largely on their utility towards tangible ends, such as worldly benefits, social bonding, creating purpose and meaning, relief from woes and misfortunes, emotional comfort and justification for their choices, and so on.

What distinguished Tantrism from Brahminism, Buddhism and Jainism? The idea that worldly temptations, cravings and physical desires are impediments to spiritual growth and enlightenment was central to the latter three, so they idealized asceticism and renunciation. At Nalanda, for instance, *kulapati* (householder) was an insult used to chastise a monk whose acts or thoughts deviated from the renunciatory ideal.

Whereas Tantrism, besides valuing non-dualism, spiritual growth and the union of one's atman with Brahman, also valued worldly success. It saw spiritual growth as compatible *and* intertwined with success in love, rather than as opposites. The Tantrics' methods for achieving their goals differed too. In *The Roots of Tantra*, Robert L. Brown writes that Tantric practitioners reach these dual goals 'by connecting themselves to a power that flows through the world, including their own bodies, a power usually visualized as female'. He adds that 'the ultimate tool in Tantra is the human body . . . both the anatomical body of arms, hands, tongue, heart, genitals, and mind, and the yogic anatomy of *cakras* and *nadis*. It is control of the body as a tool used to actuate processes that connect the practitioner with the universal power to reach his goals'.

Or as a modern practitioner in Assam put it, 'Tantra is mind and body together, the whole human being in spiritual practice.'[38] Hindu Tantrics seek to unite two poles of reality, imagined by them as Shiva and Shakti, male and female, both present in every human body. Their union produces absolute bliss and is attained through disciplined kundalini yoga and often with added sexual practices, the goal of which is not hedonism but a higher state of awakening. Other broad characteristics of Tantra include relatively 'less stress on mythology and narrative stories of deities, less stress on love of god [as in devotional Hinduism], less stress on moral action (for Buddhism), [and] less stress on temple worship and priests'.[39]

Alternatively, 'Tantra could be defined as a means of harnessing *kama*', where Kama is seen as a lot more than sexual desire and includes 'longing, love, affection, object of desire, pleasure, enjoyment, sexual love, sensuality'[40] and more. Tantra then 'is the path that seeks to harness, transform, and redirect *kama* toward the aims of both this-worldly power and spiritual liberation'.[41] The mere sating of kama is not the end, but a means to the end of transcending kama itself. 'Not primarily a means to pleasure alone, *kama* is rather a means to awaken and channel the tremendous energy that lies within the body and the cosmos.'[42]

Additionally, according to Paul E. Mueller–Ortega, a modern scholar of Abhinavagupta (950–1016 CE), who was a polymathic Kashmiri Shaivite philosopher known for, among other things, his theory of aesthetics and for being the author of the treatise *Tantraloka*,

Hindu Tantra rejects the dry vistas of traditional philosophical debate, which seek only the representation of the Ultimate [or *Brahman*] through conceptual truths. It rejects as well the self-enclosing renunciation of traditional Indian monasticism, which protectively seeks to isolate the monk from the imagined strain of worldliness. Transcending the dualities and distinctions of conventional thought and morality, the Tantra demonstrates an outward gesture of embracing delight in all of reality. The Tantric hero pushes outward into adventurous, spiritual exploration, into savoring and delighting the experience of so many varieties of blissful *ekarasa*, the unitary taste of consciousness.[43]

Tantric rituals, writes Thapar, were not only 'contrary to Vedic Brahmanism' but often 'a deliberate reversal of upper-caste practice'. Tantra was also 'open to all castes and included women in the rituals ... Goddesses were accorded great veneration [and] the Devi, or the goddess, had an individuality of her own and was worshipped for this rather than merely as a consort of a god'. This, claims Thapar, didn't sit well with Brahminical patriarchy, or the fact that 'women were permitted to establish their own *ashramas*, to act as priestesses and to teach'. As for upper-caste practices like sati, the *Mahanirvana Tantra* declares that, 'A wife should not be burnt with her dead husband. Every woman is the embodiment of the goddess. That woman who in her delusion ascends the funeral pyre of her husband, shall go to hell.'[44] This Tantric substrate was partly fed by emerging subaltern groups and 'sections of society that had hardly known the Hinduism formulated by the Brahmans'. If the Chandelas did have a subaltern lineage, that would only have raised their psychological affinity for Tantra. Thapar adds:

> Those desirous of joining a Tantric sect had to be initiated by a guru. Tantric ritual involved the ritual partaking of the five Ms—*madya*, alcohol, *matsya*, fish, *mamsa*, flesh, *mudra*, gestures, and *maithuna*, coition. In the final state of purification everything and everyone was equal. The ritual being what it was, secret meetings became necessary, especially when some other sects denounced its practices as being depraved. Gradually there was a bifurcation into the Left-Hand path that experimented with these practices, and the Right-Hand path that restricted itself to yoga and *bhakti*. Although Tantrism has often been condemned for its more extreme activities, it seems also to have been a vehicle for opposition to the Brahmanical ordering of society.[45]

Despite their similar world-affirming beliefs and emphasis on pleasure and success in life, the Tantrics also differed from the materialist Carvakas. The Tantrics worshipped (frequently female) deities, had magical rituals and practised yoga and meditation. However, as part of their non-dualistic world view, they strived to break down the walls of social convention, often through transgressive practices. They were religious but tended to oppose both caste and patriarchy. So, in some ways, despite their differences, moderate Tantrics may have got along well enough with the Carvakas.

Tantra also had many sects with differing beliefs and methods: Pashupata, Kaula, Kalamukha, Nathapanthi, Siddhanta, Sahajiya, Ganapatya, Kapalika, etc. They differed on many fronts: being less or more ritualistic, less or more invested in magic and alchemy, less or more into sexual–yogic practices, less or more permissive about drink and meat, and so on. One might as well classify them as *mild, moderate* and *extreme*.

In *mild* forms, spanning goddess worship and meditative practices, Tantric ideas broadly pervaded all Hindu, Buddhist and Jain sects. A *moderate* Tantric sect was the Shaiva Siddhanta, whose deity Sadasiva, a form of Shiva, was eminent at Khajuraho and appears often on its temple walls. Moderate Tantrics socially interacted with and lived among the masses. Shaiva Kapalika (*kapala* means 'skull') was an *extreme* Tantric sect, whose members lived aloof and solitary lives, hated Brahmins and habitually used a Brahmin's empty skull as an eating or begging bowl. No wonder the Brahmins hated them back. The Kapalikas pursued 'practices associated with cremation-grounds and polluting substances linked to sex and death',[46] as well as ritual transgressions, animal sacrifices (perhaps even human sacrifices), consumption of meat, intoxicants, ingesting sexual fluids and more (the modern sect of Aghori sadhus is believed to have descended from the Kapalikas). These extreme sects were seen as antisocial sorcerers and libertines and were usually feared and despised.

Since most Tantric sects associated sex with magical power, Tantric gurus attracted wealthy and royal acolytes, who were drawn to their supposedly superhuman abilities to confer sexual vigour and youth through their 'knowledge of alchemy,

Figure 7. Vishwanath Temple panel

aphrodisiacs and magical *mantras* for mastery over women'.[47] In theory, Tantric sexual practices had higher spiritual ends but many pleasure-loving aristocrats—and their obliging gurus—reduced it to mere hedonism (not unlike how it's popularly presented in the US today). Crooks grew rich and powerful by posing as Tantric teachers and fooling the superstitious. According to Desai, the moderate Tantric sects of Vaishnava Siddhanta and Shaiva Siddhanta 'spread Tantric practices among the aristocracy and the royal class who were responsible for the building of temples' in Khajuraho. Some Tantrics became advisers to kings and were 'given the highest positions in the temple-organization in many places of India'. In Khajuraho's temple sculptures, Desai adds, the 'completely shaven or bearded and long-haired ascetics' appearing often in orgiastic groups with royal personages 'are, without doubt, Tantrikas'.[48]

In other words, Tantra differed a lot from other dominant streams of religious thought in India. It was the pervasive presence of this substrate in both popular and elite cultures that fertilized the soil for the creation of erotic temple art in Khajuraho and other parts of India.

Fusing Erotic with the Religious

To recap, Tantra mostly had subaltern, non-Vedic roots and was associated with fertility cults, amorous motifs and symbols, magic and alchemy, sexo-yogic practices, and a higher status for women. Across India from the mid-first millennium CE, princes, state officials, landed aristocrats, wealthy merchants, clergy, artists and others began embracing new sects that mixed Tantra with Puranic beliefs.

Tantra soon furnished, or at least amplified, a world view in which sex and religion were not divergent pursuits. In Tantra, *sex was a path to the divine* (or Brahman). Its magical use of sex to propitiate the gods became a shortcut to moksha—competing directly with the moksha of orthodox Hindus and Buddhists that required the renouncing of sex. Tantra effectively normalized the idea of yogis, acharyas, and ascetics—male and female—restlessly fiddling with their erogenous zones to attain 'union with the divine' (never mind that many were likely just having a jolly good time).

The temple-building elites seamlessly fused the magico-religious aspects of Tantric sex with their sex-positive culture. Tantra's appeal and symbols, alongside Puranic beliefs, already ran deep with the masses. In this milieu, far from being dissonant, erotica and temple walls would have seemed naturally harmonious. The result: erotic art on temple walls.

Desai, however, clarifies that for the most part, this erotic art doesn't directly show Tantric sexual rituals, which were meant to be secretive; it is art influenced by Tantra but without much functional relation to it. 'A further consequence of Tantra,' she adds, was an 'attitude of permissiveness towards sex' and a 'veneration of sex in religious life in contrast to the condemnatory attitude of orthodox Hindu and early Buddhist traditions'.[49]

Once it began, other mundane factors likely drove more erotica on temple walls. For one, sex likely brought out the numbers. Temples competed with each other for visitors, prestige and funds, so they stood to gain by literally amping up their sex appeal. An Orissan *Shilpa Shastra* text of the day, a canon of architecture, seems to recognize that religion was also entertainment, and it mentions the use of sexual depictions in temple art for the 'delight of the people'.[50] Once Tantra normalized the mixing of sex with religion, how hard would it have been to conclude that having more sexual images was the way to delight more people? As a popular art motif, it also likely fuelled competition among sculptors to create more playful, enticing or even

Figure 8. Devi Jagadambi Temple sculpture

transgressive scenes: exhibitionism, masturbation, homosexuality, orgies, bestiality, etc. It's likely that stories and symbols now lost to us may have informed many of these depictions. But why do we tend to seek only pure, lofty or spiritual motives in our ancestors' expressions of popular culture when it's something we wisely avoid doing for our own?

Why Did the Erotica Disappear from Temple Walls?

Throughout the first millennium, the erotic and the celibate had been two conflicting yet coexisting ideals in Indian religiosity. In Chandela times, Tantra upheld the erotic while coexisting with the celibate ideals of devotional and Brahminical Hinduism. After Adi Shankara (eighth century), Hinduism's shift towards more sexually puritanical and patriarchal modes only increased—largely due to internal fault lines and religious developments *within* Hinduism.

Khajuraho was very much a centre of these developments, evident in the Chandela court play, *Prabodhachandrodaya* ('moon rise of true knowledge'), a philosophical allegory in six acts written by Krishna Mishra. Staged in 1065 CE, the play, set in Varanasi, defends the Advaita doctrine and Vishnu Bhakti via a contest between the noble king Viveka ('Discrimination') and the wicked king Mahamoha ('Delusion'). In the play, writes Desai, 'the forces of orthodox religion based on Vedic order unite to re-establish the ancient order against those non-Vedic heretical forces which had earlier gained ascendancy'. It rails against the extreme Kapalika Tantrics, Jain and Buddhist mendicants, materialist–*nastika* Carvakas and other anti-Vedic sects. Desai cites evidence to show that this basic conflict played out in art and literature in many parts of India across multiple centuries from Gupta to Chandela times.[51]

In parallel, Bhakti advanced among the masses at the expense of the Tantric substrate. Bhakti espoused devotion and surrender of the self to a personal god, *contempt for worldly pleasures*, and distrust in priestly rituals. It partly shared with the Tantric substrate its anti-caste, anti-ritual and female-friendly impulses—evident later in activist saints like Namdev, Janabai, Ravidas, Kabir and Tukaram, but who also differed greatly from the pleasure-affirming Tantric acharyas of the Chandela times. Bhakti's path to liberation was paved with chaste devotion, not yogic sex. In time, Bhakti helped decimate the sex-positive culture of Tantra.

In other words, a profound shift was occurring in the Indian religious market that revived Brahminism and fuelled the Bhakti movement, both of which are sexually puritanical strains of faith. This churn and puritanical shift in Hinduism began long before the coming of Islam which, arguably, only hastened the trend. Indeed, in terms of sexual puritanism, orthodox Brahminism and Bhakti were brothers under the skin with orthodox Islam and Sufism, respectively.

Consequently, by 1400 CE or so, big temples across India almost stopped placing erotic art on their walls—a very visible link between sex and religion had been broken. The very role and function of temples in public life began changing, partly also as their wealth and patronage declined under the Indo-Muslim rule. As temples leaned more on ordinary people for their survival, they started becoming mere sites of worship. But that wasn't all; other deep cultural changes were also afoot. Fewer and fewer Hindus now read the *Kamasutra*, had casual sexual escapades, wrote erotic poetry or married out of caste. The purpose of sex became more closely aligned with procreation, as the Manusmriti advocated in the early first century CE. Control of women's sexuality increased, not the least to preserve the sanctity of caste. While the status of women in Chandela times wasn't great by twenty-first century yardsticks, it arguably worsened from then on. Much of this conservative turn was led by forces indigenous to Hinduism.[52]

The masses flocked to the devotional ecstasies of Tulsidas, Surdas, Mirabai, Eknath and Chaitanya Mahaprabhu. Tantra began receding to the fringe, where it survives to this day. With its shrinking, Hindu culture too changed significantly, eventually producing men like Vivekananda, who proclaimed Sita as the ideal Hindu woman, and Gandhi, with his famous hang-ups about sex. This profound cultural change is why Hindus now find it hard to relate to the world view that inspired Khajuraho's art. That's why powerful Hindu groups now harass urban young women who date men or go to bars. That's also why they hounded out M.F. Husain for painting naked Hindu goddesses and Doniger for her book cover showing Lord Krishna sitting on the 'buttocks of a naked

woman surrounded by other naked women'.[53] Such prudery would have
drawn amused laughter from the average Chandela aristocrat.

Two responses dominate today: On the one hand, Hindu
conservatives see nothing wrong with the powerful strain of sexual
prudery in Indian society, taking it not only as good but as the very
essence of Sanatan Dharma. They usually blame 'Western culture' for
the more permissive sexual mores around them. Rather than trying
to understand how Hindu India once had a robust 'appreciation of
eroticism', they are far more invested in maintaining 'that Hinduism
was always the pure-minded, anti-erotic, ascetic tradition' they now
subscribe to.[54] On the other hand, Hindu liberals, few as they are, feel
pride in a past that produced the *Kamasutra* and Khajuraho, scratch
their heads and wonder what caused this dramatic cultural shift. They
usually blame it on the coming of Islam and the puritanical Protestantism
of Europeans.

Doniger reminds us, 'Blaming the Muslims and the British ignores
the history of native Hindu anti-eroticism. For, as we have seen, India
had its own home-grown traditions of prudery [that predate them both]
in opposition to its own sensuality.'[55] In an interview, Kakar accepts
that both Muslim and British rule had a role to play, 'but the more
fundamental factor in the rejection of the erotic has to be looked for
within the Hindu culture itself'. He adds:

It is the ascetic tradition in Hinduism that is the real counterforce
which undermined the Kamasutra legacy. The duality of
eroticism vs asceticism dialectic has been always a part of Hindu
culture. The one or the other might become dominant in a
particular period of history though the other is never submerged.
[When] the Kamasutra was composed there were other texts
holding fast to the ascetic ideal and extolling the virtues of
celibacy for spiritual progress. The ascetic ideal, that can
degenerate into puritanism, is then also quintessentially Indian,
perennially in competition with the erotic one for possession
of the Indian soul. It is very unlikely that ancient Indians
were ever, or even could be, as unswerving in their pursuit of
pleasure as, for instance, ancient Romans. That India has been

a sexual wasteland for the last two centuries is then due to a combination of British prudery, adopted by the upper classes in what may be called an 'identification with the aggressor', and our own deep-seated strain of Brahminical asceticism . . .[56]

As Doniger and others have pointed out, the reconstruction of India's past by Europeans has profoundly shaped Hindu self-knowledge. Modern Hindus began understanding their history and culture through the colonizer's eyes, using the latter's concepts, categories and judgements. Meanwhile, British orientalists—with their Victorian values, Christian sexual morality and Brahminical native informants—valorized the indigenous strains of sexual prudery in Hinduism, at whose heart they placed the most austere of Vedantic ideas and texts like the Bhagavad Gita and Manusmriti, demoting and devaluing so many other strands of folk spirituality and religious practices, including Tantrism.[57] They emphasized only a small part of the Indian story.

On my final afternoon, I overhear a newly-arrived American tourist exclaim at a temple, 'Holy shit! WTF is going on here?' He has hired a tour guide and I feel sorry for him. I grab a beer at a cafe with a view of the temples and ponder how, if I were a guide, would I convey that the erotic art of Khajuraho is a brilliant chapter in the history of Indian art and sculpture, and ought to be a perennial reminder to not buy into simplistic narratives about our past or the present.

Marco Polo's India
(1292 CE)

Returning home from China in 1292 CE, Marco Polo arrives on the Coromandel Coast of India in a typical merchant ship with over sixty cabins and up to 300 crewmen.[1] He enters the kingdom of the Tamil Pandyas near modern Thanjavur, where, according to custom, 'the king and his barons and everyone else all sit on the earth'. He asks why they 'do not seat themselves more honorably'. The king replies, 'To sit on the earth is honorable enough, because we were made from the earth and to the earth we must return.' Marco Polo documented this episode in his famous book, *The Travels*, as part of his rich social portrait of coastal India.[2]

The climate is so hot that all men and women wear nothing but a loincloth, including the king—except his is studded with rubies, sapphires, emeralds and other gems. Marco calls this 'the richest and most splendid province in the world', one that, together with Ceylon, produces 'most of the pearls and gems that are to be found in the world'. Merchants and traders abound, the king takes pride in not holding himself above the law of the land and people travel the highways safely with their valuables in the cool of the night air. In this kingdom, justice 'is very strictly administered to those who commit homicide or theft or any other crime'.

The sole local grain produced here is rice, claims Marco. People use only their right hand for eating, saving the left for sundry 'unclean' tasks. They drink fluids 'out of flasks, each from his own; for no one would drink out of another's flask'. Nor do they set the flask to their lips, preferring to 'hold it above and pour the fluid into their mouths'. They are addicted to chewing a leaf called tambur, sometimes mixing it with 'camphor and other spices and lime'. They go about spitting freely—also using it to express serious offense by targeting the spittle at another's face, which can sometimes provoke violent clan fights.

They 'pay more attention to augury than any other people in the world and are skilled in distinguishing good omens from bad'. They rely on the counsel of astrologers and have enchanters called Brahmins, who are 'expert in incantations against all sorts of beasts and birds'. For instance, they protect the oyster divers 'against predatory fish by means of incantations' and for this service receive one in twenty pearls the divers extract from the sea. Each day, people refrain from doing business during a preordained unlucky hour that differs across days of the week.

People 'worship the ox' and do not eat beef—except the *gavi*, a group of people with low social status, who 'eat cattle when they die a natural death' and are not admitted inside holy places. Marco also records a custom among some people in which a dead man's wife 'flings herself into the same fire and lets herself be burnt with her husband. The ladies who do this are highly praised by all'. People daub their houses with cow dung. In battle they use lance and shield and, according to Marco, are 'not men of any valor or spirit' and 'kill no beasts or any living thing. When they have a mind to eat the flesh of a sheep or of any beast or bird, they employ a Saracen [Muslim] or some other who is not of their religion or rule to kill it for them'. Most do not consume any alcohol, and do 'not admit as a witness or a guarantor either a wine drinker or one who sails on the sea'. They say that 'a man who goes to sea must be a man in despair'. Marco observes that people 'do not regard any form of sexual indulgence as a sin'.

Their temple monasteries have both male and female deities, prone to being cross with each other, when they also 'refrain from [sexual] intercourse'. The priests know when this happens, and since estranged deities spell nothing but trouble in the human realm, bevies of spinsters gather there several times each month with 'tasty dishes of meat and other food'. They 'sing and dance and afford the merriest sport in the world', leaping, tumbling, raising their legs to their necks and pirouetting to delight the deities. After the 'spirit of the idols has eaten the substance of the food', they 'eat together with great mirth and jollity'. Pleasantly disposed by the evening showbiz, the gods and goddesses descend from the temple walls at night and 'consort' with each other—or so the priest announces the next morning—bringing great joy and relief to all. 'The flesh of these maidens,' Marco adds salaciously, 'is so hard that no one could grasp or pinch them in any place . . . their breasts do not hang down, but remain upstanding and erect.' For a penny, however, 'they will allow a man to pinch [their bodies] as hard as he can'. Marco doesn't say how common this custom was, or whether he himself partook in it.

Dark skin is preferred by the people. 'When a child is born they anoint him once a week with oil of sesame, and this makes him grow much darker [for] I assure you that the darkest man here is the most highly esteemed and considered better than the others who are not so dark.' No wonder their gods are all black 'and their devils white as snow'. This detail is interesting though sesame oil, while beneficial for the skin, doesn't really darken it; perhaps Marco confused it with another oil. It is also worth noting that a higher value for lighter skin— correlated with the higher varnas and castes that emerged after the Indo-Aryan migration—doesn't seem to have penetrated folk culture this far south. But cultural standards have long since changed, as evidenced by all the 'Fair & Lovely' fairness cream ads in the same regions today.

A group of their holy men, the yogis, eat frugally and live longer than most, some as long as 200 years, claims Marco. In one religious order, men even go stark naked and 'lead a harsh and austere life'. These men believe that all living beings have a soul and take pains to avoid hurting even the tiniest creatures. They take their food over large dried leaves. When asked why they do not cover their private parts, they say, 'We go naked because we want nothing of this world. For we came into this world naked and unclothed . . . It is because you employ this member in sin and lechery that you cover it and are ashamed of it. But we are no more ashamed of it than of our fingers.' Among them, only those who can conquer sexual desire become monks. 'So strict are these idolaters and so stubborn in their misbelief,' opines Marco.

The king, however, aspires to a different standard. He has 500 wives and concubines, and 'whenever he sets eye on a beautiful woman or damsel, he takes her for himself'. Even then, he covets a beautiful wife of his brother—who rules a nearby kingdom and also keeps many wives—and one day succeeds in 'ravishing her from him and keeping her for himself'. Naturally, war looms between the brothers, as it has many times before. Once again, their mother intervenes, knife in hand and pointing at her breasts, 'If you fight with each other, I will cut off these breasts which gave you both suck.' Her emotional blackmail succeeds once again; the brother who has lost one of his wives swallows his pride and war is averted. But it is only a matter of time, thinks Marco, before the mother is dead and the brothers destroy each other.

The region breeds no horses but imports them from Aden and beyond. Over 2000 steeds arrive on ships each year but, within a year, all but 100 die 'due to ill usage' and lack of horse-handling knowledge. Marco believes that foreign merchants 'do not send out any veterinaries or allow any to go, because they are only too glad for many of the horses to die in the king's charge'. Further north, in a little town near modern Chennai, is the tomb of St Thomas the Apostle, a place of pilgrimage for both the Christians and Muslims of the region. It's likely that Marco also visited Mamallapuram. He marked its location on the map he carried but didn't write about it.[3]

A few hundred miles north is the port of Motupalli, writes Marco. It's part of a kingdom 'ruled by a queen, who is a very wise woman'. Throughout 'her forty years' reign she has governed her kingdom well with a high standard of justice and equity'. Never was a 'lady or lord so well beloved as she is by her subjects'. Marco is talking about Rudrama Devi of the Kakatiya Dynasty of Warangal in modern Telangana. This kingdom, he writes, is a huge producer of diamonds and buckram cotton of 'the finest texture and the highest value' and people here live on 'rice, flesh, milk, fish and fruit'.

After the eastern Coromandel Coast, Marco sails up the western Malabar Coast, but his observations here are sparse. He speaks about Quilon (Kollam), which has 'some Christians and Jews'. The people 'make wine out of [dates], and a very good drink it is, and makes a man drunk sooner than grape wine'. Skilled astrologers abound, as do physicians, 'adept at preserving the human body in health'. Marco also makes cursory remarks about Camorin and Kannur.

Of the flora and fauna on the Malabar Coast, Marco says, 'Everything there is different from what it is with us and excels both in size and beauty . . . lions, leopards, and lynxes abound, as do peacocks and scarlet and blue parrots of which there is no lovelier sight in the world.' Some monkeys in the region have 'such distinctive appearance that you might take them for men'.

He notes pepper and indigo plantations, incense, a date wine that is 'a very good drink'. Further north in Gujarat, workshops make cotton and leather goods, shiploads of which go west every year. With such precious cargo plying the sea, piracy too operates on a large scale. In Aden, the cargo is transferred to smaller ships and carried via rivers and camels to the Nile and downriver to Alexandria and beyond. These goods include cushions and 'handsome mats of scarlet leather, embossed with birds and beasts and stitched with gold and silver . . . of more consummate workmanship than anywhere in the world . . . so exquisite that they are a marvel to behold'. Marco visits Cambay and the 'kingdom of Somnath', where people 'live by trade and industry, as honest folk ought to do'. This more or less ends Marco's travels in India spanning multiple months.

Other travellers in the next two centuries would help create a richer portrait of the Malabar Coast. These include a diverse lot: Ibn Battuta of Morocco, Ma Huan of China, Abdur Razzaq of Persia, Niccolò de' Conti of Italy and Afanasy Nikitin of Russia. In 'the Malabar lands,' Ibn Battuta writes in the 1340s, there are twelve infidel kings (i.e., not Muslim, Christian or Jew), 'some of them strong with armies numbering fifty thousand men, and others weak with armies of three thousand. Yet there is no discord [whatsoever] between them, and the strong does not desire to seize the possessions of the weak'.[4] Battuta notes that the entire road from Goa to Kollam,

> runs beneath the shade of trees, and at every half mile there is a wooden shed with benches on which all travellers, whether Muslims or infidels, may sit. At each shed there is a well for drinking and an infidel who is incharge of it. If the traveller is

an infidel he gives him water in vessels; if he is a Muslim, he pours the water into his hands . . . It is the custom of the infidels in the Malabar lands that no Muslim may enter their houses or eat from their vessels; if he does so they break the vessels or give them to the Muslims. [Fortunately,] on this road there are houses belonging to Muslims, at which Muslim travellers alight, and where they buy all that they need. Were it not for them, no Muslim could travel by it.

Battuta comes to Calicut in a trading vessel. He calls it 'one of the largest harbours in the world . . . visited by men from China, Sumatra, Ceylon, the Maldives, Yemen, and Fars [Persia], and in it gather merchants from all quarters'. His shipmates receive a rousing welcome by the ruling Zamorin, with drums, trumpets and bugles, and he stays as the king's guest.

There were so many Arab merchants in Calicut that Ma Huan 'believed its entire population to be Muslim'.[5] There was also a strong resident community of Muslims, known as Mappilas, who spoke Malayalam (Muslims had been living here since at least the ninth century). Battuta describes the huge Chinese ships in the Calicut harbour, some with four decks, big cabins with chambers and lavatory, and able to carry a thousand men. Prominent merchants often travelled with their 'slave girls and wives'. At this time, the Chinese controlled all the shipping to and from China, using their own giant ships. Battuta remarks, 'There is no people in the world wealthier than the Chinese.'

A century later in 1443 CE, Abdur Razzaq visits Calicut and also reports that all men here, king and beggar alike, wear only loincloths. 'The people of Calicut are brave seafarers,' he writes. Their ships 'go to Mecca, mostly carrying pepper'. 'They venerate cows to such an extent that they rub the ashes of its dung on their foreheads' and 'if anyone kills a cow and is found out, that person is immediately put to death'. Razzaq also reports the prevalence of a matrilineal system with polyandry. When the king dies, 'his sister's son takes his place, and [the kingship] is not given to son, brother or other relative'. The king comes from a 'tribe whose women have multiple husbands, each of whom has a specific task to perform. They divide the day and night, and each one goes to the [wife's] quarters at a specified time. So long as [one husband] is there, no other can go in'.[6] Ibn Battuta also recognizes something of this custom in his writing, 'The rulers in these lands transmit their sovereignty to their sister's sons, to the exclusion of their own children.' Even the Mappila Muslims of Malabar practised matrilineal inheritance.[7]

Afanasy Nikitin visits c. 1470 and confirms the common male attire, adding, 'Women walk about with their heads uncovered and their breasts bare. Boys and girls go naked till seven years, and do not hide their shame.' In Calicut, he writes, 'there is a Muslim population resident, with two congregational mosques, and on Fridays they pray with peace of mind'. Nikitin also adds a detail that is at variance with Battuta's. He writes, 'It is the custom for foreign traders to stop at inns; there the food is cooked for the guests by the landlady, who also makes the bed and sleeps with the stranger. Women that know you willingly concede their favours, for they like white men.'

It later emerged that the only translation of Nikitin's account into English by Count Wielhorski had left untranslated certain salacious details from Nikitin, which add more context to the above remark: 'In India women are obtained by contract and they are cheap; you can have intercourse for two sitel. For four *fun* [a currency unit?] you can get a pretty one; for five [*fun*]—a pretty negress, all black with small and pretty nipples.'[8] Wielhorski also censored Nikitin's mention of his conversion to Islam. Whether Nikitin was seen as a Muslim in India is unclear but he too confirms the Hindu horror of 'impure' Muslims: 'They take care that Mahommedans do not look into their [cooking] pot, nor see their food, and should this happen they will not eat it; some, therefore, hide themselves under a linen cloth lest they should be seen when eating.'[9]

Making Sense of Marco Polo

What kind of a man was Marco Polo? Raised in the cosmopolitan and mercantile city state of Venice, Marco embraced something of its spirit and brought a merchant's pragmatic eye to bear on the world. His father and uncle—both enterprising merchants of Venice who accompanied him on his famous journey but left no records of their own—were early role models. When Marco began this journey, he was only seventeen.

He returned in his late thirties and a few years later, in 1298 CE, teamed up with a romance writer, Rustichello of Pisa, to tell his story—a vast panorama of countries largely unknown to his fellow Venetians. As his translator, Ronald Latham, says:

> Persians, Turks, Tartars, Chinese, Tibetans, Indians, and a score of others defile before us, not indeed revealed in their inner thoughts and feelings, but faithfully portrayed in all such particulars as might meet the eye of an observant traveler, from the oddities of their physical features or dress to the multiplicity of strange customs by which they regulated their lives from the cradle to the grave.

Marco was supremely inquisitive, attentive to a region's geography and natural resources, birds and beasts, climate and flora, foods and drinks. He was also drawn to the local arts and crafts, and assessed their commercial value for fellow Venetians. In Marco's day, cultures were classified by religion, and so arriving in a new place, he described the locals simply as Christians, Jews, Saracens (Muslims) or 'idolaters' (catchall for Tartars, Buddhists, Hindus, Jains and others). He admired hard-working, law-abiding people, and criticized indolent, unruly ones. There are hardly any personal incidents in the book. What makes his account truly worthwhile are his vignettes of social life, such as how the Tartars pitch their tents or go to war, how some Central Asians extract musk from gazelles, how a girl's virginity in Cathay is verified before marriage, why men in a Tibetan province prefer to take as wives women with lots of prior sexual experience, or how the Great Khan's 'admirably contrived' postal service works.

Marco was no scholar, however, and had scant interest in history, philosophy or language (unlike, say, Alberuni, the Persian traveller to India in the early eleventh century). Marco was a pious Christian and admired other cross-cultural expressions of piety. He believed in magic, incantations and the power of astrologers to 'bring on tempests and thunderstorms when they wish and stop them at any time'. He uses superlatives too readily and is prone to wild exaggeration (for example, he claims the city of Hangzhou has 12,000 bridges, the Great Khan goes hunting with 10,000 falconers, and every tree on the 7448 islands in the China Sea gives off 'a powerful and agreeable fragrance'). He was gullible too, lending credence to hearsay about giant birds that lift up elephants, men with tails as thick as a dog's and a legendary Christian king of Asia called Prester John (were some of these Rustichello's embellishments?). He could also be very naive about human relationships, relying too much on surface appearances. For instance, he claims that the multiple wives of Tartar chieftains live together happily, with no conflict whatsoever.

In Ceylon, he relates the story of the Buddha with admiration, adding that 'had he been Christian, he would have been a great saint with our Lord Jesus Christ'. While largely tolerant towards idolaters, particularly those with a developed material culture, he betrays a garden-variety prejudice against Muslims, best assessed in light of a post-Crusades Christendom. For instance, he deems Christians 'far more valiant than Saracens'. Taking sides in a conflict, he declares that 'it is not fitting that Saracen dogs should lord it over Christians'. But these and other expressions of contempt—the 'quite repulsive' women of Zanzibar, Tartars who live like 'brute beasts' because they smear food on the mouth of their gods, Indians being 'paltry creatures and mean spirited'—are vastly outnumbered by expressions of admiration, fair-mindedness and wonder. He likely had no role models in his writing and the result such as it is, warts and all, is nothing short of enthralling.

Marco Polo spent many months, perhaps the better part of a year, in India. Barring a few cursory mentions of inland areas, his account of India is limited to the coastal belt and ends with this tantalizing remark, 'Of the inland regions I have told you nothing; for the tale will be too long in the telling.' We would have happily read on, Marco.

The Innovations of **Vijayanagar at Hampi**
(c. 1336–1565 CE)

Like many children of my generation, I too had read illustrated stories of the great king of Vijayanagar, Krishnadevaraya, and his clever adviser, Tenali Raman (south Indian counterparts to Akbar and Birbal). In one episode, Raman detects thieves inside his house and fools them into 'overhearing' that his treasure lies in a trunk in his well. The thieves go looking for it and end up extracting water all night only to nourish his fields. In these stories, Raman, using his peerless wit and ingenuity, outsmarts the crooks and saves the day, while also imparting practical wisdom. I loved these stories, though 'woke' adults might question some of them today.

Years later, in 2005, I visited Hampi in northern Karnataka, where lie the stunningly evocative ruins of Vijayanagar city, the capital of Vijayanagar Empire. Between its founding in c. 1336 and sacking in 1565, the city rose to become a great metropolis famed for its wealth, military prowess and cosmopolitanism, especially during the reign of Krishnadevaraya, a great military commander and patron of the arts and culture. For long stretches in this period, Vijayanagar Empire held nearly all of the land south of the Krishna River, ruling over about 25 million people (the subcontinent then had about 150 million).

I visited again in late 2018, arriving by an overnight train from Bengaluru to Hospet. According to Domingo Paes, who visited in the early sixteenth century, Hospet, then Nagalapur, was a new satellite city

175

built by Krishnadevaraya for his favourite wife, who had also been his lover in his youth when she was a courtesan. This new city lay within a fortified wall of stone, the outermost of the seven walls to be built around Vijayanagar. All visitors from the western side passed a gateway here, continuing to Vijayanagar on a wide, tree-lined road with houses and shops where, wrote one European visitor, they sold 'everything'.[1] Medieval Nagalapur and its walls and gateway are no more. Hospet is now yet another dusty, noisy small Indian city struggling with ill-planned urban growth and traffic congestion.

The first morning in Hospet, I catch a city bus from near my hotel to Hampi, 13 km and forty minutes away. As elsewhere in south India, I notice women in much higher proportions in the bus and in other public spaces compared to northern cities. They often have fresh flowers in their braids, a custom noticed by travellers even in Vijayanagar times. We pass many villages and stretches of lovely green vistas of coconut and banana plantations, sugarcane fields and rice paddies. We cross the ruins of a few Vijayanagar-era shrines and mandapas and a large reservoir that once supplied water to the imperial city and is still in use. We then reach the tourist village of Kamalapur, close to the ruins at Hampi and home to yet another ASI site museum that prevents tourists from taking photos of its artefacts for no good reason.

Even in its ruined state, Vijayanagar is overwhelming. It's spread over 30 sq. km of a dazzling, boulder-strewn landscape south of the languid Tungabhadra River, whose wildness was tamed by a mega dam upriver, near Hospet. A wide range of stone buildings survive in various stages of repair in two primary zones: a northern Sacred Centre and a southern 'urban core', the latter largely residential and including the Royal Centre. Both zones, with all of the blockbuster sites frequented by tourists, have numerous thick walls, gateways and watchtowers. Between the two zones was, and still is, an agricultural zone, fed by a canal that's still in use.

The Sacred Centre abounds in temples and shrines, many adjacent to former bazaars and pavilions. These include the Virupaksha Temple, Vitthala Temple, Krishna Temple, Achyutaraya Temple and more. The 'urban core' has palaces, audience halls and homes of people who lived in stone dwellings (the rest lived elsewhere in homes made of perishable materials). It has the baths of elite residents as well as tanks and aqueducts. Prominent sites are the Queen's Bath and the Mahanavami Platform. Smaller religious sites exist too, including the Hazara Rama Temple and a couple of mosques. Military barracks and stables also appear in the 'urban core'.

I soon realize that the best way to experience Vijayanagar is to wander its sprawling ruins all day, beyond the tourist hotspots, armed with a water bottle, a map and guidebooks (avoiding those 'heritage pride' books that uncritically glorify its past while hiding unsavoury details[2]). The site requires much patience and study. One must linger there for days and get lost a few times before it yields itself more fully to the visitor. It then reveals new meanings and stories in its sculptures and layout, illuminating in the mind's eye the city in its heyday: its public spaces, social lives, ideas of order and beauty.

As I explore Vijayanagar's fortifications—and the concentric stone walls around its royal centre—I begin to imagine the threat of war its residents must have felt. Seeing its network of canals and tanks, I begin to see how it became a city of gardens and orchards. It is one thing to read that Vijayanagar was the sacred and commercial hub of the empire,

Figure 1. End of the Hampi Bazaar, across Virupaksha Temple

quite another to absorb the sheer number and scale of its temples and the bazaars around them, lining long streets with single and double-storeyed stone pavilions, often with beautifully carved columns.

Indeed, the people of Vijayanagar were, above all, builders par excellence. Construction work must have employed large numbers. I imagine labourers, masons and sculptors doing the hard, back-breaking work of quarrying, moving, cutting, shaping and raising stones with the basic technologies of the day: chisel and hammer, ropes and ramps, human and animal muscle. Countless must have died in accidents. Fortunately, they didn't have to fetch stones from very far—their landscape had heaps of multihued granite boulders, which, according to geologists are among the oldest exposed rocks in the subcontinent. The city they built seemed to have dazzled all those who visited—as it does even today.

North of the river from Hampi, near the Anegundi village, are prehistoric megalithic burial sites, indicating that burials were once common here. There's also cave art from 3000 years ago, though its artists remain obscure. By the seventh century CE, a local cult had arisen, centred on a river goddess, Pampa—from which, via Kannada *Hampe*,

Figure 2. Virupaksha Temple

derives 'Hampi'— whose husband was a god, Virupaskha. By the twelfth century, a temple to them had appeared with a settlement around it. Like many other village deities in the subcontinent, Pampa and Virupaksha got absorbed into the Hindu pantheon through Sanskritization.[3] Pampa was deemed a daughter of Brahma; she was said to have done hard penance to seduce Virupaksha, regarded as a form of Shiva, leading to their marriage. Pampa-Virupaksha effectively morphed into Parvati-Shiva.[4] In this new Brahminical patriarchal order, Virupaksha's star power had risen at the expense of Pampa's, who seems to have gone from a lead role to a consort—the modus operandi of patriarchy at the time.

The region of Hampi, as Kishkindha, is also prominent in the Ramayana. It is home to the *vanara* ('monkey') kingdom of Vali. Vali had exiled his brother Sugriva on charges of betrayal, driving him into hiding with his ally Hanuman. During this time, Ravana kidnapped Sita and flew her to Lanka. It was above Kishkindha that Sita dropped her jewels. They were found by Sugriva and recognized by Rama when he and Lakshmana came looking for her. The rest, as they say, is more mythology.

Local lore has cooked up an elaborate schema of Ramayana sites at Hampi: the pond by which Sita's jewels fell; the cave where Sugriva hid them; the cave where Rama and Lakshmana stayed; the rocky ledge from where Rama fired the arrow to murder Vali; Rama's giant footprint in stone; etc. Hanuman, the local hero, was a huge favourite with Vijayanagar's sculptors and appears often, usually with a raised hand and an overlarge tail. A shrine in Anegundi, atop Anjeyanadri Hill, claims to be his birthplace.

Wandering the ruins, I meet a local villager who tells me about the raja of Anegundi, a descendant of the kings of Vijayanagar, including Krishnadevaraya. This heir to the defunct throne has a city home in Hospet. The next morning, after many false starts, I find his home, a plain house on an arterial street. An attendant lets me in and soon a man in his early forties emerges and shakes my hand. His name is—no prizes for guessing—Krishna Devaraya, eighteen generations apart from his famous namesake. I ask if I could talk to him about his family history and perhaps write about it. He is gracious and polite, explains that he

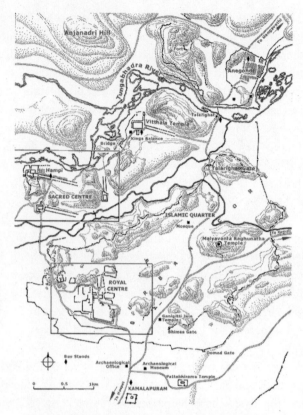

*Figure 3. Hampi site map (Courtesy of John M. Fritz and
George Michell, Vijayanagara Research Project)*

is about to head out to work and invites me to his ancestral home in
Anegundi village the next day.

The Rise of Vijayanagar

In the late thirteenth century, south India was a patchwork of small
warring kingdoms with shifting borders, many plagued by internecine
rivalries for power. The largest of them were the Hoysalas of Karnataka,
the Kakatiyas of Andhra and various dynastic claimants of the once
powerful Pallavas, the Cholas, the Pandyas and the Cheras of Tamil
country and Kerala. This fragmented political geography was jolted by a

new and formidable expansionary force in the early fourteenth century: the Delhi Sultanate, led by Ala-ud-Din Khalji, a first-generation Turko-Afghan migrant soldier into north India, and Muhammad bin Tughlak, a Delhi-born grandson of a Turkic slave father and Hindu concubine mother. Their cavalry-led armies were far more professional and ruthless than what the southern rulers were used to.

The ensuing decades saw great battles and the rise and fall of many kingdoms. When the dust cleared a bit in the mid-fourteenth century, the political map of south India had changed

Figure 4. Tungabhadra River

dramatically. A sovereign Muslim kingdom, the Bahmani Sultanate—founded by Bahman Shah, a rebellious general in Tughlak's army—had arisen in mid-peninsula. This kingdom patronized Islam as the religion of its urban centres alongside Persian language and culture. This created both cultural disruptions for some and new opportunities for others. To its south had emerged a powerful new entity, also very militaristic and expansionist: the Vijayanagar Kingdom, founded by two soldiers and brothers, Hakka and Bukka, sons of Sangama, likely a Telugu Shudra chief; though their ethnic lineage is still contested, with some claiming they were Kannadigas.

How did the two Sangama brothers found a new city? Rival accounts exist. One account claims that the two brothers, in the Kakatiya king's employ, were captured by Tughlak and taken to Delhi. The brothers converted to Islam, worked with Tughlak for a few years and imbibed the ways of the sultanate. They gained Tughlak's trust to the point that he sent them back to govern his frontier territories in the south. This began well but one day soon after, the brothers went out hunting. They came across a few hounds pursuing a terrified hare, and then saw a strange sight: the hare suddenly stopped running, turned around and began chasing the hounds instead. A sage, Vidyaranya, promptly appeared and called this a sign from high above, heralding an auspicious location for a great new city. Under the sage's counsel, the brothers betrayed Tughlak's trust, quit his employ, reverted to Hinduism and began building their own kingdom with its new capital, Vijayanagar (City of Victory). It was c. 1336 CE. Tughlak didn't seem to do much about their desertion owing to other distractions and setbacks he faced in the north.

A more mundane account claims that the brothers served a king of Kampili whom Tughlak defeated. The brothers fled and joined the Hoysala king, later gaining control of a fortress of the Kampili king at Anegundi on the Tungabhadra River. They raised an army, likely including Muslim mercenaries, and began amassing territory and building a new capital city across the river, which already had a settlement around the Pampa-Virupaksha Temple.[5] To legitimize their status, they patronized this temple. Virupaksha, now a Shaivite god, became the state deity of their new kingdom. Later, however, they broadened their appeal by patronizing Vaishnavite gods too, such as Rama, Krishna and Lord Venkateshvara of Tirupati, as well as Jain temples. They also made room for Islam in their realm—a certain Ahmed Khan built a mosque in 1439 in Vijayanagar's 'urban core'; its ruins and nearby tombs still stand.[6]

There are other variants of this origin story, but whatever the truth of its founding, there is no doubt that the Sangama brothers, first Hakka, aka Harihara I (r. 1336–56), then Bukka Raya (r. 1356–77), laid the foundations of a great capital city and empire. Bukka Raya's realm had grown large enough that he felt secure in claiming the following titles for himself: 'the prosperous great tributary, punisher of enemy kings, Sultan among Hindu Kings, vanquisher of kings who break their word, lord of the eastern and western oceans, the auspicious hero'.[7]

Thus began a new era of shifting imperial fortunes and alliances, more intense warfare with both Hindu and Muslim kings, coups and rebellions, internecine rivalries and murders. As described in the following pages, this was a time of great syncretic innovation in Vijayanagar, particularly in courtly culture, governance, military organization and architecture. People saw greater geographic mobility and economic opportunity. The city presided over a rich and diverse flowering of art, literature and culture, including the birth of Carnatic music. With perhaps 250,000 residents at its height in the early sixteenth century, Vijayanagar became one of the largest cities in the world. Four dynasties would eventually rule the Vijayanagar Empire: Sangama (1336–1485), Saluva (1485–1505), Tuluva (1505–1570) and Aravidu (1570–1652).

Chroniclers of the age report a series of brutal wars, many between Vijayanagar and the Bahmani Sultanate. Both coveted the fertile land between the Tungabhadra and Krishna rivers, whose fortress town of Raichur kept switching masters. Bloody conflicts here continued even

Figure 5. South India in 1565[8]

after Krishnadevaraya defeated the already disintegrating Bahmani Sultanate, splitting it into five Deccan Sultanates in 1518—Golkonda, Bijapur, Bidar, Berar and Ahmadnagar. Religion played a role in these wars, but was rarely the dominant cause. Examples abound of Muslims fighting Muslims; Hindus fighting Hindus; Hindus joining Muslims to fight Hindus; Muslims joining Hindus to fight Muslims; Brahmins held great sway in the governance of some Deccan sultanates. Vijayanagar's armies had lots of Muslim warriors, like the cavalry of 10,000 'Turks' recruited by Deva Raya II in 1430. Krishnadevaraya reconquered Raichur in 1520 with help from Portuguese musketeers. Many elite warriors—Hindu, Muslim and Christian—were mercenaries and often changed sides. In short, 'loyalty to family, faction, or paymaster counted for more than loyalty to land, religion, or ethnic group', writes Richard M. Eaton, a social historian of the Deccan.[9] The primary drivers of war in this age too were the imperatives of power, territory and resources, variously entangled with religion and ideology.

What Foreign Travellers Saw in Vijayanagar

Vijayanagar is 'the best provided city in the world', wrote one traveller. It is of 'enormous magnitude and population', wrote another. Our historical knowledge of Vijayanagar comes from a range of sources, such as inscriptions on stone and copper plates, archaeology, literary works, temple land grants and trade records. A Persian chronicler in the employ of Deccan sultans, Muhammad Kasim Firishta, has left many details though he wrote a generation after the sacking of Vijayanagar, and his accounts often seem dubious and lurid, especially of war.[10] At times, he seems partial to the perspective of his patrons and exaggerates their side's military exploits. Finally, a good chunk of what we know about Vijayanagar comes from the eyewitness accounts of foreign travellers.

Among the travellers whose writings on Vijayanagar have survived are Niccolo de Conti, a Venetian merchant (1420); Abdur Razzaq Samarqandi, a Persian scholar-envoy (1443); Duarte Barbosa, a Portuguese officer (c. 1515); and Domingo Paes (c. 1520) and Fernao Nuniz (1535–37), Portuguese merchant-adventurers. While much of

Figure 6. Once the royal centre

what they describe is real and useful, some of them lacked adequate language skills or cultural context to know what they were looking at. They moreover wrote for audiences back home, often relied on hearsay rather than personal observation and held various cultural biases towards the 'heathens' and 'idolaters' of the subcontinent. They were more drawn to things they found strange or shocking and they often exaggerated them. One such was the incidence of sati, writes Thapar.[11] So care must be taken in interpreting their words. From the following selections of the travellers' observations, we get a sense of Vijayanagar's rulers, flourishing economy and trade, social customs and festivals and more.

Niccolo de Conti

Years after visiting Vijayanagar in 1420, the Italian merchant Niccolo de Conti narrated stories from his Asian voyage to a scholarly scribe. Vijayanagar's circumference, Conti claims, is sixty miles and 'in this city there are estimated to be ninety thousand men fit to bear arms'. Conti says about the king of Vijayanagar, Deva Raya I:

Their king is more powerful than all the other kings of India [and has] twelve thousand wives, of whom four thousand follow him on foot wherever he may go, and are employed solely in the service of the kitchen. A like number, more handsomely equipped, ride on horseback. The remainder are carried by men in litters, of whom two thousand or three thousand are selected as his wives on condition that at his death they should voluntarily burn themselves with him, which is considered to be a great honour for them.

Conti describes temple rituals that are still performed today, but also a chariot festival in which 'young women richly adorned . . . sing hymns to the god', while others, 'carried away by the fervor of their faith, cast themselves on the ground before the wheels, in order that they may be crushed to death—a mode of death which they say is very acceptable to their god'. One practice Conti had observed in central India likely also existed in the Vijayanagar Empire: 'They have a vast number of slaves,' he claims, 'and the debtor who is insolvent is everywhere adjudged to be the property of his creditor'. This seems to describe bonded labour, then common in many parts of the world.

Conti writes that the people of Vijayanagar celebrate their weddings 'with singing, feasting, and the sound of trumpets and flutes, for, with the exception of organs, all the other instruments in use among them for singing and playing are similar to our own'. He mentions a festival during which 'they fix up within their temples, and on the outside of the roofs, an innumerable number of lamps of oil', and another festival when 'they sprinkle all passers-by, even the king and queen themselves, with saffron water, placed for that purpose by the wayside. This is received by all with much laughter'.

Conti tended to record more of the exotic or outlandish things, less so the charming or praiseworthy ones. His account also contains some odd observations, such as, 'Pestilence is unknown among the Indians.' In India, he met and married an Indian woman and had four children with her, all while travelling together. Sadly, two of the children and his wife died in a pestilence in Egypt, and Conti finally returned to Venice with his remaining children.

Abdur Razzaq

In 1443, Abdur Razzaq visited from Persia and was very impressed by Vijayanagar's 'enormous magnitude and population' and its seven concentric walled fortifications of stone. The outermost, writes Razzaq, had 'strong gates, and the guards stand watch with the eye of caution for the slightest thing'. Inside are orchards, gardens, buildings, shops and bazaars. The king is Deva Raya II, 'of perfect rule and hegemony' with 'around three hundred ports' and an army of, Razzaq guesses, 'more than a thousand elephants' and 1.1 million men.[12] 'In all of Hindustan,' writes Razzaq, 'there was no raja more autocratic than he' and in whose 'presence the Brahmins have great status'.

Razzaq is hosted in 'extremely fine quarters'. When he meets the king, Razzaq offers him 'five fine horses and two *toquzes* of damask silk and satin'. The youthful king, dressed in 'a tunic of Zaytuni silk and a necklace of lustrous pearls', receives him graciously and offers him the customary betel leaf and supari, thought to have amazing benefits for dental health and virility. He grants Razzaq a daily ration of 'two sheep, four pairs of fowl, five maunds of rice, one maund of oil, one maund of sugar, and two gold *varahas* [large coins]'.

The king has many wives, 'seven hundred ladies and concubines', and he keeps 'strict control over the affairs of each one'. Male kids, writes Razzaq, could stay with their mothers in the harem only until ten. 'Throughout his realm wherever there is a beautiful girl, he persuades the girl's mother and father and has her brought with much celebration to his harem. Thereafter no one sees her, but she is kept in great honor and veneration.'

About the city's bazaars, he writes:[13]

The bazaars are extremely broad and long. Flower sellers have tall platforms in front of the stalls, and on both sides they sell flowers . . . there are aromatic flowers continually in bloom, and as necessary as they deem food to be, they cannot bear [to be] without flowers. The practitioners of every craft have stalls adjacent to one another. The jewelers sell pearls, diamonds, rubies and emeralds openly in the bazaar . . . All nobles and commoners of the region, even the craftsmen of the bazaar, wear pearls and jewels in their ears, around their necks and on their arms, wrists and fingers.

The 'elaborateness of their brothels,' writes Razzaq, 'or of the beauty, blandishments and attraction of their courtesans is beyond my ability to express'. Prostitutes, adorned 'with costly pearls and jewels and fine clothing, are quite young and extremely beautiful, and with each stand one or two serving girls'. They ply their trade on attractive streets, waiting for customers on chairs outside rows of chambers 'as clean as can be'. Taxes on their income, Razzaq claims, pay for the city's police services. If the policemen can't find an object reported lost or stolen, they fully compensate the owner for it. Razzaq witnesses this personally. 'Several slaves that my companions had bought ran away,' he writes, and the policemen, after a futile search 'in the quarter where the poor lived', paid the fair price for each slave to the owners.

Razzaq also attended the Mahanavami festival at Vijayanagar, when a grand annual celebration was held in the royal centre for many days. He describes decorated multi-storeyed pavilions raised at the festival grounds, where mostly young female singers, dancers and reciters perform 'in an astonishingly enchanting manner'. Elephants perform circus tricks. Generous rewards are given. All the chiefs and governors of the realm are present, with their 'elephants roaring and raging like mountains and thunderclouds, adorned with weaponry and embellished with howdahs, with acrobats and pyrotechnists, and on the elephants' heads, trunks and ears amazing pictures and strange designs painted in cinnabar and other [colours]'.

Soon after leaving the city for Calicut, Razzaq heard of a shocking assassination attempt on the king by his own brother. A festival had been organized and amid the sound of drums, the king, along with his other brothers, generals and ministers had been lured into traps and stabbed. But the injured king had somehow survived and regained control. Retribution followed: 'All those who had in any way aided in the conspiracy were put to death. Men in great numbers were slain, flayed, burnt alive, and their families entirely executed. The man who had brought the letters of invitation [to the festival] was put to the last degree of torture.'

Indeed, the threat of assassination or usurpation and the need to pre-emptively strike were occupational hazards for a king—'five assassinations and four usurpations' occurred in Vijayanagar's Sangama Dynasty alone.[14] Paranoia was commonplace. According to Fernao Nuniz, Virupaksha Raya (1465–85) had summoned one of his regional governors and had him put to death solely because in his dream the governor had entered his room to kill him.

Duarte Barbosa

When Barbosa, a Portuguese officer in India for fifteen years, visited Vijayanagar in c. 1515, Krishnadevaraya was king. Barbosa describes great palaces, buildings and many water tanks 'in which is reared abundance of fish'. He was struck by the city's 'great traffic and endless number of merchants and wealthy men', including visitors 'to whom the King allows such freedom that every man may come and go and live according to his own creed, without suffering any annoyance and without enquiry whether he is a Christian, Jew, Moor or Heathen'.[15]

The markets sell diamonds and pearls in 'great quantities', and iron, copper, mercury, vermilion, opium, scented materials, pepper, fine textiles and cheaper brocades from China and Alexandria. To groom themselves, elite men grind up sandalwood, aloeswood, camphor, musk and saffron, knead it with rosewater and anoint themselves with it. They wear 'certain clothes as a girdle below, wound very tightly in many folds, and short white shirts of cotton or silk or coarse brocade, which are gathered between the thighs but open in front', with turbans, or caps of silk or brocade, earrings with pearls and rings with precious stones. These foppish gents of Vijayanagar might

Figure 7. Former market stalls in front of Virupaksha Temple

be 'accompanied by pages walking behind them with swords in their hands' and sometimes a silk umbrella in the hot sun or rain.

Elite women wear five yards long garments of white cotton or silk of bright colours. One part of it 'is girt around them below, and the other part they throw over one shoulder and across their breasts in such a way that one arm and shoulder remain uncovered'. They wear 'leather shoes well embroidered in silk, [and] necklaces, bracelets, nose and ear pieces of gold, precious stones, and fine coral beads', with uncovered heads, hair held in a knot and scented flowers in it. From childhood they are taught to sing and dance. Barbosa describes a local ceremony in which, upon turning twelve, a girl 'takes her own virginity' with a stick.

The king has a large harem, for which 'the fairest and most healthy women are sought throughout the kingdom', after which they are materially secure for life. 'They bathe daily in the many tanks', and the 'king goes to see them bathing, and she who pleases him most is sent for to come to his chamber'. Barbosa claims that 'there is such envy and rivalry among these women with regard to the king's favour, that "some kill others" and some poison themselves'.

When waging war, the king deploys the 100,000 warriors on his payroll, and also recruits 5000 to 6000 courtesans to go with them, claiming that 'war cannot be waged where there are no women'. Barbosa adds that these women 'are all unmarried, great musicians, dancers and acrobats, and very quick and nimble at their performances'.

Men of the warrior class eat all meats except beef and marry as many women as they can afford, who 'when their husbands die . . . burn themselves alive with their corpses', sometimes after ornate public rituals based on rank. 'This abominable practice of burning is so customary, and is held in such honour among them, that when the King dies four or five hundred women burn themselves with him.' Women who refuse are held 'in great dishonour, and their kindred shave their heads and turn them away as disgraced and a shame to their families'. If young, they are sent to a temple 'to earn money for the said temple with their bodies'.

Men of the priestly class do not eat meat, 'marry only one wife', and 'hold the greatest liberties and privileges and are not liable to death for anything whatsoever which they do' (Nuniz said this too). They get 'much alms on which they live' and many even 'have estates while others live in the houses of worship, as in monasteries, which possess good revenues. Some are great eaters and never work except to feed well'.

A third kind of elite men, writes Barbosa, dangle 'a stone the size of an egg' around their necks, eat no meat and are merchants and traders. They take only one wife but when the man dies, 'the wife buries herself alive' while standing in a 'hole deep enough' as others shovel in the earth around her. Two decades later, Nuniz mentioned this custom too but ascribed it only to one particular Telugu group. Barbosa marvels at the power of ideas like honour and reputation that 'induce these women to submit of their own will to such a horrible end'.

The social customs Barbosa describes were those of upper-caste elites—a small minority that dominated his milieu. It's not clear if he ever interacted with people of the lower classes in Vijayanagar, many of whom must have lived in the thatched homes he noticed in the city. He superficially equated Hindu society's divisions to European ones, i.e., nobility, priests and merchants, rather than exploring the far more complex divisions of caste and untouchability common in Vijayanagar. But that's hardly surprising; like most outsiders, he too was unable to penetrate many intricacies of Indian social life. He had spent most of his fifteen years in India in coastal Kerala working as a translator and clerk with local kings.

In 1519, Barbosa joined his brother-in-law, Ferdinand Magellan, on the first circumnavigation of the earth, but died in the Philippines before he could complete it.

Domingo Paes

When Domingo Paes visited in 1520, Krishnadevaraya was halfway into his reign. In his account, Paes calls him 'the most feared and perfect king', 'a man of much justice but given to fits of rage', who 'seeks to honor foreigners'.[16] He 'has twelve lawful wives, of whom there are three principal ones', each in her own house with other maidens and female guards who can 'handle sword and shield' and wrestle. These women 'are never seen by any [unapproved] man . . . When they wish to go out they are carried in litters shut up and closed', accompanied by hundreds of eunuchs.

Paes writes that Krishnadevaraya starts his day with a 350 ml drink of seed oil, rubs it all over his body and does weightlifting, wrestling, fencing and horse riding. A Brahmin bathes the king, after which the latter does puja and then begin his courtly duties. His palace is 'surrounded by a very strong wall' near which is an unusual temple where they sacrifice 'every day many sheep'. Down the street from this temple are many fine homes of the rich, including merchants who sell precious stones, textiles, horses and 'every other sort of thing there is on earth and that you may wish to buy'. The city's flourishing trade attracts 'men belonging to every nation and people', some of whom are even depicted on pillars and other relief sculptures in the city.

Paes visits the Muslim quarter of Vijayanagar where live many Muslim 'natives of the country and who are paid by the king and belong to his guard'. He climbs a hill for a view of the city and finds it 'as large as Rome, and very beautiful to the sight', with its groves of trees, homes with gardens, orchards and lakes. He likely climbed Matanga Hill, which still affords a sweeping view of the city's ruins and a lovely belt of coconut and banana plantations.

Paes calls Vijayanagar 'the best provided city in the world', well stocked with various grains, pulses and other seeds; poultry, mutton, pork, fish; butter, oil, milk; fruits like mangoes, oranges, lime, pomegranates, jackfruit and grapes; and vegetables like brinjals, radishes and others 'in such abundance as to stupefy one'. Religious sensibilities have clearly changed as today's traveller finds no meat in the Hampi village, not even in restaurants catering to foreign tourists.

Paes describes a Ganesh temple where 'they feed the idol every day, for they say that he eats; and when he eats women dance before him'. These women, and the daughters born to them, all belong to the temple, and who, according to Paes, are of 'loose character'. However, they 'live in the best streets in the city', are 'very much esteemed', on par with the courtesans of the elite, and 'any respectable man may go to their houses without any blame attaching thereto'.

The Brahmins of course serve as temple priests but many also work 'as officers of the towns and cities and belong to the government of them; others are merchants, and others live by their own property and cultivation, and the fruits that grow in their inherited grounds'.

Paes describes their grand nine-day Dussehra festival. All the chiefs, governors and dancing women of the kingdom attend. It's a time of feasting, ceremony, ritual and prayer, dancing, circus acts, martial parades, wrestling and other games, fireworks, gift giving and more. 'Their wrestling,' writes Paes, 'does not seem like ours, but there are blows (given), so severe as to break teeth, and put out eyes, and disfigure faces, so much so that here and there men are carried off speechless by their friends.' For nine days, people fast all day and eat at midnight, shortly before which the king witnesses the sacrificial slaughter of twenty-four buffaloes and 150 sheep, their heads severed in a single blow. After the festival is over, the king parades his forces on the outskirts of the city, both his own and of his feudatory chiefs and governors, with soldiers, horses and elephants decked out in all their finery—a noisy, fearsome, testosterone-driven display of the king's military might to all his enemies.

Fernao Nuniz

Fernao Nuniz, a Portuguese merchant and horse trader, spent three years in Vijayanagar (1535–37). His long account also covers the kingdom's early history, but he is more reliable when closer to his own time. This includes Krishnadevaraya's victorious 1513 war against the Gajapati kings of Orissa. To commemorate his win, he built the grand Krishna Temple and installed an idol of infant Krishna that he stole during a temple raid in Orissa. Nuniz also describes in fair detail the Battle of Raichur in 1520 between Krishnadevaraya and Adil Shah, the sultan of Bijapur. Nuniz must have spoken to men who participated in these wars.

Nuniz writes that Krishnadevaraya, lusting after Raichur and its lucrative hinterland, found a flimsy pretext to go to war with the sultan of Bijapur, breaking a peace of four decades. Summoning his regional 'captains', or governors, with their armies, he marched towards Raichur with 500,000 infantry—'archers, men with shields, musketeers, and spearmen'—32,000 cavalry and 500 elephants. Alongside came the support staff: 'numberless' washermen, thousands of men with water-skins, merchants with all sorts of city goods, Brahmins for 'ceremonies and sacrifices', drummers, musicians and 20,000 courtesans for the army men. Their large camps 'were divided into regular streets' with markets that sold meats, grains, vegetables and even jewellery and textiles. Tents and all other baggage and supplies were carried by bullock carts.

Adil Shah could only muster 120,000 infantry, 18,000 cavalry and 150 elephants, though he had better artillery. A brutal war followed in which Adil Shah was routed and fled for his life. Animosities among the Deccan Sultanates meant no one aided him. Vijayanagar's casualties were as high as 16,000. Their spoils of the war were 'four thousand horses of Ormuz, a hundred elephants, four hundred heavy cannons' and more. When the victorious king entered Raichur, writes Nuniz, its citizens greeted him 'with more cheerful countenances than their real feelings warranted', and many cried and begged him for mercy. Despite the king's admonition against it, his men indulged in 'great robberies' in the city. Indeed, soldiers looting a defeated city was a common practice on both sides, part of what we might call their 'package of incentives'. When Adil Shah sued for peace and implored the king to restore Raichur to him, Krishnadevaraya agreed to do so on one condition: Adil Shah must come and kiss his foot. Krishnadevaraya then marched to Bijapur, 'the best city in all the kingdom of Deccan' and 'left [it] almost in ruin'.

Interestingly, Krishnadevaraya, writes Nuniz, 'fell sick of the same illness of which all of his ancestors had died, with pains in the groin, of which die all the kings of Vijayanagar'. Given the sexually profligate ways of the kings, this sounds like venereal disease. The next king, Achyutaraya, also had some five hundred wives, mostly 'daughters of [governors] and nobles of the country'. Nuniz writes that all of these women would be burnt at the king's death but he doesn't comment on the political and social compulsions that led even powerful families to consign their daughters into such bargains.

King Achyutaraya, Nuniz says, 'never puts on any garment more than once', which are typically made of fine silk 'worked with gold'. In contrast to the sartorial tastes of the king and his courtiers, 'the common people go quite naked, with the exception of a piece of cloth about their middle', writes Ludovico di Varthema, an Italian traveller to Vijayanagar between 1502–08. Mosquitos are a menace, writes Nuniz, and the king 'always carries a mosquito net with a frame of silver'. He is so rich because all of the land belongs to him, and his regional governors are principally rent collectors. Near Dussehra time, according to Nuniz, they pay the

Figure 8. Talarigatta Gate, one of the entrances to the city

king up to half of their collection, keeping the rest for their own costs, such as for keeping armies. 'For this reason, the common people suffer much hardship, [because] those who hold the land [are] so tyrannical.'

Further, writes Nuniz, all goods that enter the city are taxed. Most of the produce and merchandise sold in the city comes from outside, and 'every day there enter by these gates 2,000 oxen' and all but a few exempted ox-carts pay tax. To get an audience with the king, a merchant has to offer a gift 'of the best that he has brought', say, textiles or a horse. Nuniz knew because he was a horse trader himself. 'And this not only to the king,' adds Nuniz. 'You must perforce pay bribes to all the several officers with whom you have to deal. They will do nothing without some profit to themselves.' Some cultural habits have deep roots, it seems.

The people of Vijayanagar do not kill or eat oxen and cows, for they worship them. But 'they eat mutton, pork, venison, partridges, hares, doves, quail and all kinds of birds; even sparrows and rats, and cats and lizards, all of which are sold in the [city's] market'.

Policing is efficient and few robberies take place. As for punishment, 'for a thief, whatever theft he commits, howsoever little it be, they forthwith cut off a foot and a hand, and if this theft be a great one he is hanged with a hook under his chin'. Ditto with rape and 'other such violence'. Traitors 'are sent to be impaled alive on a wooden stake thrust through the belly, and people of the lower orders, for whatever crime they commit, he forthwith commands to cut off their heads in the market-place, and the same for a murder'. Occasionally, 'when the king so desires, he commands a man to be thrown to the elephants, and they tear him to pieces'. Nuniz reported all this in a matter-of-fact way, perhaps because Vijayanagar was hardly exceptional—medieval European states too doled out appallingly cruel punishments.

The Political Economy of Vijayanagar

My first visit to Hampi left me with many knotty questions: How did the emperors of Vijayanagar rule such a vast region with multiple kingdoms, languages and cultures for nearly three centuries? How did their capital city acquire the riches evident in the gushing accounts of foreign travellers and what political and economic arrangements enabled this? What, if any, deep changes did Vijayanagar Empire bring about in south Indian society?

Among the scholars to tackle such questions is Burton Stein, giving us a rich yet complex portrait of the politics, society and economy of the Vijayanagar Empire in *The New Cambridge History of India: Vijayanagara* (1989). Beginning in pre-Vijayanagar times, Stein postulates the rise of broadly two kinds of settlements in south India by the thirteenth century: one along coastal riverine basins, agriculturally fecund, wealthier, with dense populations and more trades, such as those of the Cholas and Pandyas; the other in the central peninsular uplands, more arid, with limited agriculture, fewer people and a weaker economic base, such as of the Kakatiyas and Hoysalas.

This natural asymmetry, argues Stein, led the latter to desire the former's resources, partly to meet the rising costs and frequency of warfare in this age. And so, in the thirteenth century, 'hardy peasant groups, prevented by insufficient water from achieving high levels of multi-crop production, were compelled to pursue plundering expeditions with fighting skills honed by turbulent relations with herdsmen and forest people. The Reddis and Velamas of Andhra and Vanniyars of Tamil country exemplify such warlike peasantries'. It didn't help, writes Stein, that 'the superior cavalry and archery of [northern] Muslim fighters intensified this emerging martial quality, gave it an edge that doomed the older, more prosperous areas of agriculture and settlement in the river valleys to political subordination and plunder'.

Vijayanagar too was an upland peninsular settlement, very much on the frontier of the expansionist Muslim rule. As the Sangama warrior brothers and their progeny began expanding Vijayanagar's realm in the south, they fortified their dominance through new innovations. Most notably, they appointed a cadre of governors, or *nayak*s, across their realm, to assert the king's authority and extract regional rents.[17] These imperial governors—comprising dozens of trusted royal kin, noblemen and military generals—either had sole and direct authority in some regions or worked through semi-autonomous local chiefs in others. Some governors funnelled up half of their tax revenue to the king, while others kept more of it and grew quite powerful, which created its own problems.

Taxes also came from trading ports—likely sizeable since major roads linked their capital to ports on both the Malabar and Coromandel coasts, and military guards ensured the smooth flow of goods on them, including Arabian war horses (every year, writes Nuniz, the king of Vijayanagar imported 13,000 horses from Hormuz, besides others from Aden). The largest taxpayers in Vijayanagar Empire were traders, merchants, and industrial producers. Their economic importance is evident from these words by Krishnadevaraya:

A king should improve the harbours of his country and so encourage its commerce . . . make the merchants of distant foreign countries who import elephants and good horses attached to yourself by providing them with villages and decent dwellings in the city, by affording them daily audience, presents and allowing decent profits. Then those articles will never go to your enemies.[18]

What soon began emerging was a centralized state that was further fine-tuned in the early sixteenth century by Krishnadevaraya, reaching its peak performance under him—no doubt reflected in the affluence and splendour noted by foreign travellers like Barbosa and Paes in his capital city. Stein calls it 'a parasitic regime that extracted tribute from the productivity and commerce of its peoples and contributed little itself to either'. This sounds a little harsh but is mostly on the mark. Other scholars of Vijayanagar, like John Fritz and George Michell, see the capital city not 'as a natural trading center but rather as an artificially created emporium sustained by courtly patronage, to which much of the wealth of the empire was diverted'.[19]

One could also see Vijayanagar as having become 'what Nilakanta Sastri called a "war state", one ruled by warrior-chiefs whose whole being was bent on attaining ever greater military force to be applied to any enemy, Hindu and Muslim'.[20] Brute force was applied to subordinate states too. In 1544, the king of Vijayanagar, Rama Raya, sent a large force to punish the raja of Travancore, Unni Varma, who had apparently not been sending enough trade tributes. Over time, Vijayanagar had moved towards a feudal patrimonial state, especially in the sixteenth century. Scholars, however, still debate the precise nature of political and economic subordination within this imperial pyramid, especially its regional variations.[21]

The imperial governors were often outsiders to their regions—say, Telugus or Kannadigas stationed in Tamil country. They couldn't rule by force alone, at least not for long. Sustainable rule required cultivating goodwill and appeasing local power brokers. Some did this by investing in irrigation works like dams and tanks and providing competent civic administration. The locals likely also benefitted by gaining greater access to a larger market for their goods like cotton, rice, indigo, oil seeds and textiles, still transported via bullock carts and boats but now over longer distances.[22]

More shrewdly, these outsider governors patronized existing temples and funded new ones, turning their vicinities into urban centres of commerce, artisanal trades and culture. The temples, in turn, often funded irrigation works and other public goods. The imperial governors also donated land and money to priests and to mathas, the powerful monastic orders attached to big temples. Lo and behold, the governors and their descendants began gaining the religiously sanctioned right to rule, which had earlier vested in hereditary regional chiefs (like the *nayanar*s of Tamil country), who understandably resented the outsiders and their disruption of the old social order, especially in the sixteenth century. However, in many distant parts of the empire, local chiefs continued to rule almost independently and kept their hereditary privileges, either just paying ritual homage to their imperial overlords or also contributing arms and revenue.

In certain areas, the governors encountered no regional chiefs. Local power there was more decentralized, split across families of landed caste elites (Brahmins and Vellalars in Tamil country, Kammas and Reddis in Telugu country, etc.), who monopolized local resources and wealth, while exploiting the labour of untouchable castes in exchange for food and shelter. These elites, too, resented the upstarts, the governors, though some parlayed their privileges into lucrative niches in the emerging order—as scribes, bankers and accountants (much as they would with the new professions of the colonial period). Mirroring such integrative forces, even village guardian deities, often goddesses of harvests and fertility, began to be 'Sanskritized' as variants of the more majestic divinities of Vijayanagar's Hindu pantheon. This reconfiguring of older customs and political economy would continue well into the British era and beyond.

Notably, the imperial governors resided in fortified garrisons and maintained standing armies, which were expected to join Vijayanagar's wars against its external enemies and to quell internal revolts by local chiefs or the sporadic peasant revolt. Governors who broke away to set up their own sovereign domains, or 'nayaka kingdoms', also attracted the king's wrath. But after the sacking of Vijayanagar in 1565, the floodgates on this trend opened wide, leading to many independent kingdoms (a process that resembled the earlier disintegration of the Bahmani Sultanate). The largest among them were at Mysore, Ikkeri, Gingee, Tanjore and Madurai. With its complex weave of disruptions and continuities, the Vijayanagar era, writes Stein, 'saw the transition of South Indian society from its medieval past to its modern future'.

Textures of Religious and Courtly Life

One morning, I wander deep inside the Sacred Centre to the lovely and forlorn Achyutaraya's temple complex built in the 1530s. It lies in a

Figure 9. A relief carving in the Achyutaraya Temple complex

valley between picturesque hills. A street lined with ruined market stalls and a giant tank leads to a majestic gateway. Inside is a cluster of temples, pavilions and courtyards, once dedicated to Lord Tiruvengalanatha, a form of Vishnu. Their relief carvings include quirky depictions of secular life, full of charm and mystery. They not only show dancers, musicians and saints, but also people with strange robes and hats—seemingly Arab, Turkish, Persian, and Portuguese envoys and traders—and others with unusual facial hair, beards, ornaments and poses that are a delight to behold (foreigners also appear on the Mahanavami platform in the Royal Centre and on other monuments, both secular and religious).[23] It reminds me how even the most modern and grand Hindu temples of today are so lacking in such lightness of touch and cosmopolitanism. Vijayanagar also holds the distinction of evolving the pyramidal entrance architecture of early Tamil Nadu temples into the monumental Raya Gopuram gateway, which would then spread all over the south. Here too, as in much of the world, grand architecture was used to signal imperial power to their subjects and neighbouring kingdoms.

What strands of Hinduism did Vijayanagar patronize? Most successful multi-ethnic empires, despite their particular leanings, tend to adopt a pragmatic pluralism. Vijayanagar's rulers too were plural in their patronage. On the one hand, Virupaksha Temple, their state temple, was run by followers of Adi Shankara, who, in the eighth century, had boosted Advaita Vedanta—a non-dualistic interpretation of Vedanta—along with a renunciatory monasticism led by mathas. Cannibhatta, a fourteenth-century conservative logician in the Vijayanagar court, wrote a treatise defending Advaita Vedanta, 'the philosophy officially embraced by the Vijayanagar court'.[24] On the other hand, the state also patronized the opposing view of Dvaita Vedanta—a dualistic interpretation of Vedanta. This was taught by Vyasatirtha (1460–1539), a scholar, poet, devotional singer, head of the Madhava Brahmin monastic sect and *rajguru* to Krishnadevaraya himself.

One of Vyasatirtha's disciples was Purandara Dasa (1484–1564), a wealthy jewellery trader who had given away all his wealth to become a devotee of Lord Krishna. He attained great fame as a Bhakti saint and singer of devotional melodies. He was also a scholar of music, and his classical compositions laid the foundations of what became Carnatic music. In fact, so great was his influence that he's widely regarded as the father of Carnatic music. Some call him an avatar of the celestial singer Narada. He spent his later years in Vijayanagar, composing and singing devotional songs to Lord Vitthala. He lived by the scenic river in an open pillared pavilion, Purandara Dasa Mantapa, near which an annual music festival now celebrates his legacy.

This religious substrate—renunciatory monasticism plus mystical devotionalism—was part of a larger shift that had occurred in Hinduism. It helps explain why there is so little erotica on temple walls in Vijayanagar. I search thousands of relief sculptures and statues and find less than ten copulating couples—remains of a dying trend, marginal in placement and import. In fact, the Hinduism and temple art of Vijayanagar were well on their way to the far more insipid and puritanical strains of Hinduism and temple art that Hindus identify with today. These strains had been amplified by Adi Shankara and Bhakti, long before the invasions of Mahmud of Ghazni from 1000 CE. They would get reinforced by their contact with the Sunni, Shia and Sufi Islams that came from the north-west, and later with Victorian Britain (see 'The Enigma of Khajuraho' for a discussion on why erotic art disappeared from temple walls across India).

Some scholars have argued that a consequence of the state's plural patronage to temples and mathas, especially through the nayaka governors, was to raise competition between various sects of Hinduism, even as it perhaps fostered a broader Hindu identity.[25]

The language of the Vijayanagar court was Telugu. Kannada and Sanskrit were common too. For writing material, according to Razzaq, people used either coconut fronds or cloth, the latter for more durable records. In his fifties, after his aggressive military campaigns, Krishnadevaraya took greater interest in the literary arts. He wrote *Amuktamalyada*, a book of Telugu verse that relates the love of Andal, a Tamil poetess-saint, for Vishnu and their marriage. He had eight great poets in his court, including Allasani Peddana, 'grandfather of Telugu poetry', and Tenali Ramakrishna (or Tenali Raman), poet, scholar and court jester, who became the hero of many a folk story I read as a child even in north India.

Another celebrated poet in the realm was Atukuri Molla, a woman of the potter caste, who composed her own version of the Ramayana in Telugu verse, recited it in the court of Krishnadevaraya and won praise and honour from the court poets. Not far from the city lived a lower-caste poet-saint and shepherd, Kanaka Dasa, who was denied entry into temples. His songs deftly point out the absurdity of the logic that underpins caste, as in the following verse:

> To what caste does the soul belong?
> To what caste do life and love belong?
> To what caste do the five senses belong?
> If a soul is united with God, the Soul of Souls,
> What does caste have to do with it?[26]

Vijayanagar was a Hindu empire and its elites had many identities distinct from that of Muslim elites in the Deccan. Religion was one pillar of identity for both groups, but many Muslim elites, even after generations in the Deccan, also identified with their Turko-Afghan roots and the then dominant world of Persian language and culture. Notably, Vijayanagar's elites, too, had acquired many Persianate affinities. Even without conversion to Islam or syncretic religious movements, writes

Phillip B. Wagoner, a cultural historian of the Deccan, the material and political culture of the elites of Vijayanagar had been Persianized to 'a remarkably high degree'.[27]

A good example here is Vijayanagar's very Persianate courtly attire: *kabayi*, 'a long-sleeved pullover tunic with front slit', and *kullayi*, 'a high, brimless conical cap with rounded top'. This was in sharp contrast to the attire of other Hindu kings in south India, who, as Razzaq observes, went 'as naked as other Hindus', donning merely a loincloth. Wagoner argues that 'the

Figure 10. Relief carving of courtly attire

minimal dress of South Indian rulers would have appeared immodest and barbaric' by Persianate cultural standards. In a bid to be taken seriously by Muslim royalty of north India and West Asia (via traders and envoys), Vijayanagar's elites adopted a style of dress closer to Persianate 'norms of modesty and public decorum'.

Such ready embrace of Persianate culture was voluntary, writes Wagoner (he uses 'Islamicate' to mean the same thing), and went beyond 'the material culture of the court' to cover 'military technology and strategy, political and administrative institutions' as well as architecture. Indeed, 'metropolitan Vijayanagara, especially the Royal Center, is saturated with Persian architectural elements: domes, vaulted arches, parapets of merlons, corner finials, fine plasterwork, and so forth'—evident in the Queen's Bath, the Elephant Stables, the Lotus Mahal and other buildings in the mislabelled 'Zenana Enclosure'.[28] Wagoner adds that this cultural mingling 'unfolded not as some inevitable consequence of "the onslaught of Islam," but quite the opposite, as the result of conscious and deliberately calculated acts by creative individuals seeking to maximize their opportunities in an ever-widening world'. Of course, as in the Sultanate of Bijapur, syncretic cultural diffusion went both ways with elite Muslims adopting Hindu arts, such as in styles of depicting human figures in paintings.[29] Historian William Dalrymple writes that Bijapur's sultan, Ibrahim Adil Shahi II, 'visited both Shaivite temples and the monasteries of the Nath yogis, and knew Sanskrit better than Persian'.[30]

Wandering the Royal Centre, it occurs to me that perhaps another Persianate cultural import in Vijayanagar was its constraints on courtly women. Other south Indian kings, half-naked in their loincloths, didn't confine their 'royal queens and female family members' in 'segregated and strictly guarded zones' within walled compounds. In contrast, the royal women of Vijayanagar, watched over by eunuchs and carried in closed palanquins, were given no role in public life and couldn't even be seen by other men.[31] Child marriages were common among the Brahmins and certain upper castes. Add to this the custom of sati and what we have here is a very oppressive place for royal and aristocratic women even by medieval Indian standards.[32]

Yet another Persianate import in south India, it seems to me, was a markedly higher level of military violence. The fighting ferocity of Turko-Afghan horsemen of the Delhi Sultanate—born of a culture of greater military discipline, meritocracy, and battlefield innovations— meant that any ruling class of Hindus who could challenge them would also have to be equally violent, with a similarly keen instinct in pursuing and protecting its own interests. Such indeed was the ruling class at Vijayanagar.

The Fall of Vijayanagar

A great war took place in 1565 at Talikota between Vijayanagar and four Deccan Sultanates. A key personality here was Rama Raya (1484–1565), son of a prominent general of Vijayanagar. Curiously, earlier in his life, in 1512, Rama Raya had enlisted for three years 'in the service of the sultan of Golkonda', a great rival of Vijayanagar. This illustrates the high degree of mobility that elite warriors enjoyed, beyond religious considerations. Back in Vijayanagar, Rama Raya later married Krishnadevaraya's daughter, and, as regent, rose to become its de facto ruler in 1543. For the next two decades, he played a great game with the sultans, allying with some, playing one off against another. According to Stein, 'A combination of high skill and arrogance characterised [his] policies toward the Muslim sultanates of the Deccan.' K.A. Nilakanta Sastri, acclaimed historian of south India, writes, 'Rama Raya paid heavily for his miscalculations. His policy opened the direct road to the disaster of [Talikota].'[33]

One such miscalculation may have followed a war in 1558–59 in which Rama Raya had allied with Bijapur to defeat Ahmadnagar and Golconda. According to Firishta, Vijayanagar's victorious army 'left no cruelty unpractised. They insulted the honor of the mussulmaun women, destroyed the mosques, and did not even respect the sacred koraun'.[34] It's unclear if Firishta is embellishing or reporting only part of the story, but Sastri, seemingly agreeing with him, thinks 'the excesses committed by the Hindu forces against the Muslim population and sacred places in their invasions of Ahmadnagar and Golconda had no small share in rousing feelings against Rama Raya'.[35] Apparently even his Muslim allies in Bijapur were turned off by it.

This and sundry political factors soon led the sultans to realize that on their own, they stood no chance against Rama Raya, who now had enormous wealth and resources. In 1564, a peace treaty was struck between the two rival factions of sultans and sealed with a marriage deal. A military alliance was forged between four of the five sultanates (excluding Berar) to jointly tackle Rama Raya. Preparations for a great war began in earnest on both sides. With more troops at his disposal, Rama Raya felt confident of victory, though in recent years the sultanates had opened up a 'wide gap in military technology' by integrating field artillery in their ranks.[36]

A pitched battle took place using both artillery and hand-to-hand combat. Nearly 3500 Portuguese mercenaries fought on the side of Vijayanagar.[37] Vijayanagar's 'gunners were Portuguese or Muslim, just as the light horse- and foot-soldiers of the Muslim regimes were often [Hindu] Marathas'.[38] At first Rama Raya, now eighty years old, seemed to be winning. Then came a sudden reversal, according to Firishta. After a blistering artillery attack 'charged with copper coins' for shrapnel, a unit of the enemy's cavalry cut through an opening in the centre and reached

Rama Raya. They captured and decapitated him, and hoisted his head on a spear. This caused panic among his troops and they began fleeing the battlefield. A rival account from a later Italian traveller, however, claims that the decisive factor in Rama Raya's defeat was the betrayal by two of his Muslim generals. This threw their side in chaos, enabling a unit of the enemy's cavalry to reach Rama Raya, decapitate him and hoist his head on a spear.[39] It is now impossible to say which of these two accounts is true. If historians pick one over the other, they do so for their own reasons. Either way, Vijayanagar's troops were routed. Many were pursued and slaughtered, says Firishta, and a river nearby ran red with blood. All along, 'Golkonda's Telugu [Hindu] soldiery remained faithful to their Muslim ruler against the Hindu king'.[40]

Bad news quickly spread across the capital city as chiefs, generals and soldiers began straggling in, grabbing what they could of their possessions and fleeing the city with their families. Within hours, the royal family fled with hundreds of elephants 'laden with treasures in gold, diamonds, and precious stones'. Others took the few remaining ox-carts that had not been taken to the war. The citizens began realizing that this was not merely a defeat but a catastrophe. For over two hundred years, no enemy had penetrated the walls of Vijayanagar and now they were at the unguarded gates. Some buried their treasures, many fled, others waited hoping for the best.

As news of the defeat spread, the depopulating city first fell prey to nearby tribes, such as the Brinjaris, Lambadis, Kurubas and other nomadic groups, who looted its markets. One wonders what sort of relations Vijayanagar had fostered with them to invite this opportunism. The enemy troops then arrived to plunder the city, and they apparently did so for five or six months, leaving it ruined and desolate. Little would survive of Vijayangar's palaces and other residences; built using wooden pillars and beams, they were either easily burnt down or otherwise crumbled over time.

Scholars disagree about what exactly happened. On the one hand, historians Hermann Kulke and Dietmar Rothermund write, 'The victors destroyed Vijayanagar, thus taking revenge for Krishnadevaraya's devastation of the old Bahmani capital of Gulbarga in 1520. There are few comparable instances in history of such a sudden defeat and of such a wanton destruction of a large imperial capital: Vijayanagar was even more thoroughly sacked than was Delhi by Timur's army.'[41] On the other hand, historian John Keay writes, 'Despite colourful [later] descriptions of a five-month sack, wholesale slaughter, savage iconoclasm and such remorseless demolition that "nothing now remains but a heap of ruins", the impression these "ruins" convey is less of wilful destruction and more of neglect, plus some random treasure-hunting and much casual pillage of building materials.' He accurately points out, 'Temples, the bigot's prime target, prove to be the least damaged structures; and in many of them the statuary, so invitingly vulnerable, remains miraculously intact.'[42] Some of these sculptures still stand among the ruins, while many others are in the ASI museum at Kamalapur and in museums and private collections around the world.

Though their great city was gone forever, the descendants of Rama Raya would preside over a shrinking empire for a few more decades from Penukonda, a couple of hundred kilometres to the south-east, and from other towns. Within a year of Talikota, the alliance of the sultanates fell apart, descending again into a pattern of intermittent war and peace. In the following century, they would all be absorbed into the Mughal Empire.

Two years after the war, in 1567, Caesaro Federici, an Italian traveller, wrote that 'the Citie of Vijayanagar is not altogether destroyed, yet the houses stand still, but emptie, and there is dwelling in them nothing, as is reported, but Tygres and other wild beasts.' Over two centuries later, in 1799, when Colin Mackenzie came to survey Hampi, wild animals still abounded, and 'he and his team took refuge in the Virupaksha temple . . . since it was the only place that could be securely locked at night'[43]—the place from where Vijayanagar Empire had risen nearly five centuries earlier.

A Hindu Bulwark against Islam?

Modern scholarship on Vijayanagar began with Robert Sewell's influential *A Forgotten Empire* (1900), which included the first English translations of Paes and Nuniz. He described Vijayanagar as 'a Hindu bulwark against Muhammadan conquests', whose 'fighting kings' became 'the saviors of the south for two and a half centuries'. In Sewell's lifetime, as modernity spread in the subcontinent, religious revival and sectarian feeling accompanied political awakening. In this milieu, Sewell's words roused upper-caste Hindu nationalists to romantically imagine Vijayanagar as a brave and final stand of 'traditional' Hindu religion and culture against the 'darkness' of Islam.[44] Many accepted this ideological framing, including V.S. Naipaul in *India: A Wounded Civilization* (1976). This polarizing rhetoric still dominates popular histories and perceptions, especially among contemporary Hindu nationalists.

The reality, however, was far more complex. Among scholars today, Sewell's view is largely untenable. As Wagoner writes, 'The actual pattern of political conflicts and wars in South India . . . cannot be understood in terms of a simple Hindu-Muslim conflict. In the words of the Historical Atlas of South Asia, for example, "both Hindu and Muslim states fought among themselves as much as they did against one another."'[45] There is no evidence, writes Eaton, that Rama Raya's 'contemporaries saw him as a defender of Hindu dharma or the Deccan itself as a region permanently divided between a Muslim north and Hindu south'.[46] Such a framing is largely a projection of later passions and prejudices upon the past.

As we've seen, Vijayanagar's elites embraced many Persianate norms and customs and hired Turkish fighters and commanders. Likewise, the Deccan Sultanates hired Hindu officials and army men. 'In terms of court ritual, fiscal structure and imperial style,' writes historian Sanjay Subrahmanyam, 'Vijayanagara shares far more with the Bahmani sultanate and its successors at Bijapur and Golconda, than with the Pallavas and Cholas. Politically, the rulers of Vijayanagara were as often allied to these sultanates as opposed to them, while amongst their major rivals and enemies were the [Hindu] Gajapati rulers of Orissa.'[47] In the realpolitik of both rajas and sultans, religion was one factor alongside many other pressing worldly concerns. At times, much like today, religion was cynically deployed to unite people for a cause, mobilize emotions or camouflage dubious material objectives. In the 1360s, for instance, the Vijayanagar king annexed Madurai from the Bahmani Sultanate, but he cheekily claimed to have done so in the name of 'a new dharmic kingship and an end to Muslim oppression'.[48]

It's true that Hinduism and its cultural institutions got more patronage in Vijayanagar Empire than under Islamic regimes (and vice versa). In the latter case, any loss of state patronage for Hinduism was felt most acutely by upper-caste Hindus. Most others—lower-caste Hindus, the outcastes and tribal groups—either continued with their folk religiosity beyond the norms of Brahminical Hinduism, or converted to Islam to improve their lot, or evolved syncretic religious forms. Continuity, disruption and renewal were all in play, and outcomes were rarely as black and white as modern nationalists—usually upper-caste Hindus—imagine them to be. The kings of Vijayanagar were not mainly defending Hinduism against Islam; they were mainly defending their kingdom against other kingdoms, both Muslim *and* Hindu.

The Modern Raya of Anegundi

A day after meeting Krishna Devaraya in Hospet, I take a ferry across the Tungabhadra to visit his ancestral home in Anegundi, a dusty village with a population of 4000. This home, built 200 years ago, stands across a ruined fort-palace—the place from where the Sangama brothers likely launched their imperial dreams nearly 700 years ago.

Krishna greets me warmly. He is a soft-spoken man of medium height. His blue jeans and white T-shirt, bushy moustache, and red tilak convey a relaxed yet serious persona. His living room is like a tastefully renovated mini palace from

Figure 11. Krishna Devaraya's family home

another era. He asks a maid for tea as we settle down on diwan-style sofas to begin our conversation.

His personal history seems oddly commonplace. Krishna grew up in the vicinity, studied mechanical engineering from Davangere, married in his early twenties and went to the US on H-1B and H-4 visas. From 2001–08, he worked in the residential construction segment in Washington DC and suffered his share of ups and downs in the job market. His only sibling, a sister, lives on the US East Coast. After his father's death in 2008, Krishna returned to Hospet/Anegundi. His household now includes his mother, wife, son (eighteen) and twin daughters (twelve). But none live at this ancestral home: the daughters attend school in Hospet and the son attends high school in Bengaluru.

Growing up, Krishna says, he cared little about Indian history or his royal ancestry. While he himself married a 'commoner', a non-royal woman he knew since childhood, until the previous generation his family tended to marry only within other royal families. His mother is from the royal family of Narsinghgarh, a former princely state in Madhya Pradesh, and which claims descent from Raja Bhoj. It was only in the US that his family history and Vijayanagar's past began to interest him. As he discovered his roots, he began to imagine a new sense of purpose and life path for himself.

Krishna gives me a tour of his beautiful double-storeyed home. He renovated it for years after his return. It combines a traditional layout and architectural flourishes with Western-style bathrooms, skylights, a modern kitchen and a home theatre. Ornate teak wood pillars, beams and carved doors coexist with high-tech, smartphone-controlled lights. Vaastu-inspired architectural designs go hand in hand with solar panels, an inverter battery unit and a reverse osmosis water system for the whole house. His home library brims with American sci-fi and fantasy fiction that his kids read. Krishna now mostly reads books on spirituality and the history of Vijayanagar.

Krishna inherited forty acres of agricultural land on which he is trying out a new mix of crops beyond paddy, bananas and sugarcane, such as coconuts and mangoes. He keeps two desi cows to ensure pure milk. He is also reviving a dormant family business of mining iron ore. A good chunk of central Anegundi belongs to the family, including the ruined palace. The family must decide what to do with the fort and palace—turn it into a heritage hotel? A museum? An information centre on Hampi? In a partially restored corner of the palace lives his uncle, Rama Devaraya, seventy-five, a garrulous man with a sharp memory, who spends a lot of time in his veranda overlooking the ruins. When I briefly meet him later, he explains their Aravidu lineage and says the family is projecting Krishna as the principal heir and family spokesperson.

Krishna is a devout and seemingly humble man. He says they are Kshtriyas Rajputs. His *isht devata*, or personal deity, is Virupaksha, and *kula devata*, or family deity, is Tirupati Balaji. He says he is merely a subject of Virupaksha, the king of kings, and follows his every command. Krishna also has a guru and vouches for his supernatural powers, such as of mind reading, curing ailments and astrological predictions.

Anegundi seems like the sort of village that any aspiring adolescent would want to escape. But it's different for Krishna. To the locals, he still exudes the essence of a raya (i.e., raja). They give him respect, status and privilege of the kind that would have been impossible in the US, where he was just another brown man with an accent. Here he presides over festivals, temple ceremonies, a *rathotsav* (in which the local deity is taken around the village in a chariot). He feels the weight and burden of his ancestry and struggles to find his own way of embracing it. He seems stoic about it too, content to play the part of 'royalty' that fate has ordained for him.

At a festival in April, mimicking old custom, he crowns the Virupaksha temple priest using a crown from Vijayanagar days. After major festivals, villagers come to pay respects, including Muslims, about 10–15 per cent of the population. Inside a glass enclosure at his home are swords and daggers; the villagers pay homage to these during Dussehra, an echo of the martial substrate of that festival in Vijayanagar. I watch as three elderly housemaids, before taking leave, touch Krishna's feet with their foreheads. He stands, his hands raised in a gesture of blessing.

He is not currently interested in political office but doesn't rule it out. All political parties are the same, he fumes, full of corrupt politicians out to make money. If good people don't enter politics, bad people will rule. In the preceding two generations, two of his relatives were MLAs in the Karnataka Assembly. His father contested and lost on a BJP ticket in the early 1990s.

For now, Krishna is happy running Anegundi Foundation, an environmental NGO focused on local community projects and keeping

Hampi clean. He speaks passionately about raising awareness of plastic avoidance, waste segregation and recycling, renewable energy, and conservation. He is also involved with heritage restoration projects, but laments that the ASI folks often take shortcuts with restoration work, such as using cement instead of lime mortar.

'We need to be proud of our culture and heritage,' Krishna says. I wonder who his 'we' seeks to include and exclude, which soon becomes apparent. He strongly disagrees with those who idolize the West as a model for India. 'Our society was once great,' he says. 'What we have lately become is due to the Mughals and the British. We were not so corrupt back then,' he says. 'Our class divisions were once based on merit and aptitude; now, sadly, we have hereditary caste, Brahmin pride, reservations, and all that stupid stuff. We were much better, and we need to go back and reclaim that past, while avoiding the mistakes of that age.' I wonder what 'mistakes' he has in mind and how far back he wants to go, but he continues, 'We need to cultivate more pride in our own history and achievements. Here in the south, for instance, why should we read about the Mughals and the Delhi Sultanate? Our history books, he asserts, contain so little about Vijayanagar, and only praise the Mughals and the British, even though we were better. We had a great civilization and we built amazing cities like Vijayanagar. We need to tell our own stories, because, as that famous African proverb goes, until the story of the hunt is told by the lion, the tale of the hunt will always glorify the hunter.' The irony escapes him that for centuries his ancestors, running a powerful empire, were the proverbial hunters of south India.

Often when Krishna visits the ruins at Hampi, he feels a sense of wonder and awe at what happened here, and what this place must have been like in its glory days. At times, he just goes and sits on some of the higher rocks or by the riverside, lost in reflection. In this he finds a sense of peace and contentment, even happiness. I notice that it is early evening already. As I prepare to take his leave, a muezzin's call to prayer comes wafting over the village rooftops.

François Bernier's India

(1658–69 CE)

'The heat is so intense in Hindoustan, that no one, not even the King, wears stockings,' writes Frenchman François Bernier (1625–88) in a letter to a friend back home in the 1660s. For over six months, 'everybody lies in the open air without covering—the common people in the streets, the merchants and persons of condition sometimes in their courts or gardens, and sometimes on their terraces, which are first carefully watered'.[1] Bernier, a medical doctor, was then in Aurangzeb's employ in Shahjahanabad, the new capital of the Mughal Empire in Delhi.

Eager to see the world, Bernier had left France in 1654 and spent a few years in Syria, Palestine, and Egypt, from where he made his way to Surat, Gujarat, in 1658. He stayed in India for twelve years, starting as the personal physician of Dara Shikoh, Emperor Shah Jahan's eldest son. He was in Delhi during the bloody war of royal succession that saw Aurangzeb prevail over his three brothers and imprison his father Shah Jahan—a saga Bernier documented in extensive detail in a letter to a friend.

Bernier then worked for a nobleman in Aurangzeb's court, Daneshmand Khan, secretary of state for foreign affairs and grand master of the horse. In his letters to people back home, later published as *Travels in the Mogul Empire*, Bernier warmly refers to Khan as 'my Agah', 'the most learned man of Asia', 'whose thirst for knowledge is incessant', and who devotes his afternoons to 'philosophical studies . . .

Astronomy, geography, and anatomy are his favourite pursuits, and he reads with avidity the works of Gassendi and Descartes'.

In his letter, Bernier criticizes Europeans who complain that the buildings in the Indies 'are inferior in beauty to those of the Western world, forgetting that different climates require different styles of architecture; that what is useful and proper at Paris, London, or Amsterdam, would be entirely out of place at Delhi'. 'In these hot countries,' he explains, a beautiful house is capacious, 'airy and exposed on all sides to the wind, especially to the northern breezes'. He adds, 'A good house has its courtyards, gardens, trees, basins of water, small *jets d'eau* in the hall or at the entrance, and handsome subterraneous apartments which are furnished with large fans, and on account of their coolness are fit places for repose from noon until four or five o'clock, when the air becomes suffocatingly warm . . . no handsome dwelling is ever seen without terraces on which the family may sleep during the night.' Bernier then describes the typical interiors of fine houses, their carpets, painted ceilings and flower pots. He describes the beauty of a few public buildings in Delhi, such as the Jama Masjid and the Caravanserai (demolished in the nineteenth century), as grand as the Palais Royale in Paris—'the rendezvous of the rich Persian, Usbek, and other foreign merchants'.[2] 'I think it may be safely asserted, without disparagement to the towns in our quarter of the globe, that the capital of Hindoustan is not destitute of handsome buildings, although they bear no resemblance to those in Europe.' The Taj Mahal, he thinks, 'deserves much more to be numbered among the wonders of the world than the pyramids of Egypt'.

Bernier estimates the population of Delhi as not 'greatly less' than that of Paris. '[Besides] the Omrahs [noblemen], the city never contains less than thirty-five thousand troopers, nearly all of whom have wives, children, and a great number of servants, who, as well as their masters, reside in separate houses,' he notes. 'The uniform and wide streets that so eminently distinguish Dehli [sic]' from the old Mughal capital Agra, 'are crowded with people . . . and, excepting a few carts, unincumbered with wheel carriages'. 'Omrahs and Rajas ride thither, some on horseback, some on majestic elephants; but the greater part are conveyed on the shoulders of six men, in rich

Palekys, leaning against a thick cushion of brocade, and chewing their bet-lé, for the double purpose of sweetening their breath and reddening their lips.'

In summertime, a major fruit market sells expensive 'dry fruit from Persia, Balk, Bokara, and Samarkande; such as almonds, pistachios, and walnuts, raisins, prunes, and apricots; and in winter . . . excellent fresh grapes, black and white, brought from the same countries, wrapped in cotton; pears and apples of three or four sorts, and those admirable melons which last the whole winter'. Babur, who began the Mughal Dynasty, would have loved this market. He had terribly missed grapes and melons from Bukhara and Samarkand. He had tried to grow a few on the Indian soil and even had some success with it. In *Baburnama*, his urbane memoir, he writes, 'To have grapes and melons grown in this way in Hindustan filled me with content.'[3] Clearly, he and his descendants weren't able to grow on Hindustani soil all of the grapes and melons they missed.

'To be considered a Mogol, it is enough if a foreigner have a white face and profess Mahometanism,' writes Bernier. The term 'Mogol' includes Persians, Turks, Arabs, Uzbeks and their descendants. The Persians are mostly Shia, the rest mostly Sunni. He contrasts the Mogols with others of darker complexion, the largest being the Gentiles (i.e., not of an Abrahamic faith), who have 'the languid manner of this country'. There are many ethnic and religious groupings but no 'Indian' identity. A hierarchy exists in which the Mogols heavily dominate the best imperial positions, besides a few Hindu Rajputs. The cavalry at the king's disposal, including 'those in the provinces, forms a total of more than two hundred thousand horse' and 'two, or even three hundred thousand infantry'. This includes 'servants, sutlers, tradesmen, and all those individuals belonging to bazaars' who convey 'the immense quantity of tents, kitchens, baggage, furniture, and even women, usually attendant on the army', much of it using numerous 'elephants, camels, oxen, horses, and porters'. Even a subset of this army on the move is a spectacle to behold and a very disruptive—and economically lucrative—event for the locals.

Bernier describes the opulence of the emperor and his courtiers, their grand processions, bejewelled costumes, the audience hall at

Red Fort with its peacock throne and lavish furnishings of silver, gold brocade, silk and satin. He observes 'the base and disgusting adulation which is invariably witnessed there' and 'the vice of flattery [that] pervades all ranks'. He describes the luxurious but cloistered lives of women in the Seraglio. Whereas Shah Jahan invited singing and dancing girls there, 'often detained them the whole night, and amused himself with their antics and follies', Aurangzeb doesn't do so. Bernier writes that Aurangzeb 'is more serious than his father' and 'anxious to appear a true Musulman'. His 'extremely liberal' and erudite brother Dara Shikoh, who translated the Upanishads into Persian, had called him a 'Nemazi', or '"that Bigot," that ever-prayerful one'. But Dara too had many flaws. Bernier thinks he was 'very irascible; apt to menace; abusive and insulting even to the greatest Omrahs' and undervalued 'the opinions of the wisest counsellors'. Whereas Aurangzeb possessed 'a sounder judgment, and was more skilful in selecting for confidants such persons as were best qualified to serve him with faithfulness and ability' and 'whose talents for government [his father] always entertained a high opinion'.

The common man's life, however, is very different. 'In Dehli there is no middle state. A man must either be of the highest rank or live miserably.' In Paris, 'seven or eight out of ten individuals seen in the streets are tolerably well clad, and have a certain air of respectability; but in Dehli, for two or three who wear decent apparel, there [are] seven or eight poor, ragged, and miserable beings'. All in all, he tells his friend, 'I may indeed say, without partiality, and after making every allowance for the beauty of Dehli, Agra, and Constantinople, that Paris is the finest, the richest, and altogether the first city in the world.'

Among the things he misses from home is bread. Bakers 'are numerous,' he writes, 'but the ovens are unlike our own, and very defective. The bread, therefore, is neither well made nor properly baked.' Liquor is forbidden, 'equally by the Gentile and Mahometan law', but secretly consumed. Wine is rare, and those imported by the Dutch 'are so dear that, as we say at home, the taste is destroyed by the cost'. Only a few Christians 'dare openly to drink' a tipple called Arac, which is 'harsh and burning'.

On the Social and Economic Conditions of 'Hindoustan'

'Of this vast tract of country,' Bernier writes, 'a large portion is extremely fertile; the large kingdom of Bengale, for instance, surpassing Egypt itself, not only in the production of rice, corn, and other necessaries of life, but of innumerable articles of commerce which are not cultivated in Egypt; such as silks, cotton, and indigo.' Artisans manufacture 'carpets, brocades, embroideries, gold and silver cloths, and the various sorts of silk and cotton goods, which are used in the country or exported abroad'.

The king is the proprietor of all land in the kingdom, writes Bernier (Megasthenes also noted this in Mauryan times). He asks 'whether it would not be more advantageous for the King as well as for the people, if the former ceased to be sole possessor of the land, and the right of private property were recognised in the Indies as it is with us? I have carefully compared the condition of European states, where that right is acknowledged, with the condition of those countries where it is not known, and am persuaded that the absence of it among the people is injurious to the best interests of the Sovereign himself'. Lack of formal property rights, argues Bernier, deters people from investing in their lands and homes to improve their lot, since they may lose them based on the whims of power. This, in turn, depresses tax revenues and encourages people to hide their surpluses in gold. (In his day, expanding property rights and waning feudalism had in recent centuries put Europe on a heady new path of economic and cultural evolution.)

Provincial governors and tax collectors, writes Bernier, 'have an authority almost absolute over the peasantry, and nearly as much over the artisans and merchants of the towns and villages within their district; and nothing can be imagined more cruel and oppressive than the manner in which it is exercised'. Therefore, if and 'when wealth is acquired [by a commoner], the possessor, so far from living with increased comfort and assuming an air of independence, studies the means by which he may appear indigent: his dress, lodging, and furniture continue to be mean, and he is careful, above all things, never to indulge in the pleasures of the table. In the meantime, his gold and silver remain buried at a great depth in the ground'.

This 'miserable system of government', mixing despotic power with lack of private property, went beyond the Mughal realm and was said to be pan-Asian. What Bernier refers to was an Indian system of non-hereditary feudal land tenure that arose in Gupta times. This system, according to Bernier, explains why 'most towns in Hindoustan are made up of earth, mud, and other wretched materials' and the 'decline of the Asiatic states', presumably relative to Europe's rising fortunes in its age of exploration and colonization. His account reveals a powerful extractive bureaucracy concentrating riches at the top, sustaining a huge army and funding the lavish lives of the aristocrats, not to mention 'the enormous expenses of the Seraglio, where the consumption of fine cloths of gold, and brocades, silks, embroideries, pearls, musk, amber and sweet essences, is greater than can be conceived'. Millions, he writes, 'depend for support solely on the King's pay. Is it possible, [as many] have asked, that any revenue can suffice for such incredible expenditure?' They seem 'to forget the riches of the Great Mogol, and the peculiar manner in which Hindoustan is governed'.

Consequently, 'the inhabitants have less the appearance of a moneyed people than those of many other parts of the globe'. Bernier's portrait of the extreme disparities in India agrees with the testimony of Athanasius Nikitin, a Russian traveller in the fifteenth century: 'Those in the country are very miserable, whilst the nobles are extremely opulent and delight in luxury.' This is at odds with the *sone ki chidiya* (golden bird) imagery often invoked about precolonial India, likely based on the accounts of foreign travellers who hobnobbed with the social elites and reported on their great wealth—even as the commoners were no better off than in other parts of the world.

Further, as Bernier writes, much of the oft-remarked fabulous wealth of Hindoustan existed in gold, diamonds, and 'a prodigious quantity of pearls and gems of all kinds, of great size and value'. Bernier doubts 'whether any other Monarch possesses more of this species of wealth . . . But all these precious stones, and valuable articles, are the spoils of ancient princes, Patons and Rajas, collected during a long course of years, and, increasing regularly under every reign'. However, Bernier astutely points out, 'upon the security of [such wealth] the King, in a time of pressing necessity, would find it extremely difficult to raise the smallest sum'.

Given all this, Bernier asks, 'Can it excite wonder, that under these circumstances, the arts do not flourish here as they would do under a better government, or as they flourish in our happier France? No artist can be expected to give his mind to his calling in the midst of a people who are either wretchedly poor, or who, if rich, assume an appearance of poverty, and who regard not the beauty and excellence, but the cheapness of an article.' Bernier believes that the arts of the Indies 'would long ago have lost their beauty and delicacy, if the Monarch and principal Omrahs did not keep in their pay a number of artists'.

Moreover, a 'profound and universal ignorance is the natural consequence of such a state of society'. 'Is it possible,' asks Bernier, 'to establish in Hindoustan academies and colleges properly endowed? Where shall we seek for founders? Or, should they be found, where are the scholars? Lastly . . . where are the benefices, the employments, the offices of trust and dignity, that require ability and science and are calculated to excite the emulation and the hopes of the young student?' As if this wasn't enough social anthropology to reckon with, Bernier also seems to have anticipated Adam Smith, born thirty-five years after his death in 1688:

> Nor can the commerce of a country so governed be conducted with the activity and success that we witness in Europe; few are the men who will voluntarily endure labour and anxiety, and incur danger, for another person's benefit—for a governor who may appropriate to his own use the profit of any speculation.
>
> . . . to conclude briefly I must repeat it; take away the right of private property in land, and you introduce, as a sure and necessary consequence, tyranny, slavery, injustice, beggary and barbarism: the ground will cease to be cultivated and become a dreary wilderness; in a word, the road will be opened to the ruin of Kings and the destruction of Nations. It is the hope by which a man is animated, that he shall retain the fruits of his industry, and transmit them to his descendants, that forms the

main foundation of everything excellent and beneficial in this sublunary state; and if we take a review of the different kingdoms in the world, we shall find that they prosper or decline according as this principle is acknowledged or contemned: in a word, it is the prevalence or neglect of this principle which changes and diversifies the face of the earth.

Bernier accompanies Aurangzeb's large entourage to a retreat in Kashmir, 'one of the most beautiful countries in the world'. The Kashmiris, he writes,

> are celebrated for wit, and considered much more intelligent and ingenious than the Indians. In poetry and the sciences, they are not inferior to the Persians. They are also very active and industrious [and] proverbial for their clear complexions and fine forms . . . The women especially are very handsome; and it is from this country that nearly every individual, when first admitted to the court of the Great Mogol, selects wives or concubines, that his children may be whiter than the Indians and pass for genuine Mogols.

Near Kashmir Bernier also meets a leader from the 'Lama tribe' of Tibet, led by a very old 'Grand Lama', who, nearing death, 'assembled the council, and declared to them that his soul was going to pass into the body of an infant recently born'. Buddhism had disappeared from India to such an extent that Bernier didn't even recognize them as adherents of a faith with roots in India.

On Ridiculous Errors and Strange Superstitions

'Bernier was very much the educated European of the early Enlightenment,' writes historian William Dalrymple in *City of Djinns*. 'He knew his classics, was a firm believer in Reason, and had no patience with "ridiculous errors and strange superstitions".' Bernier studied physiology and philosophy under the materialist Pierre Gassendi and was a man of the emerging scientific–philosophical thought of Europe.

He felt part of a more 'advanced' civilization, both in terms of its scientific knowledge and its social and political thought.

Consequently, in his letters, he is often dismissive of Indians and their beliefs, especially Gentiles (who were more alien to him, whereas he had access to Europe's considerable body of knowledge and attitudes on Muslims). '[The] Gentiles understand nothing of anatomy,' he writes. 'They never open the body either of man or beast, and those in our household always ran away, with amazement and horror, whenever I opened a living goat or sheep for the purpose of explaining to my Agah the circulation of the blood [recently explained by William Harvey].'

In another letter, he tries to show 'that there is no doctrine too strange or too improbable for the soul of man to conceive', citing examples from Gentile India (and a few from France). During a solar eclipse, he watches 'deluded people' plunge themselves in the Yamuna and 'perform their silly tricks until the end of the eclipse'. Then they 'gave alms to the Brahmens, who failed not to be present at this absurd ceremony'. He ridicules the logic behind these acts, which, he is told, derives from the four Vedas.

These books, he writes, also 'enjoin that the people shall be divided, as in fact they are most effectually, into four tribes [that] are not permitted to intermarry, that is to say, a Brahmen is forbidden to marry a Quettery [Kshatriya], and the same injunction holds good in regard to the other tribes'. Another contemporary French traveller, Jean Baptiste Tavernier (1605–89), also writes about India's caste divisions. 'An idolater will not eat bread nor drink water in a house belonging to any one of a different caste from his own, unless it is more noble and more exalted than his own.' One caste, Haldrkkors, is 'only occupied in removing the refuse from houses, it gets the remains of what the others eat, of whatever caste they may be, and it does not make any scruple about eating indifferently of all things. [Its members] alone feed pigs and use them for food'.[4]

With barely concealed horror, Bernier also relates events from the famous 'car' festival of the Jagannath Temple in Orissa (similar to the chariot festival described by Niccolo de Conti in Vijayanagar):

A superb wooden machine [with] many grotesque figures . . . is set on fourteen or sixteen wheels like those of a gun-carriage, and drawn or pushed along by the united exertions of fifty or sixty persons. The idol, Jagannat, placed conspicuously in the middle, richly attired, and gorgeously adorned, is thus conveyed from one temple to another . . . blindly credulous [people] throw themselves upon the ground in the way of its ponderous wheels, which pass over and crush to atoms the bodies of the wretched fanatics without exciting the horror or surprise of the spectators. No deed, according to their estimation, is so heroic or meritorious as this self-devotion: the victims believe that Jagannat will receive them as children, and recall them to life in a state of happiness and dignity.

Bernier derides Brahmins who 'promote these gross errors and superstitions to which they are indebted for their wealth and consequence'. Though 'held in general veneration', 'their tricks and impostures' are 'wicked and detestable'. 'Lustful priests' even deceive and possess young girls dedicated to serve the deity at Jagannath Temple. He claims, 'The Great Mogol, though a Mahometan, permits these ancient and superstitious practices; not wishing, or not daring, to disturb the Gentiles in the free exercises of their religion.'

He then focuses on the 'melancholy fact' of sati, relating many harrowing cases that he has seen. He is certain that many widows 'would willingly have recanted, if recantation had been permitted by the merciless Brahmens; but those demons excite or astound the affrighted victims, and even thrust them into the fire'. Citing an example, he writes that a young woman on the burning pyre was 'prevented from escaping by the long poles of the diabolical executioners'. In another, the Brahmins pushed 'the unwilling victim toward the fatal spot, seated her on the wood, tied her hands and feet, lest she should run away, and in that situation the innocent creature was burnt alive'. Bernier doesn't mince words, 'I need scarcely say how much my own indignation has been excited, and how ardently I have wished for opportunities to exterminate those cursed Brahmens.' He clarifies, too, that any widow who manages to 'avoid the impending sacrifice, cannot hope to pass her days in happiness, or to be treated with respect or affection . . . she is ever afterwards exposed to the ill-treatment of her low and vulgar protectors'.

Women became satis mostly among upper-caste Hindus, especially warrior elites, who appeared more often in Bernier's milieu. Notably,

> . . . the Mahometans, by whom the country is governed, [do] all in their power to suppress the barbarous custom. They do not, indeed, forbid it by a positive law, because it is a part of their policy to leave the idolatrous population, which is so much more numerous than their own, in the free exercise of its religion; but the practice is checked by indirect means. No woman can sacrifice herself without permission from the governor of the province in which she resides, and he never grants it until he shall have ascertained that she is not to be turned aside from her purpose: to accomplish this desirable end the governor reasons with the widow and makes her enticing promises; after which, if these methods fail, he sometimes sends her among his women, that the effect of their remonstrances may be tried. Notwithstanding these obstacles, the number of self-immolations is still very considerable, particularly in the territories of the [Rajput] Rajas, where no Mahometan governors are appointed.

Tavernier too notes the official restraints Bernier describes above. A woman, Tavernier writes, 'cannot burn herself with the body of her husband without having received permission from the Governor of the place where she dwells, and those Governors who are Muhammadans, hold this dreadful custom of self-destruction in horror, and do not readily give permission'. It is then curious, writes Romila Thapar, that in the nineteenth century people would start believing that sati 'was necessitated by the "Muslim invasions" when upper-caste Hindu women had to defend their honour from Muslim marauders'.[5] In fact, the first-known cases of sati in India date from mid-first millennium BCE, long before the birth of Islam.[6]

Bernier refuses to believe, as some apologists of sati claim, that 'an excess of affection was the cause why these women burn themselves with their deceased husbands'. He believes it's 'the effect of early and deeply rooted prejudices'. 'Every girl is taught by her mother that it is virtuous and laudable in a wife to mingle her ashes with those of her husband, and that no woman of honour will refuse compliance with the established custom. These opinions men have always inculcated as an easy mode of keeping wives in subjection, of securing their attention in times of sickness, and of deterring them from administering poison to their husbands.'

Bernier also expresses his dislike for the 'endless variety of Fakires, or Derviches, and Holy Men, or Gentile hypocrites of the Indies'. He speaks of a group 'seated or lying on ashes, entirely naked [with] hair hanging down to the calf of the leg, twisted and entangled into knots, like the coat of our shaggy dogs . . . several who hold one, and some who hold both arms, perpetually lifted up above the head; the nails of their hands being twisted, and longer than half my little finger'. At first, they remind Bernier of 'the ancient and infamous sect of Cynics', but he only sees in them 'brutality and ignorance' and 'vegetative rather than rational beings'. He rues that 'novices wait upon these fanatics, and pay them the utmost respect, as persons endowed with extraordinary sanctity'.

Bernier has seen 'bands of these naked Fakires, hideous to behold', who 'shamelessly walk, stark naked, through a large town' with 'frightful hair' hung loose or 'twisted round their heads'. He recalls one 'celebrated Fakire, named Sarmet, who paraded the streets of Dehli . . . He despised equally the promises and the threats of Aureng-Zebe, and underwent at length the punishment of decapitation for his obstinate refusal to put on wearing apparel'. The fakirs' public nudity seems to curtail Bernier's sympathy for them, though he is also disgusted by what he sees as their ignorance, superstition and lack of piety, evident in their painful austerities and fasting for days in order to seek union with God.

Piety mattered to Bernier because he was also a proud Christian and shared the historical European antipathy towards Islam. From his account, it's clear that he favours the 'establishment of missions, and the sending forth of learned and pious missionaries'. 'They are absolutely necessary,' he says. Christians ought to 'supply every part of the world with men bearing the same character and following the same benign object as did the Apostles . . . promoting the glory of their REDEEMER'. Bernier expects some Gentiles to convert, but about Muslims he says, 'It is in vain to hope, however, that they will renounce the religion wherein they were born, or be persuaded that Mahomet was a false prophet . . . To counteract [Islam's] baneful progress, Christians must display the zeal.'

Bernier also had many discourses with Gentile scholars, including 'the six most learned Pendets' of Varanasi, but nothing seems to have impressed him. He concedes that some of their hypotheses 'have an affinity to the theories of Democritus and Epicurus', but he claims their 'opinions are expressed in so loose and indeterminate a manner that it is difficult to ascertain their meaning'. This leads him to think that 'the Pendets neither comprehend themselves, nor can make [themselves] intelligible to others'. Instead, they only 'make a thousand foolish and confused observations'. He is bemused by their conception of the world as an illusion, and has no patience for their 'fine similes'. 'In vain will you look for any solid answer,' he declares.

He asks the six learned pandits of Varanasi for 'their opinion of the adoration of idols'. The pandits respond, 'Images are admitted in our temples, because we conceive that prayers are offered up with more devotion where there is something before the eyes that fixes the mind; but in fact we acknowledge that God alone is absolute, that He only is the omnipotent Lord.' Bernier doubts this explanation. He suspects 'it was so framed as to correspond with the tenets of Christianity. The observations made to me by other learned Pendets were totally different'. He needles another set of Brahmins that many of their practices aren't possible in colder climes, such as bathing in rivers, clearly showing that their religion is not universal—and therefore inferior. But the Brahmins see things differently:

'We pretend not,' they replied, 'that our law is of universal application. God intended it only for us, and this is the reason why we cannot receive a foreigner into our religion. We do not even say that yours is a false religion: it may be adapted to your wants and circumstances, God having, no doubt, appointed many different ways of going to heaven.' I found it impossible to convince them that the Christian faith was designed for the whole earth, and theirs was mere fable and gross fabrication.

To the modern reader, this gives a sense of a series of frustrating engagements driven largely by Bernier's inability to step outside his own philosophical framework. He rarely doubts his own comprehension and certainties in religion. Instead, his response is to grossly misunderstand and ridicule, and declare much of what he hears as 'extravagant folly'. He doesn't read Sanskrit, yet calls all of their books full of 'fabulous trash'. In geography, he claims, 'They believe that the world is flat and triangular.' This would have been news to Alberuni, who came in the eleventh century, read texts in Sanskrit and characterized the Indians' knowledge systems far more intelligently before evaluating them.

Could it be that Bernier's views were coloured by popular beliefs and social practices—astrology, superstitions, sati, naked fakirs, otherworldly attitudes, etc.—that vexed his humanistic sensibilities, and which then led him to dismiss that entire edifice of philosophies that he saw as enablers? Perhaps he didn't meet the best scholars. In India, Bernier 'is simultaneously attentive and dismissive, curious and contemptuous', writes philosopher Justin E.H. Smith, adding another nuance in noting that 'his negative judgments flow from his status as a libertine materialist philosopher in the battle against superstition back home in Europe'.[7]

Bernier triumphantly concludes, 'If the renowned sciences of the . . . Indies consisted of all the extravagant follies which I have detailed, mankind have indeed been deceived in the exalted opinion they have long entertained of their wisdom.' This may have been a valid critique had Bernier arrived at it through an adequate understanding of the subject. Instead, he mostly illustrates the difficulties inherent in a dialogue between disparate intellectual traditions.

Bernier's world view is familiar to us for its early modernity, humanism and materialistic ethos. He had his prejudices but he was also often remarkably clear-eyed. In Europe, his account fuelled the stereotype of 'oriental despotisms' among thinkers like James Mill, Hegel and Marx, who imagined Indians as unchanging, passive and superstitious.[8] Later, some others would see in his depiction the presence of 'tolerance and coexistence of pluralistic subcultures' in India.[9]

Bernier didn't just travel through; for twelve years he worked and engaged with Indians with considerable openness. He wrote what is now a rare and insightful portrait of seventeenth-century India, decades before the arrival of European colonizers. In his account, India seems to be in a state of intellectual decay, uncreative and stunted, ill-prepared against the advancing power of Europe's scientific method, mercantilism, scholarship and the nation-state model. He expressed fondness and affection for many people and things, but a good part of his account is an indictment of Indian society—though in ways that resonate aplenty with our own liberal assessments today.

The Faiths of **Varanasi**
(800 BCE–)

'My friend, I like Banaras. It is a fine city,' writes Mirza Ghalib to a friend
in 1860. 'I have written a poem in praise of it called *The Lamp of the
Temple* [a poem of 108 stanzas in Persian],' he adds.[1] In 1827, when
Ghalib was thirty, he spent a few months in Varanasi, travelling there
from Delhi on unpaved roads and boats along the Ganga. He fell in love
with the mood and festive spirit of Varanasi and wrote to a friend, 'This
city is so beautiful and lovely that even a stranger misses counting his
sufferings. If I would have no fear of religious contempt and criticism
from my enemies, I would have left my religion . . . to count beads, bear
sacred threads, put a mark on the forehead and in this way I would have
passed my life on the bank of the Ganga.'

Nearly two hundred years later, in May 2019, I too make the journey
from Delhi to Varanasi. I take the fastest and newest train in India, the
Vande Bharat Express. Compared to Ghalib's hard journey, mine is a lot
easier, but my first response to the city is far less favourable. As on my
previous visit in 2006, Varanasi strikes me as anything but lovely, with
its chaotic traffic, deafening honks, poor urban planning, overcrowding,
too many beggars and sporadic stench from drains. It feels left behind
even by the low standards of BIMARU states. Aspiring young people
have been escaping to the metros to pursue better lives. This is despite
helpful recent investments in the city by Prime Minister Narendra Modi,
who is seeking re-election to the Lok Sabha from here. On my first

evening, returning to Godowlia Chowk from the Ganga Aarti on the river, a pickpocket steals my mobile phone. I go late at night to report the theft at the local police chowki and learn that mine is one of a dozen odd such thefts reported daily.

But the morning starts afresh; over the next two weeks, as I ease myself into the rhythms of the city and talk to a wide range of people, other aspects of Varanasi emerge to soften my first impressions.

Varanasi's present is even harder to reconcile with its ancient past—a city of gardens and groves; mini lakes, lotus ponds and kunds; ashrams and hermitages—only faint traces of which remain in isolated pockets. Long ago, its 'groves, streams, and pools provided a beautiful setting for temples and ashrams', wrote historian Diana Eck in her acclaimed account, *Banaras: City of Light* (1982). 'Here teachers could gather their students, yogis could practice their yoga, and ascetics and hermits could find a place for their disciplines.' Even in the late eighteenth century, Varanasi's riverfront 'was a long spectacular bluff crowned with trees and a few prominent temples'.[2] Most of the densely crowded cement buildings that now line the riverfront arose in the last two or three hundred years.

Varanasi brims with religious mythologies. It is claimed to be 'the place where the linga of Shiva was first established and worshipped on earth' and is now Shiva's permanent home. He dwells 'not only in the city's great temples, but in the very ground and substance of the place itself'.[3] Varanasi's mystique has long attracted foreigners; many have left vivid accounts of the city. It is also associated with famous natives and sojourners like the Buddha, Jain Tirthankaras, Dhanvantari, Sushruta, Patanjali, Sankara, Ramanuja, Kabir, Ravidas, Tulsidas, Nanak, Lakshmibai, Annie Besant, Premchand, Malviya and Radhakrishnan.

But 'timeless', a favourite trope of past travellers for Varanasi, now feels dated. As in much of India, the city's culture and ethos are changing fast. Old pillars of its economy are crumbling. Its weaving industry, which sustains nearly a quarter of the city—more Muslims than Hindus—is shrinking. Most weavers, known for their exquisite Banarasi silk sarees, are poor and typically work with a couple of looms set up in tiny spaces at home. Power looms have now mostly replaced handlooms, though some weavers still do manual *zaridosi* or intricate embroideries.

Additional innovations in technology have tilted the cost and efficiency advantage firmly in the favour of the mega textile mills of Surat (Gujarat) and China. 'Surat copies our designs, uses cheap artificial silk and often calls its products Banarasi,' a weaver told me. This has raised poverty and job loss in Varanasi—the flip side of the 'creative destruction' of economic globalization.

Indian pop culture and Bollywood associate a colourful linguistic style, diction and flamboyance with the Banarasis. Many locals speak of a Banarasi identity that often trumps other group identities. And if the city is today seen as a centre of Hindu orthodoxy and Hindutva nationalism, it's worth recalling that in the decades before the 1990s, the communist parties did very well here, winning the parliamentary seat in 1967 and coming second on four occasions (though it's also true that in India these two things are not as opposed as they ought to be; the so-called communist parties of India also have a history of being steeped in Brahminism).[4]

Modern Hindi too arose in Varanasi. Writers led by Bharatendu Harishchandra forged it out of Khariboli—infusing more Sanskrit into it at the expense of Persian—and popularized it via theatre in the nineteenth century. Often called 'the father of modern Hindi', Harishchandra was a polyglot, a 'rakish, extravagant nobleman', and a patron of the arts.[5] His old haveli still stands in a tangled gully where his fifth-

generation descendants live and warmly receive the occasional cultural tourist like me. With many old paintings on the wall, the haveli feels historic and charming, even as its younger residents chafe at its maintenance problems and dream of leaving the congested alleyways for

Figure 1. Former haveli of Bharatendu Harishchandra

a modern township. Avadhi and Braj are also widely spoken (Tulsidas wrote his version of the Ramayana, *Ramacharitmanas*, in Awadhi).

Of the millions who visit Varanasi each year, most are pilgrims. Some hope to die here in old age, or at least to be cremated beside the Ganga. This is said to be a sure-shot path to moksha—liberation from the endless cycle of rebirth—for all people, including rogues. Many find this idea silly, as did the fifteenth-century poet-saint Kabir. To illustrate its folly, in his last days, Kabir left Varanasi to die in a town called Maghar, about which it was said, 'He who dies in Maghar is reborn as an ass.' Though claimed by sections of both Muslims and Hindus as one of their own, the still-beloved Kabir is of course famous for ridiculing 'with equal vehemence the sacred books of the Muslims and Hindus, the Muslim mullas and the Hindu brahmins, the Muslim Mecca and the Hindu Kashi'.[6] A free spirit, he fought dogma and oppression in all religions with a gentle and ironic wit. One of his typical short verses goes:

Saints, I see the world is mad.
If I tell the truth they rush to beat me,
if I lie they trust me.[7]

As with so many religious rebels, who disliked all sects and went their own ways, Kabir's fans responded by forming a sect in his name, Kabir Panth (Path of Kabir), now with centres all across India and even abroad. It is led by Kabir Math, located in a part of Varanasi called Kabir Chaura, where Kabir grew up. Adjoining the math's compound is the tomb of his parents, Niru and Nima. I spend a pleasant afternoon hour with Sant Vivek Das, the head of Kabir Math, who speaks about the genius of Kabir, his life and times, and his changing reception today. I ask if he agreed with Varanasi's popular image as a stronghold of Brahminism. He replies defiantly, 'A city that produced and still loves revolutionaries like Kabir and Ravidas is not a city of Brahminism, but one that belongs to people of all creeds and classes.'

Varanasi's past abounds in such sociopolitical contestations. Take the utopian visions of two other influential bhakti poet-thinkers of Varanasi from the fifteenth and sixteenth centuries: Ravidas and Tulsidas. Ravidas, an 'untouchable', advocated social reform towards a casteless and classless society he called 'Begumpura'—ideas that later animated B.R. Ambedkar. Whereas Tulsidas, a Brahmin, advocated personal piety and the status-quoist Varnashrama Dharma of 'Ram Rajya', where all castes adhered to their respective dharmas—ideas that later inspired M.K. Gandhi. Sensing a kindred spirit in me, Das speaks openly about the grave threat that Hindutva nationalism poses to Kabir's teachings. He has made it his life's work to defend and spread them. I browse and purchase two books on Kabir from a shop at the math and leave reflecting on this verse by him and the disguises under which I live my own life:[8]

> Dropped from the belly at birth,
> a man puts on his costumes
> and goes through his acts.

The Antiquity of Varanasi

Varanasi's high perch lies between two rivers (now mere streams): Varana in the north and Asi in the south. No points for guessing the origins of the city's name. To its east flows the Ganga, which here happens to flow north in its meandering course to the sea. Among the world's oldest living cities, perhaps as old as Jerusalem, Athens and Beijing, Varanasi ('Baranasi' in Pali, from which comes Banaras and Benares) has had many other names: Ananda-kanan, Kashi, Sudarshan, Pushpavati, Molini, Jitvari, Avimuktadham, Rudravas, Mahashamshana and more.

Archaeological digs on the Rajghat plateau near the northern end of the city have turned up finds that date from the ninth century BCE (the visible ruins at the tourist complex date from a much later period). Ancient urban Varanasi likely began here. We have no precise historical sources such as inscriptions, but going by stories in the Mahabharata and Buddhist Jataka tales, the kingdom of Kashi existed here in the first half of the first millennium BCE, with Varanasi as the capital. Kashi was one of the sixteen political units in north India called janapadas, where early Aryan culture and Vedic religion took root and led to urbanization. Kashi was then famous for its shipbuilding, ivory, sandalwood and textile crafts. To Kashi's north was Koshala, to its east Magadha. Koshala later conquered Kashi and both were in turn swallowed by Magadha. With

such antiquity, it's strange that only a few archaeological excavations have been undertaken in Varanasi.

Figure 2. Remains of ancient Varanasi

In the Buddha's time, Varanasi was already a major centre of learning. Its heft as a religious and cultural centre likely drew the Buddha here to make his mark and gain a wider audience. He seems to have avoided Varanasi proper, a stronghold of Brahminism, and stayed in adjoining Sarnath, where he famously delivered his first post-enlightenment sermon to five companions.[9] In due course, a large Buddhist settlement arose here. The excavated site of Sarnath, now in a suburb of Varanasi, has beautifully evocative ruins of ancient stupas and monasteries and a museum with exquisite sculptures, including the famous Lion Capital of Emperor Ashoka, which became the basis for the National Emblem of India in 1950.

When Xuanzang visited Sarnath in c. 635 CE, it had hundreds, possibly thousands, of monks. The 'country' of Varanasi, Xuanzang wrote, has a circumference of about 1000 km. 'The families are very rich, and in the dwellings are objects of rare value. The disposition of the people is soft and humane, and they are earnestly given to study . . . a few revere the law of the Buddha. The climate is soft, the crops abundant, the [fruit] trees flourishing, and the underwood thick in every place.' He estimated thirty Buddhist monasteries and 3000 monks, and a 'hundred or so' temples with 10,000 devotees of Shiva. Some of them, he wrote, 'cut off their hair, others tie their hair in a knot, and go naked, without clothes; they cover their bodies with ashes, and by the practice of all sorts of austerities they seek to escape from [the cycle of] birth and death'. The 'densely populated' capital of this country was by the Ganga and had about twenty temples, 'the towers and halls of which are of sculpted stone and carved wood. The foliage of trees combines to shade (the sites), whilst pure streams of water encircle them'. Xuanzang saw a copper statue of Shiva 'somewhat less than 100 feet high' which 'is grave and majestic, and appears as though really living'.[10]

In the early eleventh century, Alberuni visited India during the years it was repeatedly raided by Mahmud of Ghazni. In his account, Alberuni calls Varanasi a leading centre of the 'Hindu sciences' and a place 'venerated for reasons connected with their law and religion', though he didn't visit the city. Much as 'the dwellers of the Ka'ba stay for ever in Mecca,' he writes, Hindu ascetics go to Varanasi 'to live there to the end of their lives, that their reward after death should be the better for it'. 'They say that a murderer is held responsible for his crime and punished . . . except in case he enters the city of Benares, where he obtains pardon'—a karmic pardon, Alberuni likely means—by the automatic attainment of moksha for dying in this hallowed city.

Around 1700 years after the kingdom of Kashi had fallen, Varanasi again became a capital city in 1090 CE. For a century hence, under the

Figure 3. And quietly flows the Ganga on a hot May afternoon.
View from Alamgiri Mosque.

Gahadavala Dynasty, it thrived as a capital located on the Rajghat Plateau in northern Varanasi. The kings of the Gahadavala Dynasty patronized Varanasi and Kannauj as centres of Hindu pilgrimage, funded works of religious literature and culture and made land endowments to temples and Brahmins, such as to the Kashi Vishwanath Temple and King Chandradeva's donation of thirty-two villages to five hundred Brahmins in 1100 CE.[11] At the end of the twelfth century, a weak Gahadavala dynast was defeated by the armies of Sultan Muhammad of Ghori, whose recent ancestors in Afghanistan had left Buddhism to embrace Islam. From 1192–94 CE, his Turkic commander, Qutb-ud-din Aibak—commanding a disciplined cavalry-led army of mercenaries often paid in war booty—defeated Prithviraj Chauhan and killed Jayachandra, the last Gahadavala king, plundered his capital in Varanasi and desecrated many temples. In 1206, Aibak inaugurated a new political dynasty in the north: the Delhi Sultanate.

Varanasi came under the sway of the Delhi Sultanate until 1526 and then of the Mughals. Varanasi's experience during these centuries is now a charged and contentious debate. Muslim dynasties, writes Eck, 'were far from monolithic in their policies toward the sacred sites of the Hindus'. 'There were certainly high moments in these centuries, when Kashi recaptured something of its lost glory. There were times of ambitious temple construction [in Varanasi] and stimulating scholarly activity. But for the most part these were hard centuries.'[12] Still, she adds, 'Banaras continued to be an important center of intellectual life and religious thought'.

Varanasi, in fact, became a major site of the Bhakti movement—a grassroots rejection of Brahminical orthodoxy with an alternative idea of religious piety—led by thinkers like Kabir, Ravidas and Tulsidas. It may seem paradoxical but religious sites like Varanasi and Gaya also benefitted *because* of the Mughal Empire, which created new travel opportunities for pilgrims, scholars and traders. Political unification gave the pilgrim a high 'degree of security on his journey; and the state had a positive interest in promoting this freedom of travel in that it derived substantial revenues from trade and pilgrim taxes'.[13]

Varanasi suffered setbacks too. According to historian Richard Eaton, two campaigns of temple desecration took place: one each under Shah Jahan and Aurangzeb. Hindu nationalists today allege thousands of temple desecrations in Varanasi over many more Mughal campaigns, which, while possible, lack scholarly evidence.[14] By and large, the Mughals, writes Eaton, treated temples in their domain as state property and 'undertook to protect both the physical structures and their Brahmin functionaries'.[15] The temples they destroyed, argues Eaton, were far fewer and usually politically salient for their association with rival Hindu kings, who drew their divine right to rule by patronizing these temples.[16] Most desecrations had political and not sectarian motives. Such nuance, however, remains a bone in the kebab of Hindu nationalism.

In reality, under Muslim rule, realpolitik greatly overshadowed sectarian motives. All Mughal emperors had Hindu administrators and Rajput and Maratha allies and soldiers, which curbed sectarianism. The Mughals fought brutal wars against other Muslims, such as of Bijapur and Golconda; perhaps the deadliest massacres of Hindus in this period were carried out by the Hindu Marathas in Bengal.[17] Akbar actively supported Hinduism, interfaith dialogue and multiculturalism; his Rajput allies built many temples and ghats in Varanasi. Forced conversions remained rare.[18] A sizable minority in Varanasi, especially lower-caste, voluntarily converted to Islam, drawn to its promise of spiritual equality among all believers and the mundane benefits of practising the rulers' faith, such as better job prospects, easier employment in the army and avoiding *jizya* (see below).[19] Many converts were lower-caste weavers, or *julaha*s, including Kabir's parents.

It would of course be foolish to argue that every temple desecration had purely political motives. In some cases, sectarian motives mattered too, especially with Aurangzeb, a puritanical man.[20] Selective razing and replacement of temples with mosques hurt the political standing of rival Hindu kings, but it often also signalled that the top dog was now Islam. In that non-secular, non-democratic age, most Muslim rulers patronized Islam more than Hinduism (and vice versa)—state funding to temples and Brahmins declined relative to pre-Islamic times. Though a minority population, 'Muslims numerically dominated the corps of the Mughal elite'.[21] Muslim rulers also levied jizya, a tax on non-Muslims (it exceeded *zakat,* a tax on better-off Muslims). Discriminatory and widely resented, jizya was poorly collected in practice, especially in villages where most Hindus lived, and it often only lined the pockets of the tax collectors. Akbar abolished jizya in 1579. A hundred years later, despite opposition from his nobles and family, Aurangzeb revived it for forty more years. The Brahmins, however, got their own class exempted from jizya all along.

Such adverse policies and shifts in patronage likely dampened Varanasi's Brahminical culture more than temple desecrations (averaging once in a few generations). Unintentionally, this 'may have encouraged the spread of new, more popular forms of Hinduism such as bhakti', writes historian Wendy Doniger.[22] Popular forms paid scant attention to sectarian boundaries. Wandering 'gurus, pirs and sants' of all backgrounds preached 'a religious melange that defied identification with a particular religion'.[23] Alongside, a rich new high culture arose too. An early example is that of Sufi poet Amir Khusrau, whose Turkish father—a refugee from Samarkand after Genghis Khan had ravaged it—had married the daughter of a Rajput noble and minister in the Delhi Sultanate. Khusrau was only eight when his father died; he then grew up in his mother's Rajput family in Delhi. He would later fuse multiple traditions to create qawwali music and introduce the ghazal in India. In the ensuing centuries, a syncretic Indo-Persian fusion culture arose in cities across India, including Varanasi. Its many legacies pervade modern Indian culture in art, architecture, literature, music, dance, cuisine, dress, painting, crafts, etc. Varanasi's musical syncretism, for instance, would later make the city central to the evolution of Hindustani vocal styles like Thumri, Dadra and Tappa, and produce maestros like Bismillah Khan, Ravi Shankar and Girija Devi.

In 1660, Frenchman François Bernier, a medical doctor in Aurangzeb's court, visited this 'general school of the Gentiles [Hindus]' set 'in the midst of an extremely fine and rich country'. In a letter to a friend, Bernier calls Varanasi the 'Athens of India, wither resort the *Brahmens* and other devotees, who are the only persons who apply their minds to study. The town contains no colleges or regular classes, as in our universities, but resembles rather the schools of the ancients'.[24] Bernier writes about 'a large hall . . . entirely filled' with books on 'philosophy, works on medicine written in verse, and many other kinds of books'. He describes Varanasi's guru-disciple model of schooling, with four to fifteen disciples per guru, who met 'in private houses, and principally in the gardens of the suburbs, which the rich merchants permit them to occupy'.

Most pupils, Bernier writes, had 'an indolent disposition, owing, in great measure, to their diet and the heat of the country'. 'Feeling no spirit of emulation, and entertaining no hope that honors or emoluments may be the reward of extraordinary attainments, as with us, the scholars pursue their study slowly, and without much to distract their attention, while eating their *kichery*, a mingled mess of vegetables supplied to them by the care of rich merchants of the place.'[25]

The first thing they're taught, he writes, is Sanskrit, 'a language known only to the *Pendets*, and totally different from that which is ordinarily spoken in *Hindoustan*'. Their 'scientific books' are all in Sanskrit, he notes, but it 'has long become a dead language, understood only by the learned'. (Indeed, under the Mughals, state administration and literary production in royal courts happened in Persian and vernacular tongues like Braj and Awadhi. Under the British, Persian would suffer the same fate as Sanskrit, and make room for the rise of modern Hindi, Urdu and English.)[26]

Another Frenchman, Jean Baptiste Tavernier, who passed by in the 1660s, writes that Ganga water is highly esteemed in the country and people carry it on their shoulders over long distances. 'The principal reason why this water of the Ganges is so highly esteemed,' he writes, 'is that it never becomes bad, and engenders no vermin; but I do not know whether we should believe what is said about this, taking into consideration the number of [dead human] bodies which are constantly being thrown into the Ganges.'[27] Even today many believe in the magic of the water of Ganga. 'Ganga *maiya* can never become impure,' a sadhu tells me. My arguments from the hygiene perspective are beside the point. His faith in Ganga's cleansing power comes from a metaphysical belief in its ritual purity, which transcends physical impurities like human and toxic industrial waste.[28]

After the Mughal Empire disintegrated in the eighteenth century, Varanasi was ruled again by a Hindu dynasty, though as a feudatory of the nawab of Awadh and the East India Company. Most of Varanasi's 'ancient' ghats and temples were built between 1730 and 1810 with support from the Marathas, who 'invested heavily in the major centers of Brahminical Hinduism in an attempt to legitimize their Kshatriya pretensions and supra-regional aspirations'.[29] Several royal houses built ghats, mansions and dharmashalas on the riverfront. Inside a two-hundred-year-old sandstone fort on Darbhanga Ghat stands Brijrama Palace, an elegant three-storeyed structure built around a traditional courtyard by the royal house of Nagpur; it is now a luxury hotel. In the early 1800s, the king of Nepal, Rana Bahadur Shah, commissioned a temple, Nepali Mandir, and a dharmashala on Lalita Ghat. In 1737, Maharaja Jai Singh of Jaipur built Jantar Mantar near Ganga Ghat, an observatory to study the movement of the sun, planets and the stars.

The British politician Thomas Babington Macaulay visited in the 1830s and saw Varanasi as 'a city, which, in wealth, population, dignity, and sanctity, was among the foremost of Asia' with a 'labyrinth of lofty alleys, rich with shrines, and minarets, and balconies, and carved oriels, to which the sacred apes [monkeys] clung by hundreds'. 'The traveler could scarcely make his way through the press of holy mendicants, and not less holy bulls.' Along the river 'lay great fleets of vessels laden with rich merchandise. From the looms of Benares went forth the most delicate silks that adorned the bells of St. James's and of Versailles'. Under the British Crown, Varanasi became a princely state in 1910.

Today the titular head of the dynasty, Kashi Naresh Anant Narayan Singh, still lives in the palace at Ramnagar Fort, a mile south of Assi Ghat across the river. He still claims descent from Lord Shiva and presides over the biggest religious events at the Kashi Vishwanath Temple. Built in 1750 by Kashi Naresh Raja Balwant Singh, the fort's finely sculpted sandstone buildings around a courtyard now exude a faded grandeur. A month ahead of Dussehra, Singh rides an elephant in a procession and inaugurates the famous Ramlila folk theatre festival of Ramnagar, begun by an ancestor in the nineteenth century. Each evening for a month, thousands come to watch a colourful play performed in the beloved Awadhi of Tulsidas's *Ramacharitmanas*.[30]

A City of Religious Pluralism

Varanasi is frequently associated with Lord Shiva and Brahminical Hinduism, but it has so much more. It has been home to many major and minor faiths, and exhibits a dynamic pluralism. Twenty-nine per cent of its people are Muslim.[31] Bhanu Shanker Mehta, a proud resident scholar, saw Kashi as the confluence of a plethora of sects, including 'the Vedics, Sanatanis, Vaishnavas, Shaivas, Shaktas, Sikhs, Nastiks, Theosophists, Christians, Muslims, Parsees, Arya Samajis, Neo-moderns of Lord Ford, and the Hippies'. 'It is the city of Yakshas, Birs, Barams, and Pirs. It has the office of all the sects like Kabirpanthis, Dadu-panthis, Niranjanis, Udasis, Raidasis, Awadhoots, Aghoris, and Tantrics,' he writes.[32] Muslims include Shia, Sunni, Sufi and Ahmadiyya. Many local and colourful folk religions still thrive, whose gods include animals, trees and rivers. *Matas*, or mother goddesses, abound, such as Shitala, Gauri, Annapurna, Siddheshwari and sixty-four Yoginis (most appropriated by Brahminical Hinduism). Sati stones in old town are still revered. There are caste-specific gods too, like the impressively moustachioed Nishadraj—god of Nishads, or Mallahs, the boatmen and fishermen of Varanasi. Some devotees offer liquor and meat to Kal Bhairav, a fierce form of Shiva wearing a garland of skulls. Hindus visit local Sufi shrines like Chandan Shahid ka Mazar and Muslims visit Aghori ascetics seeking relief from mundane woes. Such syncretism too has been part of Varanasi's character—a fusion Hindu-Muslim culture often referred to as the Ganga-Jamuna *tehzeeb*, exemplified by Kabir himself.

Varanasi's reputation for religious pluralism is empirically well-earned too. Given the vast range and diversity of its creeds, one would expect at least some violent conflict. What's remarkable is how little there has actually been, especially through the end of the nineteenth century. For the most part, its religious and caste groups—fragmented, self-absorbed, inhabiting separate but adjoining physical and social spaces—forged a modus vivendi for coexistence. The very diversity that could have created conflict seems to have made it harder for people to rally behind narrow religious or political ideas. 'While premodern Indians were certainly aware of religious difference,' writes Eaton, 'not a single communal riot is known to have occurred for almost all of medieval history.'[33] Absence of evidence is not evidence of absence, but this is still a startling remark. Even if Eaton is only substantially correct, it is no mean feat.

Another explanation may lie in a default 'live and let live' attitude, partly the by-product of an old otherworldly sensibility in

Figure 4. Handmade embroidery by traditional weavers

the subcontinent—evident in the unorthodox mystical and pacifist traditions of Bhakti and Sufism. This fostered pluralism, distinct from the one in modern political thought, but valuable in its own way and still extant today. A significant factor is also the thick interdependence of communities on each other's traditional trades and skills. For instance, while most weavers of Varanasi's silk sarees are Muslim, most yarn suppliers and retailers of the finished products are Hindu, creating natural incentives to cooperate, maintain peace and oppose those who seek political mileage from communal polarization—a trend yet sadly on the rise, not just in Varanasi (which was also fuelled periodically in the twentieth century as competitive electoral politics grew, notably around Partition. Today, this fragile peace is again under threat as a weakening caste system and the religious right lead more people to see others as 'just Hindus'. The new 'Hindu' identity increasingly transcends caste and ethnic identity and ironically feeds Hindutva nationalism. Stated differently, the old 'division of labourers' that Ambedkar diagnosed in the caste system is fading not to give rise to a casteless proletariat but to a sectarian nationalism).

I got a vivid sense of the city's pluralistic ethos in 2006. I was travelling there on a train from Delhi when terrorists struck Varanasi with bombs at multiple sites, including at the train station; many died. I was with my partner and two white American friends, both on their first visits to India. They seemed rattled, and I worried for their safety. What if Hindu-Muslim riots broke out? Should we abandon the trip and get off at an earlier stop? Despite my concerns, I persuaded my fellow travellers to continue. Worst case, we could stay holed up in our hotel. When we arrived, we found a part of the station cordoned off by the police, red stains on the floor. Our taxi driver had witnessed the explosions: flying body parts, screams, the ensuing melee. He had taken an injured man to the hospital. But our decision to continue turned out to be a good one—the city remained calm and we moved about freely. I felt proud of my fellow citizens.

Perhaps Shiva himself inspires the city's pluralistic ethos. Quite unlike other 'respectable' Hindu gods, he still betrays his pre-Aryan roots. 'He has none of the concern for purity, the love of the auspicious, the disdain of the polluted, the reverence for family, lineage, and status which are characteristically Hindu,' writes Eck. A half-naked ascetic yogi with shaggy hair, he dwells in the forest and is lord of the beasts, smokes ganja, hangs out in cremation grounds and covers his body with ash from the funeral pyres. He 'challenges any facile distinctions between sacred and profane, rich and poor, high and low'. He has long appealed to the rebels, misfits and renunciants in Hindu society (but not only them; his domesticated forms also appeal to conservatives). In short, not a bad presiding deity for a multicultural city.

One evening I meet Amitabh Bhattacharya, an erudite Banarasi and retired professor of journalism. A polyglot known for his deep knowledge of the city, he rattles off an impressive list of faith groups that have called Varanasi home and speaks of its long ethos of pluralism. Varanasi's cultural essence, he says, has been more spiritual than religious, which is why so many thinkers were drawn to it. It took in all kinds of groups and *mostly* avoided the four pitfalls of religion: fanaticism, communalism, fundamentalism and forced conversion. Even the strictures of caste were more fluid in Varanasi, he says, and its casteism relatively milder. 'Where else can a Shudra Yadav casually ask a Brahmin panda [priest] on the ghats to mind his shoes while he takes a dip in the river, as happens here?' His example strikes me as feeble in this day and age, but his point still seems plausible as long as we take 'relatively milder' as the operative phrase.

But recent decades have brought unwelcome changes, Bhattacharya says. A big political party and its affiliated groups are hell-bent on turning this into a parochially Hindu city. Their push to saffronize has caused immense damage already, polarizing communities and bringing out the worst in people. Communal-minded thugs and criminals now compete for the elected office. A kind of madness has taken hold. They want revenge for past wrongs against today's Muslims. Will the good people of the city defeat such forces, he wonders pensively, or will they lose much of their pluralistic soul and usher in a spiritually arid city not worth inhabiting?

Much of Varanasi, directly or indirectly, is sustained by pilgrimage and tourism. Among the professional communities central to it, and which outsiders encounter more often, are the Mallahs, the Doms, the weavers and the pandas, each a complex social world in itself. Many old Varanasi neighbourhoods above the ghats exhibit strong ethnic concentrations. Muslim areas may adjoin and overlap with Yadav, Mallah or Dhobi areas. The old town also has generations-old settlements of Tamilians, Bengalis, Gujaratis and others. I meet many people in Varanasi, but I'm especially drawn to the Mallahs and Doms and spend many hours interacting with them.

The Boatmen of Varanasi

No journey to Varanasi is said to be complete without a boat ride on the Ganga, along its 7-km arc lined by about eighty ghats. As I have been advised, I begin at sunrise and take a rowboat from Assi Ghat. My bearded young boatman rows languidly, making a rhythmic sound with his oars and the river. His aging boat creaks in places. The city is quiet; a soft morning light suffuses the ghats and their temples, dormitories and former royal houses. Many visitors have waxed poetic about this ride. In mid-nineteenth century, M.A. Sherring, a British missionary and Indologist, spent a few years in the city and wrote, 'For picturesqueness and grandeur, no sight in the world can well surpass that of Benares as seen from the river Ganges.'[34] I feel some of that magic too until I reflect on the anaemic width of the summertime Ganga and its murkiness. I try not to think about a recent estimate that three-fourths of the Ganga pollution is from untreated municipal sewage from settlements along its banks.[35]

Street dogs abound on the ghats, playing out their rich social life and territorial games denied to their pet cousins. We pass Harishchandra

Figure 5. View of the middle ghats in Varanasi, May 2019

Ghat, where a pyre burns even at this early hour. Most ghats seem tidier than they looked a decade ago. I see scores of devotees bathing, praying or offering water to the sun on Dashashwamedh Ghat, the most touristy ghat of the city. A chat with my boatman reveals that he'll vote saffron this time. We pass Manikarnika Ghat, smoky as ever, and I alight at the next stop, Scindia Ghat.

All boatmen in Varanasi belong to a single caste community, the Mallahs (or Nishads). As a group, they've been vital to the city's commerce, pilgrimage and tourist economy for centuries. They've managed to corner the profession with claims of traditional and hereditary rights, scriptural sanction and lobbying like a labour union. Consequently, while not all Mallahs are boatmen, all boatmen are Mallahs.

The Mallahs were deemed a 'criminal tribe' by the British. This assessment had two sources. First, as the East India Company began controlling the commerce on the river routes and taxing the flow of goods on them, friction with the locals led to thefts and attacks on Company boats. This was seen to be led, or at least enabled, by the Mallahs. Second, many Mallah subcastes, among them 'Bind, Chain,

Dhimar, Kahar, Kevat, Muriari, Sorahiya, and Tiyar', had dietary habits and social customs that scandalized the British. They reportedly ate rats, tortoises, crocodiles and drank alcohol in excess. The British despised the Tiyan subcaste for its 'considerable laxity of sexual intercourse'. The women of the Bind subcaste, a prudish colonial ethnographer noted, 'get drunk, dance, sing obscene songs, and indulge in rude debauchery'.[36] British data collection was usually mediated by Brahminical elites, who too historically looked down on the Mallahs. To the Victorian-era British, these were adequate grounds to see the Mallahs as unruly, criminal and depraved, and in need of discipline and reform.

The Mallahs, who the state classifies among the Most Backward Classes for its affirmative action programmes, have tried raising their marginalized social status by associating with the famous *kevat*, or boatman, of the Ramayana. Once during their exile, Rama and Sita arrived at the Sarayu River. They met a kevat from the non-Aryan tribe of Nishads. The kevat honoured them by washing their feet and ferried them across the river. When Sita offered him her ring as payment for his labour, the kevat cleverly declined, saying that people of the same profession do not charge each other for their labour. Rama and Sita were puzzled, so the kevat explained that he ferried people from one shore to the other, similar to the lord ferrying people across the ocean of samsara.

The kevat then asked Rama for passage across this ocean, i.e., moksha, which Rama generously granted him.

Scenes from this mythic story appear on walls at a few ghats, and it's clear that the Mallahs derive some

Figure 6. Nishadraj Temple on Nishadraj Ghat

dignity, pride and power from this association (another famous Nishad is Eklavya in the Mahabharata). Nandini Majumdar, author of *Banaras: Walks through India's Sacred City*, writes that as part of the colonial era 'reforms' and Sanskritization (a process by which an entire caste tries to attain upward caste mobility), 'the Nishads of Banaras deified an ancestor, Nishadraj' and built an airy temple to him on a ghat named after him. The small temple has a splendid view of the river and seems to attract mid-day slumberers on its shady mosaic floor.

The Mallahs also call themselves Ganga-*putra*s, or sons of the river goddess Ganga. In this capacity, they often perform certain lifecycle rituals for the pilgrims, especially the ones that involve offerings to Ganga Ma for childbirth, marriage or vows of propitiation. Such rituals as the Mallahs perform often resemble Brahminical ones and even include the chanting of mantras, prohibited for lower Shudra castes like the Mallahs. On the river, it seems, many rules of caste and religion exhibit a measure of fluidity.

A local contact leads me to Santosh, a leader of the Mallah community. We meet near Assi Ghat and he takes me to his tiny home in a tangled gully behind. But before that, I persuade him to stop at a popular stall where I order a round of Banarasi kachauri, jalebi and lassi, among the foods the city is justly famous for. We laugh at how adding 'Banarasi' before any item seems to raise its allure, such as paan, thandai, mangoes, pickles and papads, not to mention sarees, carpets, brassware and perfumes.

Santosh strikes me as a kind, self-effacing, god-fearing man of high-minded principles, devoted to his community's welfare. He commands much respect among his people. Over the next three hours, he talks about Mallah life and society, some of it also discussed by anthropologist Assa Doron in his excellent *Life on the Ganga: Boatmen and the Ritual Economy of Banaras*.

Santosh animatedly tells me about his community's triumphant yet rollercoaster protest campaign in early 2019 against the state government, which had licensed a private corporation to launch a double-decker cruise ship in Varanasi, the first of many planned. Called Alaknanda, the ship offered food, music, AC, toilets and on-board priests for conducting rituals. The Mallahs saw it as a Trojan Horse and protested by shutting down all boating for days. According to Santosh, the government even tried to divide them to break their strike, but the Mallahs held firm and prevailed.[37] At least for now. The cruise ships, Santosh adds, would've threatened their livelihoods, opened the riverfront to non-Mallah boatmen and destroyed the foundations of the Mallah community by exposing them to unbridled economic competition where the strong would trample the weak.

A sympathetic outsider might root for the little guys against the corporation, but the reality is more complex, writes Doron. While all Mallahs are entitled to seek a living from the larger riverfront economy, only a few have the right to own boats. These are the *ghatwar*s, who, between them, monopolize all boat ownership along the river. These rights are hereditary and pass down in patrilineal succession. The ghatwars fiercely defend these rights. Many own multiple boats. On the large and lucrative Assi Ghat, for instance, just four ghatwar families own all of the boats.[38] This inequity is a frequent source of friction in the community. While ghatwars invite other Mallahs to drive their boats on a fifty-fifty revenue-sharing basis, it's clear that theirs is the more secure, powerful and prosperous subgroup in the community.

Inheritance also obliges the ghatwars to dock their boats only at specific ghats. Santosh explains that the prevalent code of conduct requires each Mallah to pick up passengers only from the boat's native ghat. If he drops passengers off at another ghat, he must return empty to his own ghat to solicit new customers. A ghatwar's income therefore depends heavily on his native ghat. The four most popular of the eighty ghats generate far higher earnings. According to Santosh, a few hundred ghatwars own about 2000 boats across the eighty ghats, operated by over 6000 Mallah men.[39]

Why do other Mallahs put up with the unfair hereditary arrangement? Santosh, a ghatwar himself, acknowledges the unfairness. But he only supports reforming the system, not dismantling it. He favours limiting the number of boats a ghatwar can own, so more Mallah men can enjoy the hereditary right to own a boat. Outsiders might see a paradox here: the Mallahs monopolize a profession in the name of caste rights *and* chafe at the caste system for giving them a lowly status. They want the state to continue their unfair exclusive right to a caste profession *and* provide them the fairness of caste-based reservations to combat persisting social inequities. Such apparent paradoxes derive from the

Figure 7. Assi Ghat

harsh reality and inner logic of the caste system itself, and no section of its hierarchy—especially its upper rungs—is free of them.

The state, however, wants to dismantle the ghatwars' hereditary rights. In 1997, the Nagar Nigam (municipal authority) began licensing boats of anyone who qualified.[40] Even non-Mallahs were issued licenses to ply their own boats. But so far, the powerful ghatwars from the lucrative ghats have managed to defend and enforce the traditional rules of the game. They've prevented all rebellious Mallahs and outsiders from establishing themselves, even using violence at times.[41]

At the same time, certain moral obligations and reciprocity within the community also support a kind of safety net for all boatmen, writes Doron, whereby privileged Mallahs find small jobs for other Mallahs who seek work in the riverine economy. This would vanish if the state dismantled their caste-bound, hereditary arrangements by force (an option the state hasn't pursued yet). So while the system has much unfairness, the statist alternative may seem worse to most Mallahs.

The Mallah community, Santosh tells me, is also split in its political loyalties, mostly between the BJP and the Samajwadi Party. He hates the ruling party for its corporation-friendly market ethos that brought in the cruise ship, but his deeper animus springs from its championing of the Kashi Vishwanath corridor, an urban development project. Vishwanath Temple is the city's most revered shrine to Shiva, located in the old town. The project will create wide roads, parking and a modern tourist zone around the temple, leading down to the river. The project has already razed many neighbourhoods, including lots of Hindu temples and shrines (Santosh claims 350) tucked into the old town's cramped streets and courtyards.[42] Santosh, a pious Hindu, considers this sacrilege. 'God is watching,' he says. 'Any Hindu who destroys temples so callously cannot be called Hindu. Further, what kind of Hindu polarizes Hindus and Muslims to win Hindu votes? That's the one thing this party does best. They're now even targeting the Gyanvapi Mosque.'[43]

Back in my room, I continue reading Diana Eck's *Banaras: City of Light*. I've come to admire it for its wealth of information, but I've also had some trouble with it. It now strikes me that perhaps this is because Eck wallows too much in Hindu mythologies, often romanticizing their philosophical import while overlooking the lived realities of Hinduism. She fails to subject Hindu beliefs and practices to even modest rational criticism and betrays a superficial grasp of caste and its pathologies, a common weakness in both non-Indian and upper-caste accounts of Indian society. Her narrative illustrates to me why history needs to be continually rewritten.

The City of Death and Moksha

Death may be the world's greatest leveller, but no 'city on earth is as famous for death as is Banaras', writes Eck. 'More than for her temples and magnificent ghats, more than for her silks and brocades, Banaras, the Great Cremation Ground, is known for death.' And no place in Varanasi brings this home as much as its two main cremation ghats: Manikarnika and Harishchandra.

In Hindu lore, anyone who dies and is cremated in Varanasi gains instant moksha. Normally, moksha is gained either by a demanding journey of self-realization through which one dispels all illusions and comes to know one's unity with Brahman (the ultimate reality beneath the world of shifting appearances), or by surrendering one's self to God in loving devotion. In Varanasi, it is said, Shiva himself bestows 'instant moksha' by whispering the *taraka* mantra (ferryboat mantra) in the ear of all who die, granting them the requisite knowledge of Brahman.

But this apparent moksha-for-all 'backdoor' poses a major problem. It messes up the law of karmic causation central to orthodox Hinduism. In other words, our deeds in this or previous lives count for nothing. Do the scoundrels who die in Varanasi also gain instant moksha? Doesn't instant moksha also render the priest and his funerary rituals irrelevant to the departing souls (and thereby threaten the livelihood of the priest)?

These questions may seem flippant to some, but the theologians of Hinduism, the pandits, have long struggled for satisfactory answers. One such is to postulate that the moksha is not instant. Before the soul is granted liberation, a short but intense period of post-death suffering occurs in accord with karmic law.[44] So the priest is still required (phew!). In any case, given Varanasi's modest population and the thriving business of funerary priests, it's clear that few Hindus actually believe in this guaranteed 'backdoor' to moksha. Even fewer now, as most 'moksha guesthouses'—where people come to stay in their final days—have shut down or become regular tourist guesthouses.

Chants of 'Ram Naam Sat Hai' reverberate all day on both burning ghats. The bigger, Manikarnika, hosts fifty to sixty cremations a day, which happen round the clock. Some bodies are even flown in from other cities in refrigerated containers. The deceased, wrapped in white cotton and often covered by an ornamental orange shroud and marigold flowers, arrive at the ghat on bamboo biers upon the shoulders of the male kin. The mood is sombre yet business-friendly. Barges with piles of firewood from the forests of MP await unloading in a corner of the ghat. Cows and dogs negotiate the spaces between the mourning kin and funerary workers.

The funerary process is simple and unadorned. Above the ghats are shops staffed by funerary assistants. The kin of the deceased, according to their means, choose one of the funeral packages on offer—each with a certain grade and quantity of firewood, sandalwood or its sawdust, straw, ghee and other ritualistic supplies—plus a priest's services. What's sold as sandalwood is now a cheap imitation; scarcity has made the real thing unaffordable to most people. However, this custom is quite old. In the 1660s, Frenchman Tavernier observed, 'According to the wealth of the deceased, there is mingled with the ordinary wood which is collected for burning, more or less sandal-wood or other scented wood.'[45] The cheapest funeral package now costs about Rs 5000 in total. A middle-class family might spend 30,000 on a package with more wood, more lavish rituals and finer oblations for the fire.

The actual cremation—setting up and clearing each pyre, managing its burning, gathering of remains in an urn, etc.—is all done by the Doms, a group earlier classified as 'untouchable' that claims descent from a mythological figure called Kallu Dom. The Doms recognize a presumed patrilineal heir of Kallu Dom as their king, the Dom Raja. He 'rules' the burning ghats and lives with his family on the riverfront, a short walk south of Manikarnika Ghat. When I visit, I see no evidence of his rumoured fabulous wealth in their rustic,

Figure 8. View from the courtyard of the Dom Raja's home in Varanasi

two-storey, brightly painted home. In their courtyard overlooking the river are two sculpted tigers, a symbolic assertion of power by a relatively recent ancestor. Unburnt wood from the cremation grounds traditionally fuels the stove in their kitchen.

In a mythological story—a cringe-inducing morality tale—that appears in *Markandeya Purana*, Raja Harishchandra is tested by the gods for his honesty and dharmic commitments. When demanded by a devious Brahmin stranger, the 'righteous' raja donates his entire kingdom to him because a virtuous king can't refuse a Brahmin. But the Brahmin wants more. So Harishchandra, a dharmic man, sells his wife and son into slavery, then sells himself to Kallu Dom to pay the Brahmin with the proceeds. The royals suffer greatly, their son dies, but Harishchandra persists with his absurd dharma, until the gods are fully satisfied and grant him an eternal place in heaven, taking Kallu Dom along too.

This story may have charmed my ancestors, but I find nothing admirable in it. It upholds an unthinking devotion to dharma and the caste order. Instead of punishing Harishchandra for his bad judgement and inhumanity towards his wife and son, the gods grant him moksha and sing his praises for respecting a Brahmin at all costs (so hard to guess who might have written this story!). Yet today, a temple to Harishchandra stands on the cremation ghat named after him. This story is a great source of pride and honour for the Doms. Kallu Dom was a raja, the Doms argue, because only a raja could've owned another raja. Unlike the upper-caste response, the Dom response is best understood in the context of a marginalized caste seeking a measure of dignity by association and inference. In a caste order based on purity and pollution, the Doms and their work rank near the very bottom. No one else aspires to it. Yet, like the Mallahs, these Doms of Varanasi claim exclusive rights to conduct cremations on the two ghats. No one from outside their clan—even if they work on cremation ghats elsewhere—is permitted to work here.

The current Dom Raja's name is Jagdish Chaudhary. All Doms of Varanasi, as many as 5000, are his relatives and have the same surname (prevalent in both 'high' and 'low' castes). He is the sole employer of all Dom workers on the cremation ghats, a minority of all Doms. A compulsive paan chewer, the Dom Raja helps resolve disputes and offers financial aid for weddings and health emergencies to clan members.

While a Dom sets up the pyre, four kinsmen of the deceased bring in the corpse on a bamboo bier. They go down to the river, wade into it, and lower the bier to dunk the body in the 'sacred' waters of the Ganga. The Mahabharata says, 'If only a bone of a person shall touch the water of the Ganga, that person shall dwell, honoured, in heaven.'[46] Thus 'purified', they remove the orange shroud, transfer the wet body wrapped in plain whites on to the pyre and pay their final respects (women traditionally do so at home and do not attend funerals, but this is changing in urban India). If the deceased lived a healthy life well past eighty, there may even be muted celebration of his good fortune of a long life, admixed with quiet sorrow. The priest begins the rituals and the chanting—part of the *antim sanskaar*, or last rites, which vary as per the deceased's region, caste and other social factors. To attain moksha at Manikarnika, however, every pyre must be lit by the 'sacred flame' kept by the Dom Raja, for which he charges a *kar* ('tax') of Rs 500. This paves the way for Shiva to whisper the taraka mantra in the deceased's ears. Thus, in the end, even the 'purest' Brahmin requires the 'untouchable' Dom for the liberation of his soul.

The chief mourner, usually the closest male kin, sprinkles ghee on the pyre, and is then handed a straw torch to set it alight—an intensely emotional moment for the kinsmen. The first fire, *mukhagni*, is ritually lit at the mouth. A Dom funerary worker might sprinkle more ghee and insert burning straw in strategic places to ensure the fire picks up quickly and evenly. As the heat builds, the kinsmen step back, fall into groups and watch the flames engulf the body. The Dom stays close, periodically using a bamboo pole to shift the wood, or the corpse, to aid the fire. Even from a few metres away, one might see the deceased's facial skin darken and melt under the heat.

When the corpse is significantly burnt, an important ritual called *kapal kriya* is initiated: the Dom positions a bamboo pole and invites the chief mourner to deliver a quick jab to the skull, breaking it and releasing the deceased's atman to continue its journey beyond or to finally merge with Brahman.

If a family can afford only the cheapest funeral package—or none, in which case they rely on government aid or charity—the corpse is burnt in stages on a small pyre: first the middle part burns and collapses, the head and the legs stick out until the Dom deftly pushes them in. It takes about 250 kg of firewood and two to three hours to incinerate a corpse. Near the end, the Dom uses a pair of tongs to extract a piece of hard tissue, usually from the remains of the chest or the hips, for the chief mourner to toss in the river, which the fish apparently nibble at. Then the chief mourner, his back to the pyre, flings over his head a small clay pot of Ganga water on the smouldering pyre. This symbolically ends the relationship of the living with the dead.

The Dom comes in next and douses the embers with more water. He gathers ashes and bone fragments in an urn, an act called 'picking flowers' (not bad for a euphemism). He clears the burning platform to make room for a new pyre. The kin take the urn down the ghats to empty it in the Ganga. Dom men wait with wire nets to receive this, hoping to find bits of gold from a tooth or a nose ring. All of this 'found' gold officially belongs to the Dom Raja. If a worker is caught pilfering it, he can be fired. But pilfering still happens, a young Dom tells me with a grin.

As the day progresses, discarded tinsel shrouds and bamboo biers pile up. Flowers, ash, plastic waste, unburnt wood, and muddy water accumulate around the pyres, giving it a shabby look. Cows, seemingly unfazed by the heat, try to get to the marigold flowers around the burning pyres, pooping wherever they wish. Each morning, municipal workers sweep all perishable waste into the river.

Notably, a subset of Hindus is not cremated here: sadhus, lepers, small children, pregnant women and snake-bite victims. They're consigned directly to the sacred river. Their corpses, it is said, do not need further purification by fire, so they're taken in a boat to the middle of the Ganga, tied to a stone and sunk to the bottom, becoming food for fish and river turtles. Some of these corpses, or parts thereof, later float up to the surface, spooking unsuspecting tourists. The liturgy of death in Varanasi is not for the squeamish.[47]

Figure 9. Funeral pyres on Manikarnika Ghat

The funeral pyres of course cause a great deal of air pollution. It's harder on the Doms who spend hours enveloped in wood smoke. Their eyes water, one Dom says. They cough and feel short of breath. Most quit this work in middle age owing to *kamjori* (physical weakness). In 1984, to provide a faster, cheaper and less smoky alternative, the government installed an electric crematorium at Harishchandra Ghat (the Doms have resisted it at Manikarnika Ghat to protect their livelihood). The e-crematorium is widely seen as a poor man's choice that interferes with rituals like kapal kriya. Funerary rites are so central to most people's religio-cultural identity that they loathe to tinker with them—and the ghats of Varanasi are not exactly rippling with tradition breakers. On Manikarnika, I ask the Dom Raja's brother why a human corpse on the pyre doesn't smell anything like animal meat on the grill. He points at the sky and attributes this 'marvel' to Lord Shiva himself.

On a rooftop with a panoramic view of the burning ghats, I meet three Dom men, two in their twenties and one older. They openly talk about their lives and work. Every day twenty to twenty-five Dom men work at Manikarnika Ghat. They're on call 24x7 for four to five days after which they get as many days off. Each Dom conducts two or three cremations a day, earning Rs 250 for each. They get occasional tips, but sometimes also forego their wages for customers who can't afford to pay anything.

The younger Doms I speak to hate their jobs. They say they would gladly quit for another job that pays Rs 10,000 per month. Many have done so; one Dom's cousin left to work in a jeans factory in Delhi; another became an auto driver. Their caste, the younger Doms claim, isn't a big obstacle now in finding other jobs; the older one maintains that it still is, arguing that if he set up a *kirana* shop in the gullies above the ghats, a lot of people won't buy from him due to his caste. But they all agree that opportunities for overcoming caste barriers are much better today than a generation ago.[48]

When they first began this job in their teens, they had a terrible time. After each cremation, a Dom says, he couldn't eat for hours. But they got desensitized to the work over time. They burnt all sorts of bodies—of politicians, celebrities, even horribly mutilated ones. It became a mercenary job, the Dom says; now there is no feeling.

But talking to them, this doesn't ring entirely true. They seem to abuse alcohol and ganja to suppress their feelings. Intoxicants enable them to do this unpleasant, low-status work. In fact, while we talk on the rooftop, a chillum is passed around and I join in too. I learn that one Dom's elder brother died of alcohol poisoning; circumstances led him to marry his brother's widow, a common custom among them. 'I liked her too,' he says, smiling shyly. A cow interrupts our conversation by dropping a big runny load two feet away.

Countless Hindus come to this 'hallowed' spot seeking liberation, but the Doms consider it a hell they would gladly escape. Escaping isn't easy however—more Dom men are finishing high school, but most aren't educated beyond middle school; they have many young and old dependents; they also lack the skills and the confidence to transition to other jobs. Lucky breaks are a big driver of upward mobility. Can I find them a job in Delhi? they ask.

Watching the spectacle on the burning ghats from the rooftop, I feel an invigorating calm, the kind that steadies and concentrates the mind. What better way to peer into nothingness and to see our common fate, evocatively laid out in the *Book of Common Prayer*: from earth to earth, ashes to ashes, dust to dust. Why, there is nothing morbid about death. It's a basic fact of life, but one that rarely informs our daily choices and opinions. The greatest wonder, as Yudhisthira says in the Mahabharata, is that 'each day death strikes, and we live as though we were immortal'.

Acknowledgements

This book, over its multiyear gestation, has benefited from readings, discussions, meetings, and influences too numerous to mention. Foremost among the latter is Usha Alexander, my partner in life. She travelled with me twice to all of the sites I cover in this book. We agreed that I should write my narrative as a solo traveller and not bring her into it. But she was there all along, enriching my understanding of each site with her own thoughts, readings and analyses (which also informed her brilliant historical novel, *The Legend of Virinara*). She read my drafts and gave valuable advice. I'm grateful to her for all that and more. This book would scarcely be possible without her ideas, encouragement and support.

I'm grateful to Richa Burman, my editor at Penguin Random House India (PRHI), who saw value in this project and helped commission it. An extraordinary reader and listener with sound editorial instincts, she helped improve my narrative significantly. Her own curiosity and abiding interest in India's pasts enriched our editorial discussions and challenged me to produce my best work. She came up with the book's title, which I like a lot. I'm also thankful to the other talented professionals at PRHI who worked on this project, especially Saloni Mital, copy editor. It's a pleasure to collaborate with people who take pride in their work and strive for high standards.

I'm grateful to the scores of thinkers and scholars whose efforts I've leaned on in writing this book. Their diligent and often thankless work helped me synthesize a vision of India's pasts. I've quoted some of them but many others have also shaped my world view, which pervades this book. I'm grateful that several people gave me good advice, opened doors and offered contacts, aided us on our travels, and generously gave their time and attention. Among these are friends Asad Zaidi, Nalini Taneja, Vivek Menezes, Anil Kumar Yadav and Aditya Dev Sood. Krishna Devaraya kindly invited us into his home in Anegundi. Strangers—local people, taxi drivers, hotel managers, porters, waiters, cooks, guides, museum staff and others—enriched our travels and explorations. Many shared with us their stories and life worlds. I'm indebted to several friends and scholars who read advance review copies and offered comments or endorsements.

I thank my parents, Shrinath Arora and Lata Arora, for coming to terms with my pursuit of a project that is a labour of love, a far cry from the lucrative career that college prepared me for. I quit that career years ago, but it still funds my chosen life of reading, writing and travel. I think it's hard to adequately acknowledge the lottery of birth and the lucky breaks that have gone into making this possible—and, in turn, this book. But it's true and worth remembering often.

Notes

Introduction: The Lost Worlds of India

1. Genslinger, Neil, 'Hayden White, Who Explored How History Is Made, Dies at 89', *NY Times*, March 9, 2018.
2. Arora, Namit, 'Advice to a Young Artist', Shunya.net, 2000.

Chapter 1: The Mysteries of Dholavira

1. Possehl, Gregory L., *The Indus Civilization: A Contemporary Perspective*, AltaMira, 2002, p. 1.
2. 'One million' appears in Parpola, Asko, *The Roots of Hinduism*, Oxford University Press (OUP), Kindle Edition, 2015, p. vii; 'Five million' appears in Parpola, Asko (1988), 'Religion reflected in the iconic signs of the Indus script: penetrating into long-forgotten picto+graphic messages', *Visible Religion* 6: pp. 114–35; an estimate of 'up to five million' also appears in Joseph, Tony, *Early Indians*, Juggernaut, 2018, p. 184.
3. Robinson, Andrew, *The Indus: Lost Civilizations*, Reaktion Books, Kindle Edition, 2015.
4. Source: McIntosh, Jane, *The Ancient Indus Valley: New Perspectives*, ABC-CLIO, 2008; shared under CC BY-SA 3.0 by the author of the map, Avantiputra7; https://tinyurl.com/s48zbm3.
5. Possehl, Gregory L. *The Indus Civilization: A Contemporary Perspective*, AltaMira, 2002, p. 12.

6. The estimated time frame for the earliest successful migration out of Africa is still uncertain. See, for instance, Clarkson, C., Harris, C., Li, B. et al. 'Human Occupation of Northern India Spans the Toba Super-eruption ~74,000 years ago', *Nature Communications* 11, 961, 2020.

7. Vasant Shinde, et al., 'An Ancient Harappan Genome Lacks Ancestry from Steppe Pastoralists or Iranian Farmers', *Cell*, Vol. 179, Issue 3, October 17, 2019.

8. Joseph, Tony, 'Appendix: The Valley of the Ghaggar-Hakra', *Early Indians*, Juggernaut, 2018, p. 223. See also Parpola, Asko, *The Roots of Hinduism*, OUP, 2015, pp. 96–7.

9. Possehl, Gregory L., *The Indus Civilization: A Contemporary Perspective*, AltaMira, 2002, pp. 3, 15, 55, 71.

10. Parpola, Asko, *The Roots of Hinduism*, OUP, 2015, p. 21.

11. Bisht, R.S., 'Excavations at Dholavira 1989–2005', ASI, 2015 (https://www.scribd.com/document/262316120/Excavations-at-Dholavifra-1989-2005-RS-Bisht-2015).

12. Ibid.

13. Ibid.

14. Ibid.

15. Ibid.

16. Habib, Irfan, *The Indus Civilization*, Tulika Books, 2002, p. 28.

17. Parpola, Asko, *The Roots of Hinduism*, OUP, 2015, p. 21.

18. Kenoyer, Jonathan Mark, quoted on Harappa.com, https://www.harappa.com/answers/there-any-indication-slavery-or-ritual-human-sacrifice-ivc.

19. For an insightful discussion on Harappan funerary customs with a particular focus on Rakhigarhi, see Shinde, Vasant S., et al., 'Archaeological and anthropological studies on the Harappan cemetery of Rakhigarhi, India', *Plos One*, February 21, 2018,

20. Robinson, Andrew, *The Indus: Lost Civilizations*, Reaktion Books, Kindle Edition, 2015.

21. Parpola, Asko, *The Roots of Hinduism*, OUP, 2015, p. 163.

22. Farmer, Steve, et al, *The Collapse of the Indus-Script Thesis: The Myth of a Literate Harappan Civilization*, Electronic Journal of Vedic Studies (EJVS), Vol. 11, Issue 2, 2004.

23. Bisht, R.S., 'Excavations at Dholavira 1989–2005', ASI, 2015, https://www.scribd.com/document/262316120/Excavations-at-Dholavifra-1989-2005-RS-Bisht-2015.

24. Habib, Irfan, *The Indus Civilization*, Tulika Books, 2002, pp. 49–50.

25. Possehl, Gregory L., *The Indus Civilization: A Contemporary Perspective*, AltaMira, 2002, p. 143.
26. Ibid., p. 148.
27. Ibid., p. 122.
28. Wright, Rita P., *The Ancient Indus: Urbanism, Economy, and Society*, Cambridge University Press, 2010, p. 122.
29. See Jonathan Mark Kenoyer on Harappa.com, https://www.harappa.com/answers/how-can-we-justify-stating-citadel-area-was-exclusively-higher-class-or-category-people.
30. This has been proposed, pending further evidence, by Gwen Robbins Schug. See Harappa.com, https://www.harappa.com/answers/what-do-we-know-ancient-indus-government.
31. Robinson, Andrew, *The Indus: Lost Civilizations*, Reaktion Books, Kindle Edition, 2015.
32. A brilliantly lucid reference here is Joseph, Tony, *Early Indians*, Juggernaut, 2018.
33. An example here is Bisht's interpretation of the two large burial monuments with a wheel motif.
34. Kumar, Dhavendra (editor), *Genomics and Health in the Developing World*, OUP, 2012. Chapter titled, 'The Genetic Basis of Alcoholism in India', by Meera Vasani, p. 1128.
35. Abraham S., et al (editors), *Connections and Complexity, New Approaches to the Archaeology of South Asia*, Left Coast Press, 2012, p. 360.
36. 'Sri Lanka Sparks Revolution in South Asian History and Archaeology', *Sunday Times*, Sri Lanka, January 25, 2015.
37. Petrie, Cameron A., et al. 'Adaptation to Variable Environments, Resilience to Climate Change: Investigating Land, Water and Settlement in Indus Northwest India', *Current Anthropology*, 2017.
38. Future archaeology may also shed more light on the cultural continuities between the Harappans and the earliest urban settlements in south India. See Annamalai, S., 'Keeladi: Unearthing the "Vaigai Valley" Civilisation of Sangam era Tamil Nadu', *The Hindu*, November 2, 2019.
39. Parpola, Asko, *The Roots of Hinduism*, OUP, 2015, p. 305.
40. Kenoyer, J.M., *Ancient Cities of the Indus Valley Civilization*, OUP, 1998, pp. 83.
41. Jha, D.N., *The Myth of the Holy Cow*, Navayana, 2010.
42. Parpola, Asko, *The Roots of Hinduism*, OUP, 2015, pp. 96–7.

43. Marina Silva et al., 'A Genetic Chronology for the Indian Subcontinent Points to Heavily Sex-biased Dispersals', *BMC Evolutionary Biology*, 2017.

44. Sen, Sudipta, *Ganga: The Many Pasts of a River,* Gurgaon, Viking, 2019, pp. 75, 112.

45. Doniger, Wendy, *The Hindus: An Alternative History*, Penguin Publishing Group, 2009, p. 261.

46. David Reich, *Who We Are and How We Got Here: Ancient DNA and the New Science of the Human Past*, OUP, 2018. Speaking of population bottlenecks, Reich writes, 'One of the most striking we discovered was in the Vysya group of the southern Indian state of Andhra Pradesh, a middle caste group of approximately five million people whose population bottleneck we could date to between three thousand and two thousand years ago . . . It meant that after the population bottleneck, the ancestors of the Vysya had maintained strict endogamy, allowing essentially no genetic mixing into their group for thousands of years.'

47. Basu, A., Sarkar-Roy, N. and Majumder P.P., 'Genomic Reconstruction of the History of Extant Populations of India Reveals Five Distinct Ancestral Components and a Complex Structure', *Proceedings of the National Academy of Sciences of the United States of America,* February 9, 2015, 113(6):1594–9.

48. Modi, Jivanji Jamshedji, 'The Antiquity of the Custom of Sati', *Anthropological Papers*, 1929, Part IV: Papers read before the Anthropological Society of Bombay: British India Press, Seite 109–21.

49. The proponents of this theory and its variants include R.S. Bisht, B.B. Lal, S.R. Rao, Michel Danino, François Gautier, Subhash Kak, David Frawley, Georg Feuerstein, Koenraad Elst, N. Jha, N.S. Rajaram, Shrikant Talageri, Rajiv Malhotra, Kumarasamy Thangaraj, Aravindan Neelakandan and Sanjeev Sanyal.

50. R.S. Bisht revisits the Harappan site in Dholavira, *Down to Earth*, June 24, 2015, https://www.downtoearth.org.in/video/rs-bisht-revisits-the-harappan-site-in-dholavira-1291 (video interview).

51. Parpola, Asko, *The Roots of Hinduism*, OUP, 2015, p. 92.

52. Edwin Bryant in his excellent volume, *The Quest for the Origins of Vedic Culture: The Indo-Aryan Migration Debate* (2001), sympathetically and impartially evaluates the central claim of Hindu chauvinists—that India is the homeland of Indo-European languages—without condescension and based on evidence. He concludes that though gaps exist in the Aryan migration theory, 'there has been almost no convincing evidence brought forward in support of a homeland this far east'.

53. Eck, Diana L., *Banaras: City of Light*, Knopf Doubleday, 1982.
54. Joseph, Tony, *Early Indians*, Juggernaut, 2018, p. 196.
55. Robinson, Andrew, *The Indus: Lost Civilizations*, Reaktion Books, Kindle Edition, 2015.
56. I've used material from Arora, Namit, 'The Reservoirs of Dholavira', *Himal Southasian*, December 2008.

Chapter 2: Megasthenes's India

1. Herodotus, *The Histories* (translated by Robin Waterfield), OUP, 2008, pp. 211–13.
2. Thapar, Romila, *Early India*, Penguin Books, 2002, pp. 163–64.
3. Muhlberger, Steve, 'Democracy in Ancient India', 1998, https://uts.nipissingu.ca/muhlberger/HISTDEM/INDIADEM.HTM.
4. Arora, Namit, 'Ancient Indian Skepticism', *Himal Southasian*, 2009.
5. Thapar, Romila, *Early India*, Penguin Books, 2002, p. 164.
6. Keay, John, *India: A History*, HarperCollins, 2000.
7. McCrindle, J.W. (translator), 'Ancient India as Described by Megasthenes and Arrian: A Translation of Fragments of Indika of Megasthenes Collected by Dr. Schwanbeck, and of the First Part of Indika of Arrian', Trubner and Co., 1877, p. 122.
8. Keay, John, *India: A History*, HarperCollins, 2000.
9. Ibid.
10. Sen, Sudipta, *Ganga: The Many Pasts of a River*, Viking, 2019, p. 140.
11. Thapar, Romila, *Early India*, Penguin Books, 2002, p. 159. Also see a podcast by philosopher Jonardon Ganeri, 'Looking East: Indian Influence on Greek Thought', 2018, https://historyofphilosophy.net/india-greece.
12. Evans, James, *The History and Practice of Ancient Astronomy*, OUP, 1998, p. 393.
13. Keay, John, *India: A History*, HarperCollins, 2000.
14. McCrindle, J.W. (translator), 'Ancient India as Described by Megasthenes and Arrian: A Translation of Fragments of Indika of Megasthenes Collected by Dr. Schwanbeck, and of the First Part of Indika of Arrian', Trubner and Co., 1877.
15. Ibid., p. 23. McCrindle writes that these creatures 'might be more readily confounded with other creatures of the Indian imagination, who held a sort of intermediate place between demons and men', such as rakshasas, pishachas, and others. Historian Truesdell Sparhawk Brown also held that

Megasthenes 'reproduced correctly what his own eyes had seen' and 'what his Indian informants told him'. Source: Allan Dahlaquist, *Megasthenes and Indian Religion: A Study in Motives and Types*, Motilal Banarsidass, 1996, p. 28.

16. Kulke, Hermann, Dietmar Rothermund, *A History of India*, Psychology Press, 2004, p. 62.

17. Quote from an ASI information panel at the Kumrahar archaeological site museum in Patna.

18. Sen, Sudipta, *Ganga: The Many Pasts of a River*, Viking, 2019, p. 136.

19. McCrindle, J.W. (translator), 'The Indica of Arrian', Education Society's Press, Byculla, 1876, p. 32.

20. Thapar, Romila, *Early India*, Penguin Books, 2002, pp. 184–85.

21. In 1030 CE, Alberuni made a similar observation. 'The Hindus eat singly, one by one,' he wrote. See Alberuni, Edward C. Sachau (translator, 1888), *Alberuni's India*, Rupa Publications, Delhi, 2002.

22. Ibid., p. 192.

23. Ibid., p. 164.

Chapter 3: The Void of Nagarjunakonda

1. Subrahmanyam, R., et al., *Nagarjunakonda (1954–60)*, ASI, 1975, Vol. I, pp. xviii–xix.

2. All quotes in this and the previous paragraph are from Longhurst, A.H., *Buddhist Antiquities of Nagarjunakonda*, ASI, 1938, pp. 2–6.

3. Ibid., pp. 2–6.

4. Subrahmanyam, R., et al., *Nagarjunakonda (1954–60)*, ASI, 1975, Vol. I, p. 202.

5. It seems that both 'cremation and burying were practiced by megalithic people. Criteria for selecting cremation or burying the dead was probably based on age, sex and nature of the death as has been observed from the ethnographic study on mortuary variability in Vidarbha'. Mohanty, R. K. and T. Thakuria, 'Early Iron Age Megalithic Culture of Peninsular Indian and South India', *History of Ancient India*, Vol. 3, pp. 343–78, edited by D. Charkrabarti and M. Lal, Aryan Publishers and Vivekananda Center, New Delhi, 2014.

6. Sukumaran, Ajay, 'A Flame beneath the Ground', *Outlook India*, 2017, https://www.outlookindia.com/magazine/story/a-flame-beneath-the-ground/298344.

7.   'Note from Nehru to the Minister for Education, dated December 10, 1955, Guntur, Ministry of Education, C.I, 1955, file no. 3-125/55 C.I, pp. 19–20, NAI.' This source appears in Singh, Upinder, *The Idea of Ancient India*, SAGE Publications, 2016.

8.   Sarkar, H. and Mishra, B.N., *Nagarjunakonda*, 2006, pp. 19–20.

9.   Soundararajan, K.V. (editor), R. Subrahmanyam, et al., *Nagarjunakonda (1954–60)*, Vol. II, ASI, 2006, p. 143.

10. Ibid, p. 593–94.

11. Krishna Murthy, K., *Nagarjunakonda: A Cultural Study*, Concept Publishing Company, 1977, p. 16.

12. Soundararajan, K.V. (editor), Subrahmanyam, R., et al., *Nagarjunakonda (1954–60)*, Vol. II, ASI, 2006, p. 226.

13. Ibid, pp. 242–43. Other scholars, such as A.S. Altekar, have argued that sati was extremely rare during this period in India, especially in the Deccan, and was mainly a Kshatriya practice.

14. Apparently, in some monks' cells, archaeologists found 'a lump of lead ore and an earthenware die for the manufacture of coins of this size and pattern, indicating that the monks minted their own coins'. Longhurst, A.H., *Buddhist Antiquities of Nagarjunakonda*, ASI, 1938, p. 10.

15. Stone, Elizabeth R., *The Buddhist Art of Nagarjunakonda*, Motilal Banarsidass, Delhi, 1994, p. 30.

16. Soundararajan, K.V. (editor), Subrahmanyam, R., et al., *Nagarjunakonda (1954–60)*, ASI, 2006, Volume II, p. 107.

17. 'This is not a particularly far-fetched interpretation, and corroborates the suggested connection between Buddhist monasteries and healing traditions', Singh, Upinder, *The Idea of Ancient India: Essays on Religion, Politics, and Archaeology*, SAGE Publications, 2016.

18. The bathing ghat was transplanted to Nagarjunakonda Island c. 1960, next to a small canteen and museum.

19. Longhurst, A.H., *Buddhist Antiquities of Nagarjunakonda*, ASI, 1938.

20. Soundararajan K.V. (editor), Subrahmanyam, R., et al., *Nagarjunakonda (1954–60)*, ASI, 2006, Volume II, p.18.

21. Reich, David, *Who We Are and How We Got Here: Ancient DNA and the New Science of the Human Past*, OUP, 2018.

22. Ibid.

23. Singh, Upinder, *The Idea of Ancient India: Essays on Religion, Politics, and Archaeology*, SAGE Publications, 2016.

24. Stone, Elizabeth, R., *The Buddhist Art of Nagarjunakonda*, Motilal Banarsidass, Delhi, 1994, pp. 13–6.

25. Krishna Murthy, K., *Nagarjunakonda: A Cultural Study*, Concept Publishing Company, 1977, p. 10.

26. Singh, Upinder, *The Idea of Ancient India: Essays on Religion, Politics, and Archaeology*, SAGE Publications, 2016.

27. Paul, Diana Y. (translator), *The Sutra of Queen Srimala of the Lion's Roar*, Taishō, Vol. 12, No. 353, 2004, http://info.stiltij.nl/publiek/meditatie/soetras2/vimalakirti-srimala-mcrae.pdf.

28. Stone, Elizabeth R., *The Buddhist Art of Nagarjunakonda*, Motilal Banarsidass, Delhi, 1994, pp. 13–14.

29. Fogelin, Lars, *An Archaeological History of Indian Buddhism*, OUP, 2015.

30. Berger, Douglas, *Nagarjuna*, Internet Encyclopedia of Philosophy, 2005.

31. For a very good introduction to Nagarjuna's thought, see Westerhoff, Jan, *Nagarjuna's Madhyamaka: A Philosophical Introduction*, OUP, 2009, p. 207.

32. Longhurst, A.H., *Buddhist Antiquities of Nagarjunakonda*, ASI, 1938.

33. Soundararajan, K.V. (editor), Subrahmanyam, R., et al., *Nagarjunakonda (1954–60)*, Vol. II, ASI, 2006, pp. 52–54.

Chapter 4: Faxian, Xuanzang and Yijing in India

1. Spence, Jonathan, *The Search for Modern China*, W.W. Norton & Company, 1991, p.9.

2. Faxian is variously spelled as Fa-Hien and Fa-hsien. Xuanzang is variously spelled Xuan Zang, Hieun Tsang, Hsüan Tsang, Hiouen Thsang, Hsuan Chwang, Hsien-tsang, etc. Yijing is variously spelled I Ching, I-Tsing, Yijing, Yiqing, YiChing, etc.

3. Yijing, Latika Lahiri (translator), *Chinese Monks in India*, or *Biography of Eminent Monks who Went to the Western World in Search of the Law during the Great T'ang Dynasty*, Motilal Banarsidass, New Delhi, 2015. First edition, 1986.

4. Professor Liang Ch'i-ch'ao (1873–1929) identified about 180 monk-pilgrims who travelled to India during this period. Yijing, Latika Lahiri (translator), *Chinese Monks in India*, p. xxv.

5. Among these were Siksananda, Isvara and others who helped Yijing with translations. Bodhisena (704–60 CE), a monk from Madurai, went to China and then to Japan, where he had a huge impact on Japanese Buddhism, including the founding of the still active Kegon school of Buddhism.

6. But even Yijing had heard of Chinese pilgrims visiting India *before* Faxian, so perhaps he saw Faxian as a pioneer for another reason: for also writing about his travels, returning with sacred books and translating them.

7. Yijing, Latika Lahiri (translator), *Chinese Monks in India*.

8. Faxian, *A Record of Buddhistic Kingdoms / Being an account by the Chinese monk Fa-hsien of travels in India and Ceylon (A.D. 399–414) in search of the Buddhist books of discipline*, Oxford, Clarendon Press, 1886.

9. Ibid.

10. Waley, Arthur, *The Real Tripitaka and Other Pieces*, Allen and Unwin, London, 1952, p. 15.

11. In the words of L. Cranmer-Byng, author of the 1911 preface to Beal, Samuel (translator), *The Life of Hiuen-Tsiang* by Hwui Li., Rupa Publications, Kindle Edition.

12. *Xuanzang*, Internet Encyclopedia of Philosophy, July 2009.

13. Beal, Samuel, *The Life of Hiuen-Tsiang*, Rupa Publications, 2012, p. 92.

14. Tsiang, Hiuen and Samuel Beal (translator), *Si Yu Ki: Buddhist Records of the Western World*, Kegan Paul, Trench, Trubner & Co. Ltd, 1906.

15. I-ching (Yijing), J. Takakusu (translator), *A Record of the Buddhist Religion as Practised in India and the Malay Archipelago*, Oxford, Clarendon Press, 1896.

16. Asher, Frederick M., *Nalanda: Situating the Great Monastery*, Marg Foundation, 2015, pp. 12–13.

17. Chandra Bagchi, Prabodh, *India and China: A Thousand Years of Sino-Indian Contact*, 1944, p. 3.

18. Additional details about Harsha and his times appear in *Harshacharita*, the first-ever historical biography of a king in ancient India, written by his friend and court poet, Banabhatta, who Xuanzang would likely have met.

19. From 'Vasubandhu on the conditioning factors and the Buddha's use of language' by Jonathan C. Gold. Jonardon Ganeri (editor), *The Oxford Handbook of Indian Philosophy*, OUP, 2017.

20. Beal, Samuel, *The Life of Hiuen-Tsiang*, Rupa Publications, 2012, p. 139.

21. According to Gregory Schopen, quoted in Fogelin, Lars, *An Archaeological History of Indian Buddhism* (Kindle Location 3131), OUP, Kindle Edition.

22. Basua, Analabha, Sarkar-Roya, Neeta and Majumder, Partha P., 'Genomic Reconstruction of the History of Extant Populations of India Reveals Five Distinct Ancestral Components and a Complex Structure', *PNAS*, 2015.

23. I-ching (Yijing), J. Takakusu (translator), *A Record of the Buddhist Religion as Practised in India and the Malay Archipelago*, Oxford, Clarendon Press, 1896.

24. Faxian, *A Record of Buddhistic Kingdoms /Being an Account by the Chinese Monk Fa-hsien of Travels in India and Ceylon (A.D. 399–414) in Search of the Buddhist Books of Discipline,* Oxford, Clarendon Press, 1886.

25. Ganeri, Jonardon (editor), *The Oxford Handbook of Indian Philosophy*, 2017. This includes Nagarjuna, Vasubandhu, Asanga, Dharmakirti and others.

26. Beal, Samuel, *The Life of Hiuen-Tsiang*, Rupa Publications, 2012.

27. Fogelin, Lars, *An Archaeological History of Indian Buddhism*, OUP, 2015.

28. Thapar, Romila, *The Past as Present*, Aleph, 2013.

Chapter 5: The Vision of Nalanda

1. 'Woman Beaten Up, Paraded Naked in Bihar', *The Hindu*, August 22, 2018.

2. Ancient India had many quasi-democratic, or more precisely, oligarchic republics, where a single king didn't rule the roost and many stakeholders made decisions based on 'debate, consultation, and voting'. See Steve Muhlberger, *Democracy in Ancient India*, 1998, http://www.nipissingu.ca/department/history/muhlberger/histdem/indiadem.htm.

3. Yijing, Latika Lahiri (translator), *Chinese Monks in India*, Motilal Banarsidass, Delhi, 2015 (first edition, 1986), p. 58.

4. Beal, Samuel (translator), *Hiuen Tsiang Si Yu Ki: Buddhist Records of the Western World* (629 CE), 1906, p. 170.

5. Yijing, Latika Lahiri (translator), *Chinese Monks in India*, pp. 58–9.

6. In *Chinese Monks in India*, Yijing writes that Nalanda's population was 3500, p. 61.

7. Sankalia, H.D., *University of Nalanda*, B.G. Paul & Co., second revised edition, 1973.

8. Asher, Frederick M., *Nalanda: Situating the Great Monastery*, Marg Foundation, 2015, p. 26.

9. Thapar, Romila, *Early India: From the Origins to AD 1300*, Penguin, 2003, p. 482.

10. Dutt, Sukumar, *Buddhist Monks and Monasteries of India: Their History and Their Contribution to Indian Culture*, Motilal Banarsidass, 1988.

11. I-ching (Yijing), Takakusu, J. (translator), *A Record of the Buddhist Religion as Practiced in India and the Malay Archipelago A.D. 671–695*, 1896.

12. Ibid, pp. xxxi–ii, pp. 112–13.

13. Hartmut Scharfe, *Handbook of Oriental Studies*, BRILL, 2002, p. 153.

14. I-ching (Yijing), Takakusu, J. (translator), *A Record of the Buddhist Religion as Practiced in India and the Malay Archipelago A.D. 671–695*, 1896, pp. xxxi–ii.

15. Yijing writes that additional authors whose works monks had to study included 'Nagarjuna, Deva, Asvaghosha, Vasubandhu, Asanga, Sanghabhadra, Bhavaviveka, Gina, Dharmapala, Dharmakirti, Silabhadra, Simhakandra, Sthiramati, Gunamati, Pragnagupta, Gunaprabha'.

16. It is sometimes claimed that Plato's Academy and Aristotle's Lyceum (fourth century BCE Greece) were the first universities in the world. Besides physical and military training in their gymnasiums, they offered intellectual training to young men in philosophy, politics, statecraft, religion and more. However, compared to Nalanda, they were fairly small and informal centres of learning and inquiry with no known admission criteria, curriculum, academic milestones or structured progress through stages of learning. At best, they are an even earlier precursor to the idea of the university.

17. Tillemans, Tom, 'Dharmakīrti', *The Stanford Encyclopedia of Philosophy*, Edward N. Zalta (editor), https://plato.stanford.edu/archives/spr2017/entries/dharmakiirti/.

18. On Sarvastivada, Samvirti.com, September 14, 2010, http://www.samvriti.com/2010/09/14/on-sarvastivada/.

19. From 'Santideva's Impartialist Ethics' by Charles Goodman in Ganeri, Jonardon (editor), *The Oxford Handbook of Indian Philosophy*, OUP, 2017.

20. From 'Consciousness and Causal Emergence' by Christian Coseru in Ganeri, Jonardon (editor), *The Oxford Handbook of Indian Philosophy*, OUP, 2017.

21. Scharfe, Hartmut, *Handbook of Oriental Studies*, BRILL, 2002, p. 160.

22. *Xuanzang*, Internet Encyclopedia of Philosophy, July 2009.

23. Klostermaier, Klaus, *A Survey of Hinduism*, Third Edition, State University of New York Press, 2007, p. 40.

24. John Keay writes that 'Instead of "Hinduism", scholars sometimes use the term "Brahmanism" to distinguish the pre-Bhakti orthodoxies of the post-Vedic era from the teachings of the heterodox sects like the Buddhists and Jains'. Keay, John, *India: A History*, HarperCollins, 2000.

25. Fogelin, Lars, *An Archaeological History of Indian Buddhism*, OUP, 2015. Fogelin uses architectural evidence to persuasively argue that the Buddhist *sangha* progressively withdrew from the laity, and this led to its eventual undoing.

26. Singh, Upinder, *The Idea of Ancient India: Essays on Religion, Politics, and Archaeology*, SAGE Publications, 2016, pp. 3–42.

27. Fogelin, Lars, *An Archaeological History of Indian Buddhism*, OUP, 2015.

28. Thapar, Romila, *Early India: From the Origins to AD 1300*, Penguin, 2003, p. 488.

29. Kusuman, K.K, *A Panorama of Indian Culture*, Mittal Publications, 1990, pp. 151–58.

30. Sadasivan, S.N., *A Social History of India*, APH Publishing, 2000, p. 207.

31. Omvedt, Gail, *Buddhism in India*, SAGE Publishing, 2003, pp. 160–61.

32. Ibid., pp. 166–67.

33. Or, more accurately, what's now Bihar, Jharkhand, West Bengal and parts of Bangladesh.

34. Ghosh, A., *Nalanda*, published by the Director General ASI, Seventh Edition, New Delhi, 2006, p. 13.

35. Minhaj al-Siraj and H.G. Raverty (translator), *Tabaqat-i-Nasiri*, pp. 551–52. The text quoted in this paragraph also appears in D.N. Jha's sharp critique of Arun Shourie's claim, whether made in error or deceit, that Bhaktiar Khilji destroyed Nalanda. See Jha, D.N., 'Grist to the Reactionary Mill', *Indian Express*, July 9, 2014, http://indianexpress.com/article/opinion/columns/grist-to-the-reactionary-mill/.

36. Historian Richard Eaton has argued that in the vast majority of attacks on temples or other religious institutions, Muslim kings were selective, strategic and materially or politically motivated—not indiscriminate, and not chiefly led by religious or iconoclastic fanaticism. The primary goal of most Indo-Muslim rulers too was evidently to 'delegitimize and extirpate defeated Indian ruling houses'. See, Eaton, Richard M., 'Temple Desecration and Indo-Muslim States', *Journal of Islamic Studies*, 11:3 (2000), pp. 283–319 © Oxford Centre for Islamic Studies.

37. Scharfe, Hartmut, *Handbook of Oriental Studies*, BRILL, 2002, p. 150.

38. Chos-dar, Upasaka, *Biography of Dharmasvamin: A Tibetan Monk Pilgrim* (translated by George Roerich), 1959. Travelling around Magadh, Dharmasvamin observed that 'if a person of low caste looked at a person of high caste eating, then the food had to be thrown away ... If a person of low caste approached the place where one was taking one's food, that person

had to say, "Duram gaccha", i.e. "go away".' Source archived at https://ia801605.us.archive.org/32/items/in.ernet.dli.2015.505613/2015.505613.Biography-Of.pdf.

39. Mentioned in Ghosh, A., *Nalanda*, published by the Director General ASI, Seventh Edition, New Delhi, 2006, p. 15. Source archived at https://archive.org/details/pagsamjonzang00jorgoog/page/n11. Also mentioned in Bakshi, S.R., *From Aryans to Swaraj*, Sarup and Sons, 2005, p. 231.

40. Elverskog, Johan, *Buddhism and Islam on the Silk Road (Encounters with Asia)*, University of Pennsylvania Press, 2011, pp. 1–3.

41. Ibid.

42. Quote cited in Eaton, Richard M., 'Temple Desecration and Indo-Muslim States', *Journal of Islamic Studies* 11:3 (2000), pp. 283–319 © Oxford Centre for Islamic Studies.

43. Fogelin, Lars, *An Archaeological History of Indian Buddhism*, OUP, 2015.

44. Ambedkar wrote, 'There can be no doubt that the fall of Buddhism in India was due to the invasions of the Musalmans . . . by killing the Buddhist priesthood, Islam killed Buddhism. This was the greatest disaster that befell the religion of the Buddha in India.'

45. Omvedt, Gail, *Buddhism in India*, SAGE Publications, 2003, p. 175.

46. Elverskog, Johan, *Buddhism and Islam on the Silk Road (Encounters with Asia)*, University of Pennsylvania Press, 2011, pp. 1–3.

47. Sircar, Jawhar, 'How Buddhism Was Rediscovered in Modern India', ABP, June 22, 2015.

48. Thapar, Romila, *Somanatha: The Many Voices of a History*, Verso, 2009, p. 209.

49. See 'Nalanda University Design', Vastushilpa Foundation, YouTube.com, February 17, 2017, https://youtu.be/eR9brN9eLZA.

50. Chowdhury, Shreya Roy, 'It Is a Closed Place': Why Students Are Quitting Nalanda University, Scroll.in, October 29, 2017.

51. Devraj, Ranjit, 'Political Meddling Causes Nalanda University Turmoil', University World News, December 9, 2016.

52. Rajghatta, Chidanand, 'Nalanda to Move from Ruins to Riches', *Times of India*, May 11, 2008.

Chapter 6: Alberuni's India

1. Alberuni and Sachau, Edward C. (translator, 1888), *Alberuni's India*, Rupa Publications, Delhi, 2002. All quotes from Alberuni in this essay come from this book.

2. The languages Alberuni knew well include Arabic, Persian, Turkish, Hebrew, Sanskrit and Syriac. Erik Gregersen (editor), *The Universe: A Historical Survey of Beliefs, Theories, and Laws*, Britannica Educational Publishing, 2009.

3. Sachau in his Introduction, Alberuni and Sachau, Edward C. (translator, 1888), *Alberuni's India*, Rupa Publications, Delhi, 2002.

4. Kulke, Hermann and Rothermund, Dietmar, *A History of India*, Psychology Press, 2004, p. 165.

5. Thapar, Romila, *Early India: From the Origins to AD 1300*, Penguin, 2003, p. 427.

6. This is Sachau's speculation in his introduction to the translation. See Alberuni and Sachau, Edward C. (translator, 1888), *Alberuni's India*, Rupa Publications, Delhi, 2002.

7. Saliba, George, 'Al-Bīrūnī', *Encyclopaedia Britannica*, retrieved August 12, 2017.

8. Arora, Namit, *Early Islam: The Golden Age*, 3 Quarks Daily, October 12, 2009.

9. Saliba, George, 'Al-Bīrūnī', *Encyclopaedia Britannica*, retrieved August 12, 2017.

10. Gregersen, Erik (editor), *The Universe: A Historical Survey of Beliefs, Theories, and Laws*, Britannica Educational Publishing, 2009.

11. Sachau, in his introduction, also notes that Alberuni accused the original Arabs of destroying the syncretic civilization of Persia, a view that would find adherents among later historians. See, for instance, Hitti, Philip Khuri, *The Arabs*, Macmillan & Co. Ltd., 1965, p. 71.

12. Kulke, Hermann and Rothermund, Dietmar, *A History of India*, Psychology Press, 2004, p. 165.

13. Thapar, Romila. 'Somanatha and Mahmud', Frontline, Vol. 16, Issue 8, April 10–23, 1999.

14. Thapar, Romila, *Early India: From the Origins to AD 1300*, Penguin, 2003, p. 427.

15. Eaton, Richard M., *India in the Persianate Age 1000–1765*, Allen Lane, 2019, p. 22.

16. Ibid., p. 431.

17. Thapar, Romila, *Somanatha: The Many Voices of a History*, Verso, 2005.

18. Thapar, Romila, *Early India: From the Origins to AD 1300*, Penguin, 2003, pp. 431–32.

19. Alberuni and Sachau, Edward C. (translator, 1888), *Alberuni's India*, Rupa Publications, Delhi, 2002.

20. Kunitzsch, Paul, 'The Transmission of Hindu-Arabic Numerals Reconsidered', in *The Enterprise of Science in Islam: New Perspectives*, edited by J.P. Hogendijk and A.I. Sabra, MIT Press, 2003, pp. 3–22.
21. Dutta, Amartya Kumar, 'Aryabhata and Axial Rotation of Earth', Resonance, Vol. ll, No. 4, 2006, pp. 56-74.
22. Eaton, Richard M., *India in the Persianate Age 1000–1765*, Allen Lane, 2019, p. 388.

Chapter 7: The Enigma of Khajuraho

1. Desai, Devangana, *Erotic Sculpture of India: Socio Cultural Study*, Munshiram Manoharlal Publishers, 1974, reprinted 1985, p. xv.
2. Punja, Shobita, *Khajuraho: The First Thousand Years*, Penguin UK, 2010.
3. For an extensive image gallery of erotic art from Khajuraho, see http://www.shunya.net/Pictures/NorthIndia/Khajuraho/Khajuraho.htm.
4. Sullerey, S.K., *Chandella Art*, Aakar Books, Delhi, 2004, p. 31.
5. Ibid.
6. Ibid.
7. Ibid.
8. Punja, Shobita, *Divine Ecstasy: The Story of Khajuraho*, Viking, 1992. Punja sees the wedding of Shiva and Parvati as the key to understanding Khajuraho's temple art. Absurdly far-fetched though her theory is, at least it has some imaginative allure.
9. For example, the famous Palace of Wheels luxury train offers an add-on tour package to 'the UNESCO World Heritage Site of Kama Sutra Hindu Temples'.
10. Desai, Devangana, *The Religious Imagery of Khajuraho*, Franco-Indian Research Pvt Ltd, 1996, p. xxvi.
11. Punja, Shobita, *Divine Ecstacy: The Story of Khajuraho*, Viking, 2000, p. 11.
12. Desai, Devangana, *Khajuraho: Monumental Legacy*, Oxford India Paperbacks, 2000, p. 8.
13. Kusuman, K.K. (editor), *A Panorama of Indian Culture*, Mittal Publications, 1990, p. 154.
14. Desai, Devangana, *Khajuraho: Monumental Legacy*, Oxford India Paperbacks, 2000, p. 8.
15. Desai, Devangana, *Erotic Sculpture of India: Socio Cultural Study*, Munshiram Manoharlal Publishers, 1974, reprinted 1985, p. 151-54.
16. Ibid., p. 159.

17. Rana P.B. Singh with a Foreword by John McKim Malville, *Cosmic Order and Cultural Astronomy: Sacred Cities of India*, Cambridge Scholars Publishing, 2009, p. 57.

18. Nath, Vijay, 'From "Brahmanism" to "Hinduism": Negotiating the Myth of the Great Tradition', *Social Scientist*, 2001, 29 (3/4): 19–50.

19. Doniger, Wendy, *The Hindus: An Alternative History*, Penguin Publishing Group, 2009, p. 443.

20. Joseph, Tony, *Early Indians*, Juggernaut, 2018, pp. 188–89.

21. Desai, Devangana, *Erotic Sculpture of India: Socio Cultural Study*, Munshiram Manoharlal Publishers, 1974, reprinted 1985, p. 26.

22. Ibid.

23. Ibid., p.198.

24. Thapar, Romila, *Early India: From the Origins to AD 1300*, Penguin, 2003, p. 474.

25. All quotes in this paragraph are from the Introduction to Vatsyayana Mallanaga, *Kamasutra* (translated and edited by Wendy Doniger and Sudhir Kakar), OUP, 2002.

26. Ibid.

27. Vatsyayana, *The Kamasutra* (translated by Lars Martin Fosse), YogaVidya.com, 2012.

28. Thapar, Romila, *The Past as Present*, Aleph, 2013.

29. Vatsyayana, *The Kamasutra* (translated by Lars Martin Fosse), YogaVidya.com, 2012.

30. All quotes and many other details in this paragraph are from the chapter 'Sex in Society' in Desai, Devangana, *Erotic Sculpture of India: Socio Cultural Study*, Munshiram Manoharlal Publishers, 1974, reprinted 1985, pp. 166–82.

31. Ibid.

32. Ibid.

33. Ibid.

34. A modern-day festival of fertility is *Teej*, though it is now thoroughly cloaked in the sexual morality of our own age.

35. Thapar, Romila, *The Past as Present*, Aleph, 2014.

36. Desai, Devangana, *The Religious Imagery of Khajuraho*, 1996, p. 49.

37. Anne Harper, Katherine and Robert L. Brown (editors), *The Roots of Tantra*, SUNY Press, 2002, pp. 1–7.

38. Urban, Hugh B., *The Power of Tantra: Religion, Sexuality and the Politics of South Asian Studies*, I.B. Tauris, 2009, p. 5.

39. Anne Harper, Katherine and Robert L. Brown (editors), *The Roots of Tantra*, SUNY Press, 2002, pp. 1–11.

40. Urban, Hugh B., *The Power of Tantra: Religion, Sexuality and the Politics of South Asian Studies*, I.B. Tauris, 2009.

41. Ibid.

42. Ibid.

43. Anne Harper, Katherine and Robert L. Brown (editors), *The Roots of Tantra*, SUNY Press, 2002, pp. 1–11.

44. Thapar, Romila, *The Past as Present*, Aleph, 2014.

45. Thapar, Romila, *Early India: From the Origins to AD 1300*, Penguin, 2003, p. 486.

46. Samuel, Geoffrey, *The Origins of Yoga and Tantra: Indic Religions to the Thirteenth Century*, Cambridge University Press, 2008, p. 9.

47. Desai, Devangana, *Erotic Sculpture of India: Socio Cultural Study*, Munshiram Manoharlal Publishers, 1974, reprinted 1985, pp. 120, 126, 135, 144, 176, 200–01.

48. Ibid.

49. Ibid.

50. Ibid.

51. All quotes in this paragraph are from Desai, Devangana, *The Religious Imagery of Khajuraho*, 1996, pp. 51, 218–20.

52. For instance, the Sena dynasts of Bengal, as we saw in 'The Vision of Nalanda', had been reviving caste and an orthodox Brahminical order—as well as persecuting *nastika* orders—in the century preceding their first encounter with Muslims, i.e., Turkish invaders c. 1200.

53. 'Your Approach Is That of a Woman Hungry of Sex': The legal notice sent by Dina Nath Batra to Wendy Doniger, Penguin Group (USA) Inc. and Penguin Books India Pvt. Ltd, printed in *Outlook*, India, February 11, 2014.

54. Doniger, Wendy, *On Hinduism*, Aleph, 2013.

55. Ibid.

56. '"India has been a sexual wasteland for two centuries": An interview with psychoanalyst Sudhir Kakar', Scroll.in, 2016.

57. For more on this, see the chapter 'The Moral Universe of the Bhagavad Gita' in Arora, Namit, *The Lottery of Birth*, Three Essays Collective, 2017.

Chapter 8: Marco Polo's India

1. A precursor to this essay appeared in 2010. Arora, Namit, 'Marco Polo's India', *Kyoto Journal*, Silk Roads Special Issue, June 2010.

2. Polo, Marco (translated and Introduction by Ronald Latham), *The Travels of Marco Polo*, Penguin Books, 1958.

3. Ramaswami, N. S., *Seven Pagodas: The Art and History of Mahabalipuram*, Uma Books, 1970.

4. Ibn Battuta (translated and selected by H.A.R. Gibb), *Travels in Asia and Africa, 1325–1354*, London: George Routledge & Sons, 1929.

5. Asher, Catherine B., Cynthia Talbot, *India before Europe*, Cambridge University Press, 2006, p. 78.

6. Samarqandi, Abd al-Razzaq, *Narrative of My Voyage into Hindoostan, and the Wonders and Remarkable Peculiarities Which This Country Presents.* Written after his 1442–45 voyage and translated from Persian into English in 1857.

7. Eaton, Richard M., *India in the Persianate Age 1000–1765*, Allen Lane, 2019, p. 188.

8. Scott, David, 'Nikitin's Conversion in India to Islam: Wielhorski's Translation Dilemma', 2001, No. 3: 132–61.

9. Athanasius Nikitin of Twer (translated by Count Wielhorski), *Voyage to India* (1466–72), Medieval Russian Series, Cambridge, Ontario, 2000.

Chapter 9: The Innovations of Vijayanagar at Hampi

1. From Domingo Paes's account in Sewell, Robert, Fernão Nunes, Domingo Paes, *A Forgotten Empire (Vijayanagar): A Contribution to the History of India*, Swan Sonnenschein & Co. Ltd, 1900, republished by Asian Educational Services 2001, pp. 247–53.

2. An example here is Gupta, Subhadra Sen, *Hampi: Discover the Splendours of Vijayanagar*, Niyogi Books, 2010. A much better guidebook is Fritz, John M. and Michell, George. *Hampi Vijayanagara*, Jaico Publishing House, 2011.

3. See the definition of Sanskritization here: https://www.oxfordreference.com/view/10.1093/oi/authority.20110803100441148.

4. Eaton, Richard M., *The New Cambridge History of India, A Social History of the Deccan, 1300–1761: Eight Indian Lives*, CUP, 2005, pp. 81–82.

5. Ocean trade had brought Arab, African and other Asian Muslims to south India long before the north. These cosmopolitan Muslim communities, including fighters employed by Hindu kings, were ethnically and culturally distant from the Turkic-Afghan warriors and the new converts of the Delhi Sultanate.

6. On a 'hill to the northeast of the city are some Muslim tombs. The area below this hill was known as Gorikelaganagrama (village below Muslim tombs), inhabited by Muslims. An inscription refers to the construction of

a dharamsala by Ahmad Khan in A.D. 1439'. Source: Patil, Channabasappa S.,. 'Vijayanagara City: An Inscriptional Study', P. Shanmugam, Srinivasan Srinivasan (editors), *Recent Advances in Vijayanagara Studies*, New Era Publications, 2006, p. 77.

7. Wagoner, Phillip B., 'Sultan among Hindu Kings: Dress, Titles, and the Islamicization of Hindu Culture at Vijayanagara', *Journal of Asian Studies*, Vol. 55, No. 4, 1996, pp. 851–80.

8. From A Social History of the Deccan, 1300–1761 by Richard M. Eaton. © Cambridge University Press 2005. Reproduced with permission of The Licensor through PLSclear.

9. Eaton, Richard M., *The New Cambridge History of India, A Social History of the Deccan, 1300–1761: Eight Indian Lives*, CUP, 2005, pp. 87–88.

10. Firishta writes, for instance, that in 1419, Vijayanagar's troops marched against the Sultan. 'The Hindus made a general massacre of the mussalmans, and erected a platform with their heads on the field of battle ... They followed the sultan into his own country, which they wasted with fires and sword, took many places, broke down many mosques and holy places, slaughtered the people without mercy.' Three years later, a new sultan led a revenge attack on Vijayanagar. He 'overran the open country, and wherever he came, put to death men, women, and children, without mercy . . . Laying aside all humanity, whenever the number of the slain amounted to twenty thousand, he halted three days, and made a festival in celebration of the bloody work. He broke down the idol temples, and destroyed the colleges of the Brahmins'. See Sewell, Robert, Fernao Nunes, Domingos Paes, *A Forgotten Empire (Vijayanagar): A Contribution to the History of India*, 1900, pp. 65–68.

11. Thapar, Romila, *The Past as Present*, Aleph, 2014.

12. Such high numbers in the armies were reported on both sides by many chroniclers. Of course, all kingdoms stood to gain from officially inflating the size of their armies, and it wouldn't have been easy for passing travellers to verify them. François Bernier, writing in the 1660s about the army of Aurangzeb, who controlled far more resources and territory than Vijayanagar, reported much smaller numbers for the Mughal army.

13. Samarqandi, Kamaluddin Abdul-Razzaq, *Mission to Calicut and Vijayanagar*. Thackston, W.M. (selected and translated), *In a Century of Princes: Sources on Timurid History and Art*, Cambridge, Massachusetts: Aga Khan Program for Islamic Architecture, 1989.

14. Stein, Burton, *The New Cambridge History of India: Vijayanagara*, CUP, 1989, p. 92.

15. Barbosa, Duarte (translated by Dames, Mansel Longworth, 1812), *The Book of Duarte Barbosa: An Account of the Countries Bordering on the Indian Ocean and Their Inhabitants*, 1518.

16. Sewell, Robert, Fernão Nunes, Domingo Paes, *A Forgotten Empire (Vijayanagar): A Contribution to the History of India*, Swan Sonnenschein & Co. Ltd, 1900, republished by Asian Educational Services, 2001.

17. Fernao Nuniz, in Robert Sewell's translation, calls them 'captains', and the British 'poligars'.

18. Sarasvati, A. Rangasvami, 'Political Maxims of the Emperor Poet, Krishnadeva Raya', *Journal of Indian History 6*, 1925.

19. Fritz, John M., Michell, George, *Hampi Vijayanagara*, Jaico, 2011, p. 33.

20. Stein, Burton, *The New Cambridge History of India: Vijayanagara*, CUP, 1989, p. 110.

21. For an interesting discussion here, see Subrahmanyam, Sanjay, *Agreeing to Disagree: Burton Stein on Vijayanagara,* South Asia Research, Vol. 17, No. 2, 1997.

22. W.H. Moreland (1868–1938), an economic historian of medieval India, including of Vijayanagar and Mughal times, concluded that 'in the matter of industry India was more advanced relatively to western Europe than she is today'. However, he also claimed that lower-class Indians under British colonial rule had a better standard of living than their medieval counterparts. See Chand, Tara, *History of Freedom Movement in India*, Vol. 1, Publications Division Ministry of Information and Broadcasting, 1967.

23. Verghese, Anila, 'Depictions of Foreigners at Vijayanagara', P. Shanmugam, Srinivasan Srinivasan (editors), *Recent Advances in Vijayanagara Studies*, New Era Publications, 2006, pp. 198–208.

24. Ganeri, Jonardon, (editor), *The Oxford Handbook of Indian Philosophy*, OUP, 2017, p. 20. Cannibhatta wrote *Sarvadarśanasaṃgraha* ('The Compendium of All Viewpoints'), a treatise summarizing many systems of Indian thought, but ultimately defended Shankara's Advaita Vedanta.

25. This argument is developed by Stoker, Valerie, *Polemics and Patronage in the City of Victory*, University of California Press, 2016.

26. Nikhil, 'Kanaka Dasa's Musical Critique of "Caste, Caste, Caste"', March 2017, https://nikhiletc.wordpress.com/2017/03/07/kanaka-dasas-musical-critique-of-caste-caste-caste/.

27. Wagoner, Phillip B., 'Sultan among Hindu Kings: Dress, Titles, and the Islamicization of Hindu Culture at Vijayanagara', *Journal of Asian Studies*, Vol. 55, No. 4, 1996, pp. 851–80.

28. Eaton, Richard M., *The New Cambridge History of India, A Social History of the Deccan, 1300–1761: Eight Indian Lives*, CUP, 2005, pp. 101.
29. Jain, Anshika, 'Bijapur's Art—A Melting Pot', Live History India, June 2019.
30. Dalrymple, William, 'The Untold History of Hampi', *Open*, July 26, 2018.
31. Fritz, John M., Michell, George, *Hampi Vijayanagara*, 2011, p. 36. Contrast this with the Kakatiya kingdom (in modern Telangana), where a queen, Rudramadevi, ruled from c. 1262–89.
32. For more on women's lives at this time, see Katragadda, Sri Lakshmi, *Women in Vijayanagara: Women in Sixteenth Century (A Study of Tuluva Dynasty)*, Delta Publishing House, 1996.
33. Sastri, Nilakanta K.A., *A History of South India*, OUP, 1958, p. 279.
34. Quoted in Sewell, Robert, Fernão Nunes, Domingo Paes, *A Forgotten Empire (Vijayanagar): A Contribution to the History of India*, Swan Sonnenschein & Co. Ltd, 1900, republished by Asian Educational Services, 2001, p. 194.
35. Sastri, Nilakanta K.A., *A History of South India*, OUP, 1958, p. 283.
36. Eaton, Richard M., *India in the Persianate Age 1000–1765*, Allen Lane, 2019, p. 171.
37. Shanmugam, P., Srinivasan, Srinivasan (editors), *Recent Advances in Vijayanagara Studies*, New Era Publications, 2006, p. 199.
38. Stein, Burton, *The New Cambridge History of India: Vijayanagara*, CUP, 1989, p. 119.
39. According to Caesaro Federici, who visited Vijayanagar two years after the battle of Talikota.
40. Stein, Burton, *The New Cambridge History of India: Vijayanagara*, CUP, 1989, p. 80.
41. Kulke, Hermann, Dietmar Rothermund, *A History of India*, Psychology Press, 2004, p. 192.
42. Keay, John. *India: A History*, HarperCollins, 1999.
43. Fritz, John M., Michell, George, *Hampi Vijayanagara*, Jaico, 2011, p. 51.
44. Eaton, Richard M., *The New Cambridge History of India, A Social History of the Deccan, 1300–1761: Eight Indian Lives*, CUP, 2005, pp. 103–04.
45. Wagoner, Phillip B., 'Sultan among Hindu Kings: Dress, Titles, and the Islamicization of Hindu Culture at Vijayanagara', *Journal of Asian Studies*, Vol. 55, No. 4, 1996, pp. 851–80.
46. Eaton, Richard M., *The New Cambridge History of India, A Social History of the Deccan, 1300–1761: Eight Indian Lives*, CUP, 2005, p. 103.

47. Subrahmanyam, Sanjay, 'Golden Age Hallucinations', *Outlook*, August 2001.
48. Stein, Burton, *The New Cambridge History of India: Vijayanagara*, CUP, 1989, p. 28.

Chapter 10: François Bernier's India

1. Bernier, Francois (translated by Archibald Constable), *Travels in the Mogul Empire: AD 1656–68,* Second Edition revised by Vincent. A Smith, Low Price Publications, Delhi.
2. The Caravanserai was demolished in mid-nineteenth century. In its place now stands the Town Hall building and a clock tower (Ghantaghar) in Chandni Chowk.
3. Babur; Hiro, Dilip (editor), *Babur Nama: Journal of Emperor Babur*, Penguin Books India, 2006.
4. Tavernier, Jean Baptiste, Valentine Ball (translator), *Travels in India* (1676), Macmillan and Company, 1889.
5. Thapar, Romila, *The Past as Present*, Aleph, 2014.
6. See the chapter 'The Mysteries of Dholavira' for the earliest mentions of sati in India.
7. From 'Philosophy as a Distinct Cultural Practice: The Transregional Context' by Smith, Justin E.H., (edited by Jonardon Ganeri), *The Oxford Handbook of Indian Philosophy*, OUP, 2017.
8. Sharma, R.S. (edited by Basham A. L), 'The Socio-Economic Bases of "Oriental Despotism" in Early India', *Kingship in Asia and Early America: 30. International Congress of Human Sciences in Asia and North Africa*, México D.F.: Colegio De Mexico, 1981, pp. 133–42.
9. Tambiah, S.J., 'What Did Bernier Actually Say? Profiling the Mughal Empire', *Contributions to Indian Sociology*, 32(2), 1998, pp. 361–86.

Chapter 11: The Faiths of Varanasi

1. Singh, Rana P.B., *Cultural Landscapes and the Lifeworld: Literary Images of Banaras*, Indica Books, pp. 128–38.
2. Eck, Diana L., *Banaras: City of Light*, Knopf Doubleday Publishing Group, 1982.
3. Ibid.
4. Teltumbde, Anand, 'To the Self-Obsessed Marxists and the Pseudo Ambedkarites', Sanhati.com, 2013.

5. Sandria B. Freitag (editor), *Culture and Power in Banaras: Community, Performance, and Environment, 1800–1980*, University of California Press, 1989, pp. 78–91.

6. Eck, Diana L., *Banaras: City of Light*, Knopf Doubleday Publishing Group, 1982.

7. Kabir (translated by Linda Hess and Shukdeo Singh), *The Bijak of Kabir*, OUP, 2002, p. 4.

8. Ibid. p. 13.

9. Pankaj Mishra writes that the Buddha avoided Varanasi because of its dominance by the Brahmins, who 'despised sramanas, whom they saw as likely competition'. Mishra, Pankaj, *An End to Suffering*, Farrar, Straus and Giroux, 2004, p. 214.

10. Hiuen Tsiang, Samuel Beal (translator), *Si Yu Ki: Buddhist Records of the Western World*, Kegan Paul, Trench, Trubner & Co. Ltd., 1906, pp. 44–45.

11. Sen, Sudipta, *Ganga: The Many Pasts of a River,* Gurgaon, Viking, 2019, p. 251.

12. Historian Sudipta Sen writes that during the Delhi Sultanate period, many grand new temples were built in Varanasi, such as Vishweshwar Temple during the reign of Iltutmish, the temple of Padmeshwar during the reign of Alauddin Khalji, the temple of Manikarnikeshwar during the Tughluq rule and more. See Sen, Sudipta, *Ganga: The Many Pasts of a River,* Gurgaon, Viking, 2019, p. 266.

13. Parry, Jonathan P., *Death in Banaras*, Cambridge University Press, 1994, pp. 39–40.

14. Eaton, Richard M., 'Temple Desecration and Indo-Muslim States', *Journal of Islamic Studies,* 11:3, pp. 283–319 © Oxford Centre for Islamic Studies 2000.

15. Ibid.

16. For instance, Aurangzeb had issued a farman in 1659 to protect all Hindu temples and their staff, but when political circumstances changed ten years later, he ordered Varanasi's Bindu Madhav and Vishwanath temples destroyed, replacing them with Alamgiri and Gyanvapi mosques. In particular, Vishwanath temple, 'built by Todar Mal, Akbar's finance minister, was torn down to punish Hindus who were supporting Aurangzeb's arch enemy, the Maratha Shivaji'. See: Asher, Catherine B., Cynthia Talbot, *India before Europe*, Cambridge University Press, 2006, p. 231.

17. Daniyal, Shoaib, 'Forgotten Indian History: The Shoaib Brutal Maratha Invasions of Bengal', Scroll.in, December 21, 2015.

18. Implicit and explicit material incentives for conversion were much preferred. Aurangzeb often 'gave out robes of honor, cash gifts, and promotions to converts'. Richards, John F., *The New Cambridge History of India: The Mughal Empire*, CUP, 1993.

19. Relatively few upper-caste Hindus converted, suggesting that more than access to jobs, escaping caste was a bigger motivator for conversion—the same desire that later fuelled mass conversions to Sikhism, Christianity and Navayana Buddhism.

20. Aurangzeb too has a mixed record and wasn't the cartoonish villain he's often made out to be. For a portrait of Aurangzeb's complexities and contradictions, see Truschke, Audrey, *Aurangzeb: The Life and Legacy of India's Most Controversial King*, Stanford University Press, 2017.

21. This was true even as Hindus too held high offices 'and were entrusted with critical state business'. Ibid.

22. Doniger, Wendy, *The Hindus: An Alternative History*, Penguin Publishing Group, 2009, p. 468.

23. Thapar, Romila, Noorani, A.G., Menon, Sadanand, *On Nationalism*, Aleph, 2016.

24. Bernier, Francois (translated by Archibald Constable), *Travels in the Mogul Empire: AD 1656–68*, second edition revised by Vincent A. Smith, Low Price Publications, Delhi.

25. Ibid.

26. Eaton, Richard M., *India in the Persianate Age 1000–1765*, Allen Lane, 2019, p. 392.

27. Tavernier, Jean Baptiste, (translated by Valentine Ball), *Travels in India (1676)*, Macmillan and Company, 1889.

28. For a discussion of this phenomenon, see Sen, Sudipta, *Gangā: The Many Pasts of a River,* Gurgaon, Viking, 2019, p. 31.

29. Parry, Jonathan P., *Death in Banaras*, Cambridge University Press, 1994, pp. 39–40.

30. For a vivid and informative account of the Ramlila Festival of Ramnagar, see Ede, Piers Moore, *Kaleidoscope City: A Year in Varanasi,* Bloomsbury, 2015, pp. 31–50.

31. Varanasi City Census 2011 data, https://www.census2011.co.in/census/city/153-varanasi.html.

32. Mehta, Bhanu Shankar, *Unseen Banaras*, Pilgrims Publishing, 2013, p. 21.

33. '"We will never know the number of temples desecrated through India's history": Richard Eaton', Scroll.in, November 20, 2015. The only communal riot that Diana Eck mentions in *Banaras: City of Light* took place in 1809, when 'the Hindus had attempted to construct a shrine on the neutral ground between the Jnana Vapi Mosque and the Vishvanatha Temple'.

34. Sherring, M.A., *Benares: The Sacred City of the Hindus* (1868), Pilgrims Publishing, 2016, p. 7.

35. Despite many expensive projects, cleaning the Ganga has remained an elusive problem. For a good introduction, see Doron, Assa and Jeffrey, Robin, *Waste of a Nation: Garbage and Growth in India*, Harvard University Press, 2018.

36. Doron, Assa, *Life on the Ganga: Boatmen and the Ritual Economy of Banaras*, Cambridge University Press India, 2013, pp. 27–40.

37. Srivastava, Piyush, 'Narendra Modi Upsets Ganga's Sons', *Telegraph*, January 3, 2019.

38. Doron, Assa, *Life on the Ganga: Boatmen and the Ritual Economy of Banaras,* Cambridge University Press India, 2013, p. 104.

39. The six to seven thousand boatmen are drawn from the city's total Mallah population of perhaps 150,000. If we assume three to four dependents per Mallah, it seems that a fifth of the Mallahs rely on the boating business, while the rest have taken up other professions.

40. Doron, Assa, *Life on the Ganga: Boatmen and the Ritual Economy of Banaras*, Cambridge University Press India, 2013, p. 114.

41. Ibid.

42. Agarwal, Kabir, 'In Modi's Varanasi, the Vishwanath Corridor Is Trampling Kashi's Soul', Wire, March 8, 2019.

43. See these reports for further details: Kumar, Sushil, 'How Modi's Kashi Vishwanath Corridor Is Laying the Ground for Another Babri Incident', *Caravan Magazine*, April 27, 2019; Husain, Yasra, 'Kashi Vishwanath Project Makes Muslims Worried about Mosque', *Times of India*, May 10, 2019.

44. This puzzle and its various answers are discussed in Parry, Jonathan P., *Death in Banaras*, Cambridge University Press, 1994, pp. 27–30.

45. Tavernier, Jean Baptiste (translated by Valentine Ball), *Travels in India* (1676), Macmillan and Company, 1889.

46. Ede, Piers Moore, *Kaleidoscope City: A Year in Varanasi,* Bloomsbury, 2015, p. 10.

47. This essay uses text from a smaller precursor essay by the author. See Arora, Namit, 'As Though We Were Immortal', 3 Quarks Daily, January 30, 2012.
48. Rare for commercial films in India, a Dom character was portrayed in *Masaan*, a French-Indian co-production directed by Neeraj Ghaywan (2015).

Index

288 Index

Deccan Sultanates, 184, 194; alliances fell apart, 207; divided between Muslim north and Hindu south, 208; hired Hindu officials and armymen, 208; and Vijayanagar, great war, Talikota, 1565, 204–07
Delhi Sultanate (1206–1526), 120, 147, 181, 212, 235, 237
dependent origination, concept of, 69, 70
Desai, Devangana, 136, 146, 149, 150, 152, 153, 154–55, 160–61
design planning, Dholavira, 22
designs and motifs in jewellery, pottery and seals, Harappan, 29, 39
Deva Raya I, 185–86
Deva Raya II, 184, 187
devadasis, 154–55
Devasena, 60
'development versus heritage' debate, 55
Dhanvantari, 229
Dharamshala, 117
Dharma Vijayin, an inscription, 65
Dharmakirti (550–610), 113
Dharmanandi, 62
Dharmapala, 112, 113–14, 269
Dharmasvamin (1197–1264), 116, 120
Dholavira (2600–1900 BCE), mysteries of, 6, 10–39, 148; beyond the city walls, 23–27; the great metropolis of the South, 16–23; seven cultural stages, 16–18. *See also* Harappa; Mohenjo-daro
di Varthema, Ludovico, 194
Dibali/Diwali festival in India, 11th Century, 123
Dignaga (480–540), 113
Diodorus Siculus, 44, 46
disparities in India, 218
DNA analysis of Harappans, 36
domestication of animals, Harappan, 14
Doms, Dom workers, 9, 131; of Varanasi, 243, 251–56
Doniger, Wendy, 151–52, 163–64, 165, 237
Doron, Assa, 246–48
drainage, Harappan civilization, 16; Mohenjo-daro, 32
Dravidian Movement, anti-Brahminical, Tamil Nadu, 54
drought in Andhra Pradesh, 55
Durga, 103
Dussehra festival, Vijayanagar, 193
Dutt, Sukumar, 68, 104

East India Company, 239, 244
Eaton, Richard M., 184, 208, 235–36
Eck, Diana, *Banaras: The City of Light*, 229, 235, 242
economic liberalization in India, 96
Egypt, 12, 13, 28, 29
Egyptians, 37

Ehuvala Chamtamula (c. 270–300 CE), 65
Eklavya, 245
Eknath, 163
Eksteins, Modris, 4
Elamite, 33–34
elephants in India, 44
Ellora, 150
Elverskog, Johan, 121
endogamy, 89; based on occupation, India 300 BCE, 4; Harappan, 35, 36; Vijayapuri, 66
engineering, Harappan, 39
Enlightenment in Europe, 9
epistemology, 111, 113
eroticism, 135–65; erotica in religious art, 148–51
errors and strange superstitions, India, as observed by François Bernier, 220–27
ethnocultural distinctiveness, 82 Euclid, 131
European: antipathy towards Islam, 121; imperialism, 9
Europeans, 214; reconstruction of India's past, 165
exhibitionism, 162, 161

Failaka and Bahrain, Persian Gulf, 25
farmers, 48
fashioning of ornaments, Harappan civilization, 15
Faxian (Fa-Hien, C. 337– 422 CE) in India, 7, 75–76, 77–78, 81, 85, 87–88, 89–90, 92, 98–99. *See also* Xuanzang (Hiuen Tsang); Yijing
Faxiang school of thought, China, 115
Federici, Caesaro, 207
female Budhhas, Vijayapuri, 68
female figures, Harappan, 38
Fertile Crescent, 14
festivals in India, 123, 135, 136
figurines: Harappan, 19, 29, 34; at Vijayapri, 60, 62
Firdausi, 124
fire rituals, 38
Firishta, Muhammad Kasim, 184, 205–06
Fogelin, Lars, 93, 117, 121
folk: beliefs, 146; and Puranic deities, religious profusion, 116; religiosity, 156; spirituality and religious practices, 165
food in India: 300 BCE, 47; 13th century, 166–68
fortifications, fortification walls: at Dholavira, 17, 18, 21, 22, 39; at Vijayanagar, 177, 187, 195
four varna divisions. *See* varna system
Fritz, John, 198
funerary customs in India: Harappan, 23, 37; 11th century, 134; in Vijayapuri, 53–54

Gadhavi, Shambhudan, 26
Gahadavala Dynasty, 235
Gajapati rulers of Orissa, 73, 193, 208